LIVING IN SOUTH LONDON

Living in South London

**Perspectives on Battersea
1871–1981**

SANDRA WALLMAN

*in association with
Ian Buchanan
Yvonne Dhooge
J. I. Gershuny
Barry Kosmin
Mai Wann*

Published for
The London School of Economics and Political Science
by Gower

British Library Cataloguing in Publication Data

Living in South London.
    1. Battersea (London, England)—Social life and
    customs
    I. Wallman, Sandra
    942.1'66081   HC257.B/

Published by
Gower Publishing Company Limited,
Gower House, Croft Road, Aldershot, Hants GU11 3HR,
England

ISBN 0 566 00600 6

Printed in Great Britain by
Biddles Ltd, Guildford, Surrey

Contents

LIST OF MAPS

CHAPTER APPENDICES

LIST OF TABLES AND FIGURES

ACKNOWLEDGEMENTS

This study was supported by funds from the Social Science Research Council (SSRC) under the auspices of its Research Unit in Ethnic Relations at the University of Bristol (1975-1980). The SSRC also provided grants for the analysis of the London diaries of the 1961 Time Budget Survey which are incorporated in Chapter 7, and for the Resource Options Programme which is to build on this work in The London School of Economics and Political Science (LSE). The manuscript was prepared for the camera in the LSE. All the typing was done by Carol Evans; the graphics were produced by Barbara Duffy. The British Library of Political and Economic Science (BLPES) gave permission for the reproduction of entries from the New Survey of London which appear at the end of Chapter 3.

Our debt to all those who responded to the neighbourhood survey questionnaire and to the 22 residents who interviewed for it is enormous. We have tried to present the history and ethnography of Battersea and to represent the style of Battersea people without distorting the lives or the views of any of them. But neither they nor the sponsors of this research are responsible for the interpretation put on it here.

1 Introduction

SANDRA WALLMAN

INNER CITY

This book is about living in the inner city. Specifically it is about living in London, just south of the Thames, in the area which was entered in the Domesday Book (in 1086) as 'Patricery' and has been known as 'Battersea' long since. (McCulloch 1866). The boundaries of Battersea have changed many times since the names first appeared on any map, and the implications of living in Battersea have always varied according to who is defining it and for what purposes. Changes of both kinds are inevitable: new administrative fashions and responsibilities regularly alter official notions of how big a local government unit should be; and even if boundaries on the ground are fixed, their significance to the way people define themselves and others is not. Change is not, of course, the whole story. Some aspects of the life and identity of Battersea have certainly been characteristic of it for more than a century and probably for much longer. Our descriptions of the livelihood of several generations of Battersea people show both the change and the continuity of it quite clearly.

The definition of Battersea as 'inner city' is more problematic and much more recent. Although the phrase was occasionally used by Victorians, its current meaning seems not to have been sealed until the 1960s. The inner city label now stands for so much more than itself that it affects peoples' expectations of any area it is applied to, whether they are participant residents or official observers of the scene.

In the literal sense 'inner city' is still no more than a spatial or geographic referent. Once an urban centre has been defined then the urban districts which make up the city can be mapped or visualised in ever wider circles around it. In relation to the centre, any part of the city is then more or less close in or far out; and the <u>inner</u> city is simply that part of town which falls within the circle designated, usually by urban planners, to mark a significant change of

1

population density, housing stock, business activities, traffic patterns and the like.

But the reason for the rather sudden focus of public and academic enquiry on these areas in the recent past is not so bland. It reflects the fact that they have come to be associated with particular kinds of social and economic failure and with a concentration of urban problems. In ordinary use therefore, the inner city is now defined less by where it is than by the excesses of disadvantage and distress so often found in it. In this perspective any 'inner city' is widely assumed to be the kind of area in which no one with any options would choose to live. The assumption implies not only that inner city areas are uniformly non-viable, but also that inner city residents are inevitably worse off than people living, say, in the suburbs of the same town. If they were not they would surely have organised themselves to move to the suburbs too.

The picture is complicated by factors of colour and ethnicity. It is observed in Britain and the USA, indeed in polyglot cities everywhere, that ethnic minorities - although not always the same ethnic minorities - tend to be over represented in inner city areas. Relative to their proportion in any urban population there are said to be too few minority group members in the 'nice' suburbs, too many in the 'blighted' centre. On this basis, and with a little help from the media, the three elements - disadvantage, the inner city and minority ethnic status - have come to be associated together. Hence the popular idea that ethnic minorities (who happen to live in the inner city) are disadvantaged, and that inner city areas (which happen to have sizeable minority group populations) are unpleasant places to live.

Although there is no doubt that both these statements are or have been true in some contexts of place and history, the point to be made is that they cannot properly be applied to all ethnic minorities in all inner city areas at this time.

DIFFERENCE AND DIVERSITY

If the implications of minority status and urban decline had no bearing on practical concerns it would not matter very much how they were defined. But quite the contrary: a good part of current political and social argument rests on assumptions about the differences between people and the uniformity of inner city areas which combine to obscure the realities of urban livelihood. Because the ways in which we classify people and places both reflect and confirm these assumptions, the terms we use and the way we use them do not simply affect our understanding of events, they may actually influence those events to the extent of moving them in directions that no one intended.

It is important therefore to stress that our findings on living in a south London area go against the assumptions of current usage in two respects. The first is that although this book is about an inner city area, it does not tell a bleak tale of deprivation and disadvantage. A striking feature of Battersea is its resilience in the face of economic and social changes that might have pushed some other inner city area into irreversible decline. This resilience goes so much against popular expectations that we have felt it crucial to try to account for it - whether as a rare but lucky accident of history and demography, or as the predictable development of one type of urban industrial structure. The first possibility is fully explored in this book; the other will be pursued by comparison with an industrially different London area, begun in 1982, which is to be reported separately.

The second point to be made is that although this book is about a 'mixed' inner city area it does not find 'race' or ethnic relations to be a central or even a consistently important local issue. We take national/regional/ethnic origin into account throughout, but only as one of a number of characteristics which may, or indeed may not, affect the way people organise themselves and relate to the south London area. In this sense the gloss put on 'ethnic difference' in this book matches the experience of people as participants in ordinary life but does not fit the frames those same people might use as non-participant observers or reporters of current events. In the participant's perspective, ethnic or other origins are, of course, fixed, but the significance of these origins (as of any other human characteristic) varies with context and situation. The real life actor is aware that his relationships with the people around him are many stranded and his classifications of them multi-purpose. The official or observer's perspective, on the other hand, demands only a single purpose classification; and in the popular and popular academic view of inner city life, a mixed inner city population is likely to be classified by its cultural or genetic origins alone.

English social scientists have paid attention to ways in which the English classify people around them - to colour, class, citizenship, competition etc. as markers of social boundary. But given the English epistemology of difference, it is inevitable that they have tended to ignore the flexibility of those boundaries. And since ethnic minorities in the inner city are assumed to be deprived (because they live in a depressed area) and deprivation is, in a welfare state, the government's responsibility, it is also perhaps inevitable that more attention has been paid to 'vertical' relations, between ethnic communities and the majority establishment than to 'horizontal' relations among the people sharing any one residential space.

Certainly we still know very little about the integration of ethnic minorities into ordinary life in London - i.e. in relation to the English majority amongst whom they now live. This means that we do not know how far people of different origins living in the same area have similar goals and expectations at similar life stages, and whether they behave differently in the management of livelihood; nor do we know how or when their non local identities become locally significant.

To balance the picture we have here analysed ethnicity as a resource which individuals can, for some purposes and in some situations, mobilise to their own advantage; which will have no value or relevance to them in other situations; and which will, in still others, in which other objectives and identities are paramount, become a liability to be escaped or denied as far as possible. In effect we have set out to discover what part ethnic origin plays in the total system of resources necessary to the management of livelihood in one inner London area.

THE BUSINESS OF LIVELIHOOD

This effort leads us into a number of commonsense questions. What kinds of people live in the inner city? How do they manage? Who do they know? Who do they depend on? Where do they work? Where do they shop? What do they buy? Who does the household chores and how much time does it take them? If some households manage 'better' than others, what 'better' resources do they have? Does everyone use or even try to use the local environment in the same way? Who defines the community interest? Which forms of official intervention affect it for good and which for ill? In what circumstances does the bond of local loyalty or local identity override the divisions of ethnic, cultural or regional origin? Is every part of any one inner city like every other in these respects?...

Questions of this kind might usefully be asked of any polyethnic urban area, but the answers expressed or implied in this book apply only to a very specific part of London over a relatively short period of its history. Nevertheless it takes a theoretical perspective on the practical business of living in Battersea which could readily be applied in other settings. As much as the details of livelihood vary from one area to

another and one household to another, the necessities
of life are remarkably similar: people everywhere
need food, shelter, companionship and self esteem.
They do not organise them in the same way, either because
they do not all have optimal access to the same resources,
or because they do not evaluate those resources in
the same way. We have therefore set out to define
the resources necessary to a decent livelihood; and
to identify the various styles of resource management
used in a single urban environment.

These issues concern native south Londoners as much
as any incomer. Living in the city is for everyone
a matter of balancing a household economy and getting
on with the neighbours. Not everyone achieves these
objectives in the same way; some do not achieve them
at all. Inner city areas differ in the options they
offer, and inner city residents have different resources
to deploy and different priorities to order them by.
But the general issue is uniform: What makes for viability
in contemporary urban life? In how many ways do ordinary
people manage a livelihood?

NECESSARY RESOURCES

In the conventional economic view livelihood depends
on access to land, labour and capital and on the relations
between them; when it is the realities of ordinary
life rather than the abstractions of an analytic model
that are in focus, land becomes housing, labour becomes
people and services, and capital becomes goods and
money. There is no doubt that these three resources
are necessary to survival - even to survival without
frills - and we have described the distribution and
management of housing, services, consumer goods and
incomes at length in the chapters following.

But these resources are not sufficient to livelihood
even when they are abundantly available. Livelihood
is never 'just' a matter of finding or making shelter,
transacting money and getting food to put on the family
table or to exchange in the market place. It is equally
a matter of the ownership and circulation of information,
the management of skills and relationships, and the
affirmation of personal significance and group identity.
The tasks of meeting obligations, of securing identity
and status and of organising time are as crucial to
livelihood as bread and shelter.

A realistic description of living in the city ought
therefore to take notice of social as well as economic
tasks, and of all the resources necessary to their
performance. But how are necessary resources to be
defined? As soon as the range extends beyond the
narrowest economic bounds it is hard to know where
to stop it: not everyone has the same notion of necessity,

5

and social resources are anyway impossible to quantify.
On these grounds even socially oriented resource surveys
are likely to rule anything that cannot be measured
out of account (see e.g. Townsend 1979: 55, 116).
We have chosen instead to compromise by adding three
(and only three) other resources to the land-labour-
capital trio. They are referred to as time, information
and identity. The role of each is specifically indicated
wherever possible in the body of the book.

In some respects these extra resources are like the
others. If, for example, we want to know when and
how age or household structure or ethnic origin affect
livelihood in the inner city, we can ask when and how
each is relevant to the way people spend time, get
information or identify with their neighbours just
as readily as we can consider its significance to the
getting and keeping of land-labour-capital resources.

In other respects the two sets of three remain distinct.
Land, labour and capital resources are not only material,
they are also structural: their form and scarcity
provide the framework for action by deciding which
options are available in a given setting at a given
time. Together they make up what has been called
the 'objective structure' of livelihood. By contrast,
time, information and identity have more to do with
organisation. It is these resources that decide what
is done with or within the objective structure and
that limit 'the conditions of possibility'. In so
doing they account for who does better within the constraints of a single environment - who finds the opportunities, who solves the problems, who takes best advantage
of the options available (Bourdieu 1977, see also Firth
1951, 1964).

The two kinds of resources are not here ranked against
each other. Our approach requires only that they
be given equal weight in the analysis of livelihood.
But we should note that writers on industrial society
in general have suggested that non-material/organising
resources become more crucial than material/structural
resources as industrialisation proceeds, even that
their prior importance is a defining feature of industrialisation itself. (Apter 1967 and Gellner 1982 have
argued the case for identity and information; Gershuny
1979 for time).

It is also important to notice that the various resources
do not function separately. All the elements of the
resource system are interconnected and the viability
of the whole system is dependent on the appropriate
functioning of all its parts. A proposition originally
formulated by physical scientists also makes the socio-
logical point: the viability of any resource system
is limited by the availability of the least available

resource. For example, plenty of labour or labour incentive but a shortage of the necessary information about job opportunities or the necessary time to go and look for them, and the economic value of the labour or of the willingness to work cannot be realised. The same is true of any of the necessary resources. It accounts for the failure of 'well-off' households to cope with unplanned change or to take up options and opportunities which they themselves regard as desirable. In the particular matter of some new residents' failure to find the house or the job they want, our evidence shows that such 'failure' is better explained by their lack of access to some necessary local resource or resources, i.e. by their non local status, than by local attitudes to their ethnic origin.

BOROUGH, NEIGHBOURHOOD AND HOUSEHOLD

This book reports on a local study. It refers to the local system, local resources, local status, local attitudes, local involvement and local livelihood at various points in the various chapters. But these locally based items and ideas do not belong to a fixed local unit. They may pertain to a context as large as London or as small as one individual's network. The units referred to most importantly throughout the book are, from largest to smallest, the borough, the neighbourhood and the household - specifically: Battersea, the LARA area within Battersea, and the households which make up the LARA area. In each case the larger unit provides a context for the smaller and the smaller illustrates aspects of the larger. Since the perspectives of the study depends on the interrelations between them, it may be useful to indicate how each is defined.

The historical chapters (Chapters 2 and 3) deal specifically with Battersea, even though the official identity of the old Metropolitan Borough was erased with the reorganisation of London's local government in 1965. Battersea (with a population of about 75,000) was then absorbed by the new and much larger London Borough of Wandsworth (with a population of about 250,000) and it no longer appears by name in official census enumerations. Its constituent small areas are not, however, affected. It has therefore been possible to reconstruct the old Battersea boundaries from small area statistics of the 1971 census, and so to complete a time series of census data on the Battersea area which stretches back to 1901 and forward into the present.

The livelihood chapters (Chapters 4, 5, 6 and 7) refer to a particular small neighbourhood in south Battersea. One documents the progress of its housing action, the rest are based on material collected by ethnographic survey in 1978. The neighbourhood then contained approximately 1,300 people in just over 500

7

households.   Our material refers to 1,167 people in
446 households;   the shortfall is made up of those
who could not be contacted or did not want to answer
the survey questionnaire.   Their number is unusually
small for inner city studies - probably reflecting
the fact that we employed neighbourhood residents to
do the neighbourhood interviewing (Appendix A).

The neighbourhood is referred to throughout the book
as 'LARA' or 'the LARA area'.   It covers the Louvaine
Area Residents Association Housing Action Area as defined
by the London Borough of Wandsworth.   The boundaries
of this area do not however match the boundaries of
census enumeration districts (the smallest areas retrie-
vable from census Ward Library/small area statistics).
Seeking the maximum amount of census information over
the longest period we identified the four 1971 census
districts which are wholly contained within the LARA
area and which account for about two thirds of the
total LARA population (Map 1.1).   These make up what
we have called the core area of LARA (Tables 1.1, 1.2).

Whether this selection changes the profile of the
area can be judged by a comparison between the core
area and the total area in the 1974 and 1978 surveys
(Table 1.2).   What it does achieve is the creation
of a body of data on the area covering the period from
1961 which is drawn from the 1961, 1966 and 1971 Census
Small Area Statistics;   the 1974 local authority Housing
Action Survey and our 1978 Neighbourhood Survey.

Households appear in different guises in all the
livelihood chapters.   They are presented as explicit
units only in the chapter on household tasks and the
use of time (Chapter 7).   The chapters dealing with
local involvement and with employment and work (Chapters
5 and 6) describe the ways households manage in various
contexts of livelihood.   As the social context shifts,
so do the boundaries of the household unit: like all
social boundaries they depend on who is defining them,
what they are defined for, and whether they are defined
from inside or outside.

The ordinary dynamic of households in the LARA area
is not within the scope of this book;   it is explored
in case studies in another volume (Wallman 1983).
We have nevertheless tried here to reflect the fact
that the household is a unit of livelihood in process,
not a static material/structural block.   The effort
alone distinguishes this from the official approach.
In all UK census enumerations 'the household' is that
unit of people who live together under one roof and/or
share a common pot of food on the night of the census,
and the head of household is automatically assumed
to be the eldest economically active male person in
that unit.   For official statistical purposes this
snapshot of the nation may well be adequate.   But

in real life it is possible that the number of people
who regularly eat together varies.   What of grandpa
who regularly eats Sunday lunch or the neighbour's
child who regularly comes to tea after school?   And
the number of people who regularly sleep under a given
roof is bound to change as children become adult or
kin buy a second house which they share like the first.
The head of household assumption is equally misleading:
it can only misrepresent single parent households,
collectives and extended families, is quite inappropriate
to the livelihood of households in which women share
or have taken over the breadwinner role from their
husbands or fathers, and takes no account of the fact
that different members of the household are likely
to head it in respect of different resources - as,
for example, when a man handles money or housing matters
and his wife deals with services and information.

These variations cannot be uncovered by answers to
any single question about 'household'.   A survey which
instead asks each household a large number of questions
about several aspects of its livelihood makes for less
tidy definitions and a complex questionnaire (Appendix
B), but it does begin to identify the different styles
of resource management characteristic of the survey
neighbourhood.

THE NEIGHBOURHOOD IN 1978

The 1978 Neighbourhood Survey took place at the end
of a period of great change.   Most inner London areas
suffered a loss of people during the 1960s and 1970s;
LARA also experienced the upheaval of housing action.
Between 1961 and 1978 the core area population fell
by about half (Table 1.1).   Despite these losses however
the area is not at all homogeneous: perhaps the variety
of its housing maintains the original mixture of people
and household types.

The age structure of the area has not been affected
and remains unremarkable (Table 1.2).   The lack of
change in this respect runs contrary to expectation:
in most inner city areas the number of old people increases
proportionately as the population declines.   The stability
of the age ratio in this case may be a product of housing
action which can influence the population structure
through the bureaucratic allocation of housing; certainly
housing action has had an indirect effect by making
the area relatively more attractive to families.

Although many of the 446 households in the LARA area
contain only one or two people, almost two thirds of
the population live in households containing three
or more and the average household size is 2.6 people
(Table 1.3).   Couples and nuclear families make up
over half of all households.   The nuclear family is

the commonest household type, followed closely by single person households. A small proportion of households are collectives, either of unrelated individuals or collateral kin (e.g. brothers, sisters or cousins in the same generation), and there is a handful of extended families. The only other numerically significant type is the single parent family which accounted for 14 per cent of households. In some of these the resident children are themselves adults; only one household in ten is a single parent family with dependent children under the age of sixteen (Table 1.4). Nor has there been any major change in the birthplaces of the population of the LARA area during the 1970s. The New Commonwealth born population has accounted for about a quarter of the total throughout the decade. By 1978 the LARA area was no longer the destination of a recently arrived migrant population. Most of the Caribbean born, who are the largest immigrant category in the area, had by that time been settled for a generation; over half had lived in the UK for twenty years or more.

Although the birthplace data tell us that in-migration from the New Commonwealth has not been numerically important in the 1970s, the proportion of residents of New Commonwealth ethnic origin, largely a non white population, has increased by natural means. In 1978, in addition to the 26 per cent of the LARA area population who were born in the New Commonwealth, a further 15 per cent were people born in Britain with one or both parents born in the New Commonwealth.

The label New Commonwealth ethnic origin appears to take both cultural factors and birthplace into account. In effect it classifies people by skin colour, allowing only the superficial observation that 41 per cent of the LARA population was black or brown and 59 per cent was white in 1978. But colour has no direct effect on ethnicity or on livelihood, and the option of an ethnic identity applies equally to everyone in the population. Thus people of Caribbean and African origin have been distinguished, even the British born are classified by birthplace, and among these a south London ethnic origin category is defined to indicate those who have special ties through long association with the area. It is limited to people born in south London of south London parents (Table 1.5).

Like the household, the ethnic group is a unit in process; but the implications of ignoring the difference between inside and outside views of it are politically more relevant. We have referred to the question of ethnicity several times in earlier paragraphs and can deal with it very briefly here. People of the same ethnic origin do form an ethnic category once an ethnic category has been designated from the outside - i.e. if people are sorted on the basis of their origins without reference to how they behave or feel. The same people do not form a group unless they identify together from the inside, whether for purposes of action or affect. Both category and group, ethnic category and ethnic group can be respectable units of study or ways of defining aggregates of people, but they imply very different things about what is happening on the ground. Throughout this book we have been careful to make that difference plain.

THE FORM OF THE BOOK

The two chapters immediately following this introduction sketch a social and economic portrait of Battersea as a whole: Chapter 2 underlines the special style of its politics and its elected politicians, and describes the waxing and waning of Battersea identity; Chapter 3 expands the background to cover its economic history and demography and brings the survey neighbourhood into focus. The next four chapters deal each with an aspect of livelihood and illustrate combinations of structural/material resources (housing, people and services, goods and money) and organising resources (time, information and identity) which make it feasible.

Each of these six chapters is introduced by a short statement, printed in italics, which indicates what it is about and how it fits into the whole. Their contents are not therefore summarised here, but one point needs to be stressed: Chapters 2 and 3 refer to the whole of Battersea; Chapters 4 to 7 are concerned only with the ethnographic survey neighbourhood.

The last chapter is both conclusion and epilogue. It restates the themes of the book and reports a follow up survey carried out three years after the main survey and completed shortly before the book went to press.

Because the procedures of the neighbourhood survey were unusual and unusually fruitful, they are described in detail in a three part appendix to the volume. Part A which covers the way the survey was done is probably of general interest; Part B, the questionnaire, and Part C, the data processing are specialised.

Tables and maps are listed by title at the front of the book. They are numbered in a separate sequence for each chapter: the tables to this first chapter are 1.1, 1.2, 1.3 etc. Each set appears at the end of the chapter to which it refers so that those readers who are interested in figures know where to find them, and those who are not may pass them by just as readily. An index of names and a bibliography of works cited are given at the back of the book.

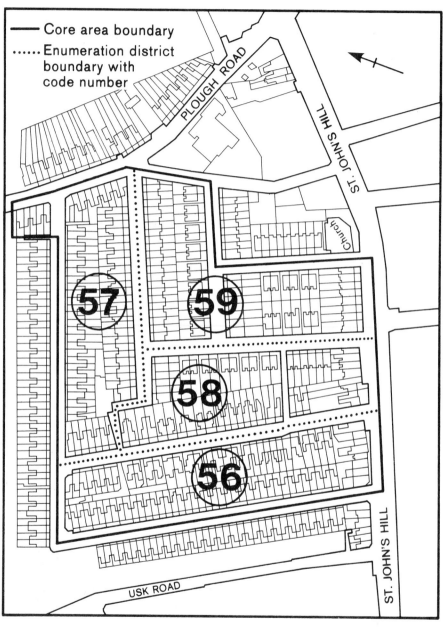

Map 1.1

TABLE 1.1

POPULATION OF THE CORE AREA OF LARA, 1961-1978

	1961	1971	1974	1978
Men	785	654	494	361
Women	807	651	506	392
Total Population	1,592	1,305	1,000	753

Sources: 1961, 1971 Census
1974 Housing Action Survey
1978 Neighbourhood Survey

TABLE 1.2

AGE AND SEX OF THE LARA AREA POPULATION, 1978

Age	Men	Women	All	Core Area only
0-14 yrs	137	128	265 (23%)	182 (24%)
15-59 yrs	357	375	732 (63%)	461 (61%)
60 and over	66	102	168 (14%)	108 (15%)
No info.	-	-	2	2
Totals	560	605	N = 1,167	N = 753

TABLE 1.3

HOUSEHOLD SIZES IN THE WHOLE LARA AREA, 1978

HOUSEHOLD SIZE	NO. OF HOUSEHOLDS	NO. OF PERSONS
1	123	123
2	136	272
3	78	234
4	53	212
5	30	150
6	15	90
7	4	28
8	5	40
9	2	18
	___	___
	446	1,167
	___	___

Average Household Size: 2.6 persons

TABLE 1.4

FAMILY STRUCTURE OF HOUSEHOLDS

IN WHOLE LARA AREA, 1978

	Number	% of all Hh
Single person Hh	123	28
Couples	97	22
Nuclear families	130	29
Single parents alone with children under 16	39	9
Single parents alone with all children over 16	16	4
Extended families including single parents with children	4	1
Other extended families	11	2
Collectives with family links	7	2
Collectives without family links	19	4
	___	
Total (N)	446	
	___	

14

TABLE 1.5

BIRTHPLACES OF WHOLE LARA AREA POPULATION, 1978

UK Born		769 (66%)
S.L.E.O.*	161 (14%)	
N.C.E.O.	179 (15%)	
NC Born		303 (26%)
Africa	101 (9%)	
Asia	44 (4%)	
Caribbean	158 (14%)	
Eire		51 (4%)
Other European		28 (2%)
Other Foreign		6 (-)
No information		10
	N=	1,167

* SLEO: South London Ethnic Origin =
       South London born of south London parents.

  NCEO: New Commonwealth Ethnic Origin =
       UK born of New Commonwealth parent(s).

Chapter Two sets the background for Battersea's distinctive political style with a history of important local personalities and events over the last hundred years. Two aspects are characteristic: the local area is the prime focus of identity and loyalty and there · is a tolerance of political and social minorities such that racist or extremist political movements tend to be ignored or actively rejected.

These traditions are reflected in Battersea's turn-of-the-century reputation as the only place in Britain where anti-imperialist opinions could be voiced; in its refusal to fly the Union Jack over the town hall in 1901 because of local disagreement with national policy abroad; and in its election of a black Pan-Africanist mayor in 1913 and an Indian Communist to parliament in 1926. They did not change when the electorate expanded to include poor men (1918), women (1918, 1928) or immigrants (1950s), and there are echoes of the same traditions in contemporary patterns of livelihood reported in later chapters.

But the extraordinary vitality of Battersea was rooted in its distinctive political culture. Both have been undermined by recent changes in London's administrative boundaries and the shift of political power away from the grassroots towards career politicians and 'faceless' bureaucrats. The last section of the chapter describes the decline of 'Batterseaness' as the loss of a valuable local resource.

2 Political identity in Battersea

BARRY KOSMIN

IDENTITY AND A SENSE OF PLACE

There are all kinds of identity points that people living together can use to give them a sense of place, unity and distinctiveness. Some residential groups or 'villages' use physical or geographical features like Dover's white cliffs, Plymouth's Hoe or in London, Hampstead's Heath or Greenwich's riverside. In other places a particular industry associated with a particular social system can provide a deep sense of identity: in Lancashire there are the cotton mills and in County Durham the coal mines, while parts of London focus around Dockland, or the Shoreditch furniture industry. A social institution such as a football team can serve the same purpose - Tottenham and West Ham without their clubs would be unthinkable. In other areas it is a certain class or social climate which provides the character: Londoners all know what to expect on a number of key social indicators when Chelsea, Surbiton or the East End are mentioned.

What then of Battersea? What is its focus of identity and source of 'self image'? It has no dominating landmark or famous football club, and has never based 'Batterseaness' on Battersea Park and its now defunct funfair (which was built after World War II), nor the enormous Power Station, or the Dogs' Home. For many its identifying feature has been instead its political tradition. Battersea was famous for its radical leftist politics and its assertive working class and labour movements. 'Republican Battersea', which refused to fly the Union Jack for 6 years or pay the 1902 Coronation expenses, which elected a republican working man to Parliament in the 1890s and an Asian Communist in the 1920s, and which had a black mayor in 1914, is surely unique in a country noted for its traditional approach to politics, its political moderation and its distrust of change, whether in the shape of new ideas or the presence of newcomers and outsiders. Battersea incorporates and excludes ideas and individuals in its own way and demonstrates an independence of thought and a sharp political awareness throughout its political development.

The uniqueness of Battersea was recorded in 1924 by a contemporary journalist on the patriotic British Week. His aim was to investigate why 'the Parsee revolutionary' Shirapurji Saklatvala should have defeated 'his Constitutionalist opponent', an English gentleman, in a straight fight during a sweeping Conservative General Election victory nationally. He wrote that 'districts outwardly much alike may differ profoundly in their mental atmosphere; and the psychology of a Borough that sent the only Communist to Parliament... should certainly be interesting'. He discovered that Battersea had 'a feeling for the underdog...an instinct to repudiate authority and commonly accepted standards... It is predisposed to support anyone who prefixes his creed with "anti". It backs the minority, whether wise or otherwise' (11.xii.24). In 1902, following the Borough Council's opposition to the South African War and the Coronation expenses, the Daily Chronicle reached a similar conclusion proclaiming: 'It is a case of Battersea against the British Empire' (22.v.02).

This chapter is devopted firstly to recording the political dimension which composes 'Batterseaness' by examining its politics over the last century in terms of politicians, elections and political campaigns. Secondly, it looks at the way in which the electoral process and enfranchisement can provide insights into local, social and economic developments, and into levels of morale, efficacy, or 'affect' among several generations of Battersea residents.

LOCAL POLITICIANS

Battersea has been described as 'a place where the Left Wing took root, and flourished exceedingly' (Williams 1975: 105). Its early leader was Thomas Atkinson, an apprentice to George Stephenson, who organised one of the first successful modern style industrial actions at the Battersea engineering works of the London, Chatham and Dover Railway Company in 1874. But it was undoubtedly John Burns who set the tone and tenor of 'Battersea-ness' for nearly forty years. Burns was born in South Lambeth in 1858, the 16th child of his parents, and went to live in Lavender Hill as a boy. According to his latest biographer 'his political views were forged in the mean streets of Battersea which were his playground, and by what he had himself undergone in the struggle to support his widowed mother' (Brown 1977: 193). These streets were close to the Shaftesbury Estate described by Charles Booth in 1891 as the area where 'the intelligent portion of the Socialism of the district is to be found, and the colony represents perhaps the high water mark of the life of the intellectual London artisan' (Booth 1902: 294).

Burns' experiences and lifestyle not only largely explain his attitudes but also have some similarity with the life of many Battersea young people over a century later. Burns left school early because of his family's poverty and took a number of short term jobs, including spells as a page boy in Hampstead and at a bakery in Lavender Hill. At the age of 12 he began work at Price's Candle Works, and two years later he moved to Wilson's in Wandsworth as a rivetter. On Sundays the lifelong teetotaller and nonsmoker worked in a local pub, the Winstanley Arms, in order to pay for his night school classes and earn enough to become indentured as an apprentice engineer. In 1873 he succeeded and joined Horn's, an engineering firm on the river at Millbank. In his restricted leisure time Burns enjoyed cricket and played football for Wandsworth Clarence Rovers. He ran into trouble with the law at Clapham Common in 1878, was arrested, but acquitted of breaking a ban on public speaking imposed by the Metropolitan Board of Works. One witness to the incident was a local girl, Martha Gale, who worked in his defence. He married her at St. Philip's Church, Battersea in July 1882, following a short period working abroad in West Africa.

Battersea people came to identify with Burns because his background and lifestyle was typical of the area, he was able to build on Battersea's strong sense of particularism and was altogether 'a remarkably appropriate person to be the focus of the desires of working class representation at this time' (Brown 1976: 227), when the newly enfranchised and organised workers began to show an interest in supporting politicians from their own class. Of what then did this working class representation consist? John Burns was one of Battersea's local members on the London County Council (LCC) from 1884 to 1908 and the Member of Parliament from 1892 to 1918. Apart from being the first Labour represen- tative on the LCC, he was also the first working man to become a Cabinet Minister in 1910.

In a predominantly working class constituency Burns was a popular and well known champion of working class interests; he had even served a six week prison sentence for sedition in 1888. He was an active member of the Amalgamated Society of Engineers and Battersea was highly unionised by London standards of the time. He was also a Londoner, with London-wide urban interests. In an interview given to The Star newspaper late in life, Burns stated that he had always dreamt of a 'digni- fied, beautiful London, free from poverty, and uncontrolled by selfish interests' (2.iii.39).

For his committee work on the LCC he spent a whole month in August 1897 inspecting what he described as 'my district - condition of roads, streets, sewers, gullies, and many dustbins'. Such mundane affairs were important to the everyday life of his constituents and his interest was recognised and appreciated. He believed in the local community as the source of political identity and legitimacy and 'his belief was that the municipality rather than the state was the right body to deal with social problems'. The upshot was that Burns organised an essentially local party to fight his LCC and parliamentary elections - a party which also formed the backbone of the Progressive alliance in the Battersea municipal seats. This political organisation was the famous Battersea Labour League. It was born out of Burns' own experiences with Tom Mann in the Docker's Strike and the fratricidal affairs of the Social Democratic Federation. Reared in the secular rationalist climate of London radicalism and a member of the Battersea Secular Society, Burns was highly suspicious of the mystical-cum-nonconformist socialism of the north . His socialism, unlike that of most Fabians and Social Democratic leaders, was a matter of personal experience rather than intellectual conviction , hence it was much closer to that of his constituents and a more genuine expression of their views. Indeed the local people supported him beyond the ballot box. He had been a working engineer right up to his election to the LCC, but he gave up his job to fight the election on the assurance of a local wages fund, funded by local trade unionists and socialists under the title of the Battersea Workmen's Association. The members paid sixpence a month and assisted with money raising activities such as the popular smoking contests. The Labour League arose in 1889 as an extension of the Workmen's Association. It was the party of radicalism and a local focus for all opposition to the ruling class. As Burns declared, 'we have cooperated with teetotallers, Radicals, Liberals, Trade Unionists, costermongers. Everyone with a grievance. This policy has done more for socialism than all the preaching about class war'. (Quotes in this paragraph are from Brown 1977, pp.57, 200, 72, 193 and 53 respectively.)

These diverse political strands were evident at his inaugural platform for the 1892 Parliamentary election. In attendance were the retiring Liberal member, O.V. Morgan, the Fabian, Bernard Shaw, and the Woolwich Labour Councillor, Will Crooks. Telegrams of encouragement were read from the international Socialists Kautsky, Engels and Aveling. Burns declared that 'in things electoral he was a Radical, in things with government, a Republican, in things social and economic, he was a Socialist, but in all things he was for labour night and day' (Kent 1950: 50).

This was too mixed a bag for some intellectual purists of the Left, but it demonstrated the route by which the Labour Party was to become a major political force electorally. Yet it is significant that this openness led to a concern with things beyond Battersea, with London, with the British constitution, and even with developments abroad - an interest which laid the basis of the wider internationalist, working class dimension which was to be a feature of the Battersea political tradition.

Though Burns was undoubtedly the dominant force in Battersea radical circles for more than three decades, he was not the only political focus. There is no doubt that the prime source of local inspiration and education for the left as a whole was the local branch of the Social Democratic Federation (SDF), founded in 1884, although Burns and others were later to reject its ideas. In its early years its membership included, apart from Burns, Tom Mann, the prominent trade unionist and dockers' strike leader, and Mary Grey, who in 1892 founded the first English Socialist Sunday School in Battersea. The legacy of early politicization in the SDF was to prove a strength and weakness for Battersea leftists. Not only did they gain an education in political practicalities from older members such as an elderly Chartist, they also learnt the fractious ways of the leftist sects. Disputes about theoretical and ideological issues led Burns out of the SDF in 1889, but the personal bitterness over this and other disputes remained long enough to cause a three way split in the Progressive Party's ranks as late as 1909. This had devastating effects in the council elections of that year: the right gained control of the Town Hall for the first of only two short periods in Battersea's municipal history and the number of Progressives was reduced from 39 councillors to only two.

Yet in its early days, the Social Democratic Federation, like the Fabians, placed an emphasis on local government affairs and when the local franchise changed in 1894 the leftist elements immediately won control of the Vestry. One SDF inspired outcome was the foundation, in 1898, of one of the earliest direct labour undertakings in the world - the Battersea Vestry Works Department. After the formation of the Metropolitan Borough in 1900, the Edwardian era was to witness Battersea's municipal socialism extended into excellent public baths, libraries, lighting, housing, milk supplies and winter concerts.

An area with Battersea's reputation attracted radically minded people such as the wealthy widow Catherine Despard. In the years after 1890 she graduated from a local antipoverty campaign in conjunction with her work with Mary Grey on the Wandsworth Union Board of Guardians, to socialist agitation and leadership of the Women's Freedom League. In the 1920s she joined the support for Sin Fein, even while her brother Lord French was Viceroy in Ireland, and at the age of 80 she joined the Communist Party.

Despard's political progression is characteristic of anti-imperialist and socialist Battersea in those years, but the mass of the working class probably still held to the more prosaic outlook of John Burns. One man whose career epitomises the working class intellectual and politician's journey from 'SDFer' to stalwart of a respectable Labour Party Government was W. Stephen Sanders. Born in 1871, he had an early life similar to that of Burns. He described himself as being 'brought up in the wilderness of mean streets in which workers in South London live' (Sanders 1927: 17). He joined the SDF in the late 1880s and learned from it 'with much trepidation, how to speak in the open air' at its 'pitch' •at the south gates of Battersea Park. Again, like Burns, he was self educated at Westminster Libraries. Sanders' political education became very cosmopolitan after he left the SDF to join Burn's Labour League in 1890. Despite having rejected Marxism, as a member of the League he was introduced to Frederick Engels by Mark's daughter, Eleanor Marx-Aveling and to other prominent French and German Social Democrats (such as Bebel, Liebknecht and Lafarge) as the League's representative at the 1891 International Socialist Congress in Brussels. Despite this cosmopolitan connection, Sanders kept in close touch with the ordinary, hum drum affairs of Battersea politics. He was Secretary of the Trades Council, of Burn's election committee, and of the Labour League. And it was he who organised the Progressive alliance which dominanted Battersea's municipal politics until 1919.

Whereas the Battersea Parliamentary Constituency could be won by Burns and his Labour League acting alone, Battersea as a local government area was a larger unit which included much of the pre 1918 Clapham Constituency which was a Tory stronghold. In any case before 1948 the municipal franchise was less favourable to working class interests than the parliamentary. In order to win at borough level therefore, it was necessary to bring together an alliance of non Tories composed of Trades Unionists, Socialists, Radicals, Liberals, temperance advocators and cooperators. This expediency was described by some of Burns' more idealistic former comrades as 'John Burns notorious whelk stall', 'a veritable Tammany Hall' (The Battersea Vanguard Dec. 1907).

Because of his passion for committee and organisational work, Sanders was dubbed Burns' 'factotum' and a 'secretarial monopolist' (Thompson 1967: 185). True to this form he became Secretary of the Metropolitan District Council of the Independent Labour Party in 1903 and an LCC Alderman in 1904. By 1907 he was also Chairman of the Union of Ethical Societies and in the same year he became organising Secretary of the Fabian lectures. By 1913 he was General Secretary of the Fabian Society. All this bureaucratic activity led him eventually to fall foul of the vitrolic tongues of Beatrice Webb and Ramsay Macdonald. His reputation in such circles was not helped when he rejected his early pacificism and internationalism and took a commission in the army; Burns on the contrary was the only Cabinet minister to resign on the declaration of war in 1914.

After the Great War Sanders worked in the Administrative Section of the League of Nations International Labour office until his election as MP for Battersea North in 1929. Yet he did not lose touch with local affairs and was very much involved in the local Labour-Communist debate and rivalry of the 1920s. As we shall see it was he, along with John Archer, Battersea's Pan-Africanist mayor, who eventually destroyed the Communist Party's power in Battersea North. By 1930 the self educated Battersea boy was Financial Secretary to the War Office. But he did not follow his former critic, Ramsay Macdonald into the arms of a Tory controlled National Government and instead joined the staff of the severely shaken Labour Party. In 1935 he won back Battersea North for the Labour opposition in a John Burns style campaign which concentrated on London issues such as the cost of the new Waterloo Bridge. Ill health forced his resignation as an MP in 1940 and he died the following year.

The tendency for Battersea Labour Party to select veteran local politicians also worked in the favour of Caroline Ganley. Born in 1879, she was an early member and secretary of the Women's Socialist League in 1907-8 having joined the Social Democratic Party (the successor to the old SDF) in 1906. In 1918 she joined the Labour Party remaining a member of the Battersea Herald League, one of the founding organisations of the Communist Party of Great Britain (CPGB). Though accused by friend and foe alike of being a Communist, she was elected a member of the Labour Party's national executive for the years 1921-3. She was also active in the cooperative movement and a long time member of the Board of the London Cooperative Society, becoming its first woman president in 1942.

Yet it was for her local government work that she was really famous in Battersea. She served as borough councillor for Church Ward and chairman of the Health and Maternity Committee in 1919-25. She went on to represent Battersea in the LCC during 1925-29 and again in 1934-37. It is not surprising that she was adopted

as the Labour and Cooperative parliamentary candidate
for Battersea South in 1945, a seat she won and held
until 1951.   Not content to let this 1951 General
Election defeat end her work for her party or the borough,
the former suffragette and pioneering woman politician
returned to municipal politics in 1953.   She won a
council seat in Stormont Ward which she continued to
represent on behalf of the Labour Party until Battersea's
final demise in 1964, two years before her own.

One Labour Party politician who served Battersea
for many years and in the process gained a knighthood
and a hereditary peerage was F.C.R. Douglas.   He was
born in Canada in 1889 but educated at Glasgow University,
becoming variously a journalist, accountant and solicitor.
Known for his publications on land tenure and taxation
he filled the role of technocrat the local party needed
in the increasingly complex world of local and national
government after the Great War.   He was a member of
Battersea Council from 1919-45, serving it as mayor,
unelected alderman and Labour leader.   In the same
period he was elected to the London County Council
(LCC) becoming chairman of its powerful Finance Committee.
He succeeded Sanders to the Battersea North seat in
1940 but continued on the LCC until 1946 when he was
appointed Governor of Malta and his career changed
direction.   He left Battersea to serve on the Corby
Development Corporation and eventually became Deputy
Speaker of the House of Lords in the early 1960s.

It is clear that many of Battersea's early parliamentary
representatives were deeply immersed in the local political
tradition.   Its continuity was maintained not only
by the likes of Sanders and Ganley, but also by some
purely local politicians whose long careers link the
world of John Burn's Labour movement to that of Wilson,
Callaghan and Foot.   J. F. 'Jimmy' Lane (Senior),
who was elected to the first borough council in 1900
as a Progressive in Park Ward is an obvious example.
He fought eight council elections in Park, Winstanley
and Vicarage Wards, winning the latter for Labour for
the last time in 1953.   His local government career
straddled more than half a century, setting a tradition
of local political involvement continued by his son
J. F. Lane (Junior), who served as a councillor from
1934 until the abolition of Battersea Council in 1964,
except for the years 1945-9.   The Pritchards were
another local family with a long Labour tradition.
D.A.G. Pritchard first won Latchmere Ward for Labour
in 1919 and represented it until 1964 apart from a
break in the years 1937-49.   N.G.M. Pritchard was
elected alongside him for Latchmere in 1928 and again
in 1934.   He served as a councillor for St. John's
Ward during 1937-45.   Pritchard's career extended
into the age of the Greater London Council where he
was elected as a Wandsworth representative in 1964,

1967, and 1970, the year he was knighted for services to local government.

All these careers demonstrate the affection and service which Battersea could elicit from its public spirited citizens. They also show how the deep roots of many Labour movement politicians could, when set in a local network of political activists who shared common experiences and a similar political education, be converted into a valuable political resource. It was a resource which, once created, tended to perpetuate itself through a local political tradition. However, in the careers of Burns, Sanders and Douglas we can see how concern for 'their borough' was weakened and the ties which bound Westminster to Battersea loosened when Labour became a national ruling party with wider national interests and pretensions. This decline in the affective strength of the local political tradition is explored below: first it is necessary to investigate the evolution of its internationalist outlook and its spirit of tolerance towards political and social minorities. These were the crucial elements of Battersea's unique 'broad church' leftist tradition to which these essentially local politicians contributed.

INTERNATIONALISM AND THE SPIRIT OF TOLERANCE

Lack of insularity and a rejection of narrow patriotism were distinguishing features of the Battersea tradition. People were aware of a larger world beyond south London: Burns' experience of foreign travel as a young man was not unique. Although Burns' Labour league was a local organisation on the political as well as the personal level, it had wide international contacts, particularly with French and German socialists. The fact that Sanders was sent to study at Berlin University in the years 1899-1903 with the aid of financial assistance from the Independent Labour Party (ILP) is an indication of the practical nature of the borough's internationalism.

Because Battersea was one of the few places where the working class and the Left had assumed some measure of political control at this time, it became a public relations centre and focus of morale for international causes. Battersea's Council Chamber provided one of the rare means of gaining publicity for opinions which were normally suppressed or scorned by the national press and right wing controlled legislatures. The most important international cause, and the one which made Battersea notorious in jingoist circles at the time, was the 'Boer Cause' during the South African War of 1899-1901. Battersea had a Stop the War Committee during 1900 which organised protest meetings attended by up to 5,000 people in Battersea Park. Apart from Burns and Keir Hardie, the speakers included Afrikaners such as Cronwright-Schreiner, J. X. Merriman and J. W. Saver. They found that Battersea was the only place in Britain where anti-imperialist opinions could be voiced. Thus it was to the Town Hall in Lavender Hill that the Afrikaner delegates went in August 1901 to be greeted by a pro-Boer crowd of 1,400. During this apogee of British imperial feeling and jingoism which produced 'mafficking' type public hysteria in most of London, the South Western Star reported that 'only in Battersea could there be such a meeting...it was demonstrated that Battersea in patriotism as in everything else, is unique' (7.vi.01).

Battersea Council's Progressive majority pursued resolutions condemning the methods of the British authorities and demanding independence for the Boer states. In May 1901 it named a street after the Boer general, Joubert, and its Finance Committee recommended against giving maintenance allowances to families of men serving with the Reservists. Things got to such a pitch that the council even opposed flying the Union Jack over the Town Hall because it had become 'the symbol of grasping commercialism...believing that the true interest of an industrial population lies, not in the display of bunting but in a steadfast adherence to the principles of social and economic freedom' (ibid. 29.vi.01).

A writer on the working class reaction to the Boer War, trying to account 'for the marked absence of a group of jingoists...in the mainly working class suburb', suggested that what Battersea had 'and what most other places lacked was a strong tradition of radicalism' manifested in the 'socialist-trade union-Progressive combination' of the Labour League (Price 1972: 70-1).

This view is borne out by the facts of higher than average voter registration among working people in Battersea and the occupational composition of the council's Progressive majority. In 1906 these councillors included a majority of artisans - a marble polisher, a bricklayer, a foreman platelayer, a harness maker, a tailor, labourers and engineers - with a leaven from the middle classes including a merchant, a civil servant, school masters and gentlemen of private means.

The anti-Boer War agitation led to only minimal decline in political support for the Progressives in the 1900 Borough elections but fierce opposition from the Municipal Alliance and the local and national press. Nor did the issue of republicanism which arose in 1902 lose the Progressives much working class support. On this occasion the council again achieved national notoriety when it refused to send a loyal address to Edward VII on the occasion of his Coronation. The anti-monarchical sentiments expressed by working class councillors were very strong and their constituents appeared, at least, to condone them. The Standard reported that a Public

Address to the King organised for 'loyal citizens' to sign gained response only from middle class commuters 'in the tunnel to the station at Clapham Junction' (24.v.02). Anyway the Battersea electorate as a whole was not much worried by their councillors' actions and opinions: at the 1903 elections the Progressives won over the 'Moderates' by 38 to 16 seats, thereby increasing their majority by one.

Given this background we should not be surprised to find that Battersea's dominant Progressive Party supported Irish nationalism and in return gained the Catholic vote. In 1917 Battersea again opposed the national trend of opinion by its open support of Sinn Fein and the Bolsheviks in Russia. Support for the revolutionaries led to a local 'Hands Off Russia' campaign and Battersea Council resolutions against British intervention on the White Russian side in the Civil War.

Commitment to the anti-imperialist cause was such that, as we shall see later, sentiments and activities hostile to the British Empire associated with a black Pan-Africanist mayor (Archer) or an Indian Communist (Saklatvala), did not appear to affect their local political standing. The latter's involvement in the unique struggle for the soul of the local Labour movement in the inter war years is both complex and intriguing. Moreover, the fact that the personality at the centre of the debate about Communism and its relationship with democratic socialism and trade unionism was an Indian revolutionary underlines the linkage between an internationalist outlook and tolerance of minority groups characteristic of Battersea.

The Great War had a radicalising effect on Battersea as it did in the rest of the world. A new idealism and a determination to change the old order prevailed. Locally, the wartime dislocations of food rationing and higher taxation intensified political debate and eventually split the Progressive alliance permanently in 1916. In 1919 a new Labour Party emerged and won an overwhelming victory at the municipal elections. The new Labour Party was in fact a loose coalition similar to that of the Progressives, except that it was several steps more to the left. The old Liberals had been replaced by Communists and with the introduction of licensing hours during the war the temperance issue had ceased to be relevant and the dissenter influence reduced. The 1919 local election victory following a disappointment in the 1918 'Khaki Election' when the new constituency of Battersea North had been won by R. Morris, a Coalition Liberal and an old friend of John Burns, on a low poll of under 44 per cent. The defeated Labour candidate had been Catherine Despard who had only received a third of the vote.

The severe postwar depression, unemployment and a

local housing crisis were drastically to change this situation and bring the electorate into line with the leftward progression of the leadership of the local labour movement. The outcome was the adoption of the Indian Communist Shirapurji Saklatvala as the united left candidate at the general elections of 1922, 1923 and 1924. Battersea was the only constituency in the country in which revolutionary socialists and reformist or democratic socialists were able to work together in alliance and agree to compromise. It was probably Burn's legacy of political realism as well as the unique structure of the local labour movement which allowed Saklatvala to be adopted and become the only CP member not to have a Labour opponent during these three elections and thus to win two of them over a Liberal-Constitutionalist opponent. The Communist put this point quite clearly:

> What assisted the Labour Candidate most was the very genuineness of his Communist principles; as in a truly proletarian spirit, he got by his side members of all sections of the Labour Movement in Battersea to stand as solid as a rock...The comrades of the I.L.P., the comrades of the Battersea Labour League (a creation of John Burns), the comrades of Trades Unions and Labour Party Wards, and the Irish Rebels stood solid as a rock without one woman or one man in the active Labour ranks making an exception (25.ix.22).

The Battersea compromise formula was to forego the establishment of a Constituency Labour Party and to rely on its traditional method of organisation. Thus Battersea Trades Council became the sponsoring body and pledged itself to the Labour Party constitution. Unlike other CP members, Saklatvala agreed to seek membership of the Parliamentary Labour Party once elected. Only the presence of experienced politicians such as Sanders or John Archer, the Pan-Africanist former mayor and local Labour agent, made such a policy possible. Battersea continued its compromise formula right up to 1926 despite bitter opposition from the national Labour Party which had banned individual membership of Communists in 1925. Powerful northern trades' union interests eventually obtained the disaffiliation of the local Labour Party affiliates in February 1926 because of their loyalty to Saklatvala.

But the transformation of an idealistic movement of international brotherhood into an instrument of Stalin's oppressive Soviet bureaucracy was already evident to some by the mid twenties. Moreover the attitude of the CPGB to the railway strike of 1924 and its stance on the General Strike of May 1926 provided real local grievances to add to the disillusion with Moscow dominanted Communism. Thus in July 1926 the dream of a united left was finally abandoned by men

such as Archer and Sanders who saw that the only hope
for a strong viable democratic labour movement was
to adopt the national Labour Party line and reject
Saklatvala. The result was the formation of North
Battersea Divisional Labour Party with Sanders as the
new prospective Labour candidate and Archer as the
Party secretary and agent.

Saklatvala's communism was not an issue for local
Labour politicians and the working class while it remained
rooted in social and economic realities. Battersea
folk did not care that their council again refused
to fly the Union Jack on the town hall for the seven
years following 1919 and were quite willing to see
the municipal 'tricolour' used instead. Nor were
they particularly concerned when the Tory Morning Post
berated them for lack of national patriotism, or for
Saklatvala's statement that the national flag was a
'symbol of enslaved labour all over the world' (20.x.24).
References to 'Battersea Bolshies' (Evening Standard
19.xi.23) or to Battersea as 'the mecca of communism'
(Daily Telegraph 20.x.24), because its town hall was
the scene of so many far left meetings in fact encouraged
local patriotism and raised morale. It was Saklatvala's
unrealistic and wild rhetoric which eventually grated
against the very practical local tradition of concern
with ordinary people's problems of the moment such
as TB cure, local education and lodging house conditions.
When the Morning Post could quote him saying 'on behalf
of the revolutionary workers, the class conscious workers
and the international workers' that Battersea's Labour
candidates aimed to convert the LCC 'into an instrument
of communist propaganda' he was clearly ignoring these
issues (28.ii.26). Saklatvala also encouraged rowdyism
by the unemployed, much of which was directed against
trades union leaders, in anticipation of the Communist
Party's (CPGB) anti-Labour 'new line' policy of 1928.
This, along with incidents like calling Sanders 'a
murderer' because of his war service, did not help
to retain a significant local following for an independent
CP candidature.

Thus the reason for the rejection of communism by
the majority of the Battersea working class was Saklatvala's abandonment of the local spirit of 1922, and
the CPGB's growing intolerance and cynical manipulation
of people and events in response to Moscow's directives.
Sanders understood this well enough to forecast the
outcome:

> His perpetual attacks on local as well as
> national Labour leaders, have wearied Battersea
> workers and his avowed object of smashing the
> Labour Party is only too obvious. If he has
> any support it will only be from a few disgruntled
> elements. Practically everyone of the local trade
> union branches has promised me support (Daily

Most Battersea workers were aware that their real
enemy lay across the river among Chelsea's rentiers
or among the tight fisted and hard nosed Wandsworth
bourgeoisie who had the majority in the local Board
of Guardians Union. The appeal of Communism declined
from Saklatvala's remarkable triumph in 1924 to its
ignominious performance after World War II; by 1931
working class voters had moved back to support of the
moderate left which was the only real hope against
Toryism. More recent evidence of the contemporary
rejection of revolutionary socialism in Battersea is
the fact that it took three Marxist sects to muster
a total of 181 votes in 1979 (Table 2.1). Of perhaps
equal significance is that no Communist Party candidate
has ever been fielded in Battersea South.

In view of the controversies surrounding Saklatvala
it is significant that no mention has been made of
his ethnic origin. The fact is that neither his Indian
background nor his English wife's adoption of the Parsee
religion aroused anything like the interest they would
have done half a century later. 'Constitutionalist'
opponents of Saklatvala did try to arouse prejudice
during the general election campaigns of the early
twenties but they were unsuccessful. Though these
campaigns reached the pitch of window breaking and
fisticuffs between the rival supporters of left and
right, the Battersea working class remained impervious
to racism. When during an election meeting in 1923
'Captain Godfrey, representing Mr. Hogbin' was reported
saying that 'the electorate have an instinctive preference
for an Englishman' he was shouted down with cries of
'shame'. Saklatvala's achievement was that he won
the 1924 election in a straightforward competition
with his respectable middle class English opponent
in the biggest interwar election turnout, a 73 per
cent poll.

The following report from the Daily Graphic is particularly revealing of the lack of colour prejudice of
ordinary people in Battersea. Its emphasis on the
candidate's exoticism along with allusions to the contemporary cult of the film star Valentino is typical of
the different - and somewhat patronising - view taken
of local Battersea events by the national press:

> The Parsee might be a Svengali or an Indian fakir
> with a knowledge of black magic. He wields a
> magnetic influence over his audiences that verges
> on hypnotism. I met a Battersea charwoman
> yesterday who was almost in tears because she
> lived on the wrong side of her street and couldn't
> vote for Saklatvala. And I saw excited women
> waving his handbills and actually kissing his

portrait printed on them.   Nor is it only hyster-
ical women that he captures, but solid British
workingmen.   A burly taxi driver stood for twenty
minutes at his door arguing, politely but stubbornly
with Colonel H.V. Combs, who had come up from the
country to help his friend Hogbin.   One of the
taxi man's arguments was that he had fought side
by side with Indian regiments, and that their
soldiers   were   as   brave   as   any   white   soldiers.
That the Oriental firm of which Saklatvala is a
departmental manager pays very capitalistic
dividends didn't matter to him - nor apparently to
the rest of his supporters.   It's not a question of
logic (Daily Graphic 29.x.24).

Saklatvala was not the only political figure to benefit
from   Battersea's   traditional   acceptance   of   minority
group members.   It was one of the first London boroughs
to   have   a   significant   number   of   Catholic   councillors.
In   the   Edwardian   era   when   there   were   only   a   dozen   or
so Catholic councillors in all London, Battersea incorporated the 'Irish rebels' into the local labour movement.
In the same period Battersea elected two Catholic mayors:
the   black   Liverpudlian,   John   Archer   became   mayor   in
1913, succeeding another Catholic, T. P. Brogan.

In   many   ways   the   case   of   John   Archer   epitomises   the
tradition.   Not   only   does   his   career   incorporate   the
internationalist   theme   and   the   spirit   of   tolerance
which we have outlined, but he also operated as a quin-
tissential   local   politician.   Born   in   Liverpool   in
1863 to an Irish mother and West Indian father he arrived
in Battersea in 1890 with his black Canadian born wife.
They set up home in Brynmaer Road, off the Albert Bridge
Road, in Park Ward where they were to live for over
forty   years.   Archer   attended   the   first   Pan-African
Conference   which   took   place   in   London   in   1900,   but
locally he first came to prominence as a public speaker
against   spiritualism   and   a   keen   supporter   of   John   Burns
in   the   1905   General   Election.   In   the   November   1906
municipal   elections   he   topped   the   poll   in   Latchmere
Ward   as   the   Progressive   candidate   in   a   three   cornered
fight.   At this time he was reported as being a medical
student.   His   first   term   as   a   councillor   ended   as
it did for nearly all the Progressives in the electoral
annihilation of 1909.

But, by 1909 Archer was deeply involved in local
affairs and had been elected, again at the top of the
poll,   to   the   Wandsworth   Union   Board   of   Guardians.
On the Council Works Committee he was active in securing
a   minimum   wage   for   council   and   Board   of   Guardians'
workers.   Perhaps because of these political commitments
he   finally   gave   up   his   medical   studies   and   opened   a
photographic   studio   in   Battersea   Park   Road.   When
he   returned   to   the   council   on   the   reformation   of   the
Progressive   Party   alliance   in   1912   he   was   senior   enough

31

to join the powerful Finance and Valuation, as well
as the Baths, Committee. In October 1913 he won party
nomination for mayor at the Progressive caucus over
two other nominees.

Until this moment there had been no reference to
Archer's colour or origins in the local press, but
the news of his adoption and the fact that a former
Progressive mayor, Watts, and the opposition Municipal
Reform group were to oppose him again led the national
press to take a major interest in Battersea's affairs.
Archer was besieged in his studio by journalists who,
seizing on the colour issue, concocted an array of
exotic origins for him, some of which fixed on Rangoon,
Burma. Sections of the Tory press took this as an
opportunity to attack the 'lower orders'. The Globe
wrote: 'Battersea does not care what people outside
think says a Progressive ornament of that riverside
district. It keeps on electing Mr John Burns, you
notice' (3.xi.13). Punch was fascinated by the 'coloured
gentleman...Anything would be better than the present
monotonous arrangement by which all our Mayors are
of the same hue' (12.xi.13).

Battersea deeply resented this ridicule. Willis,
the leader of the Council told the Daily Mail: 'We
are united in supporting the election of Mr Archer.
He has proved himself a most capable guardian and councillor and we do not recognise colour prejudice in Battersea,
and Battersea does not care what people outside think'
(3.xi.13). Even local political opponents of Archer
were quick to agree that he was 'quite as entitled
to occupy this position as any "white man". While
I hate his political policy, I cannot allow that to
bias my mind, knowing him for so many years as I do'.
(Letter from J. A. Beaumont to the South Western Star
7.xi.13).

The boundary between insiders and outsiders in Battersea
was such that anyone who genuinely identified with
the area and its people could become fully part of
it. Thus the Battersea reaction was to stress Archer's
23 years of residence and local involvement, and the
fact that he closed his business every Wednesday afternoon
to attend to Board of Guardian affairs. Even the
fiercely anti-Progressive local newspaper, the South
Western Star, rallied to him on the grounds that he
was 'entitled to the distinction which has been marked
out for him. After all, the personality of a Mayor
of Battersea is not a matter of national concern, though
some people think it is' (7.xi.13).

So on November 10th 1913 John Archer was elected
14th Mayor of Battersea by defeating the deputy leader
of Municipal Reform, a West End tailor. His party
support held together despite Fleet Street and other

outside attentions.   As Archer said for the local
working class 'the greatest thing it has done is to
show that it has no racial prejudice and that it recognises
a man for the work he has done' (Wandsworth Borough
News 14.xi.13).   Congratulations poured into Battersea
from Archer's overseas contacts in America, France,
Germany and the West Indies.

Archer's commitment to Pan-Africanist ideals took
him to the Pan-African Congresses in Paris in 1919
and London in 1921.   On the latter occasion he chaired
a session on colonial freedom and introduced to the
delegates his Battersea colleague Saklatvala, who made
a statement of solidarity on behalf of the Indian Nation-
alist Movement.   The popular Archer went on to become
an Alderman, deputy leader of the Labour group on the
council, Labour leader on the Guardians and Labour's
local agent.   His local appointments included management
of St. Joseph's Roman Catholic School, Governor of
Battersea Polytechnic and president of the Nine Elms
Swimming Club.   His humanitarian concern for the daily
life of Battersea folk was merged with his long concern
with employment and health.   He was chairman of the
council's Whitley Staff Committee and a member of the
Unemployment, Health and T.B. Care Committees.   At
the Guardians he was 'always ready to take up requests
for help and get maximum help for the needy (South
Western Star 15.vii.32).

Archer died suddenly in July 1932.   The local labour
activists attended a requiem at his local Roman Catholic
Church and then followed the cortege to Morden where
Labour's Council leader, F.C.R. Douglas, later Lord
Douglas of Barloch, praised his work for Battersea
and his reputation 'as a very ardent worker for the
benefit of the coloured races and particularly of the
Negro races' (ibid).   The Battersea labour movement
did not see anything threatening in Archer's interest
in Pan-Africanism or colonial affairs.   These interests
did nothing to detract from his devotion to the Labour
Party and to the wellbeing of his fellow citizens of
Battersea, and it did nothing to alienate him or them
from each other.

It is a feature of the political traditions of Battersea
that local involvement counts more than colour in local
assessments of political worth.   When in 1945 another
long term black resident was elected for Labour in
Nine Elms Ward his colour created no impact whatsoever.
More generally, Battersea has remained unusually resistent
to the xenophobic and racist appeals of fascism and
the extreme right until the present.

Battersea leftists were in conflict with fascists
long before Mosley and his British Union of Fascist
(BUF) blackshirts came to the fore on the streets of

London in the mid thirties. The fact that people calling themselves 'National Fascists' adopted the Union Jack as their party symbol in the 1920s was one of the reasons given for the council's refusal to raise the flag on the town hall in 1925. As early as 1933 it was reported that 5,000 local people turned out to 'demonstrate' their hostility to all brands of Fascism - Italian, German or English. This is the first of a series of regular meetings in the campaign to build up a united front in North Battersea against Fascism' (Daily Worker 1.vii.33). In February 1934 a 'Grand Communist rally' of 1,200 workers in the town hall saw disturbances 'started by a group of 30 Fascists, who had managed to get into the meeting' (ibid. 13.ii.34).

This early mobilisation against Fascism meant that Mosley made very little impact locally in the 1935-40 period but that Battersea was a prime target of blackshirt hostility. BUF meetings only took place on Clapham Common when there was police protection or, as one Battersea leftist said when arrested, 'public money for Mosley's protection'. It is indicative that each time Communist Party's Peoples' Bookshop in Lavender Hill was raided by blackshirts the culprits were not local people but East End toughs, mainly from Bethnal Green, many with criminal records. On the other hand police protection of a BUF meeting a Comyns Road, Battersea in April 1938 led to a riot and the arrest of a large number of irate locals who had objected to their territory being invaded by blackshirts. The situation can be gauged from the following court evidence:

> P.C. Hannaford said that about 200 people came towards him shouting altogether: 'Kick out Mosley's dirty rats'. He shouted he was a police officer and turned to walk away but he was struck in the neck...Witness again said he was a constable and Winter (the accused) said 'There's no ——— difference. You are still a rat. (Borough News 24.iv.36).

While the Metropolitan Police had a reputation for sympathy towards the BUF, Battersea Council had, as one would expect, a very creditable record for anti-fascism and sympathy for its Jewish citizenry. In 1936 the following was white washed on the walls around Clapham Junction:

> 'All out August 16 for Pogrom' and in a street close by 'Kill the Jews on August 16th'. There was also a Fascist sign of a streak of lightning in a circle surmounted by the letters 'B.U.F.' and 'P.J.', the latter being an abbreviation for 'Perish Judea'.

Local Jewish residents and shopkeepers were naturally concerned by this and, led by a local dentist and community

leader, J. Harrison, a delegation went to the police
the following morning. When the police said they
would 'look into it' he and others approached a Battersea
councillor:

> Together we went to the Town Hall and there saw
> the Assistant Surveyor...I understand that he
> personally attended at the Police Station and
> lodged a complaint, and he said the matter would
> be dealt with by Scotland Yard. At about 4.30 p.m.
> the Council's water-carts etc. were on the spot,
> and completely obliterated the objectionable
> writing. (Board of Deputies of British Jews
> Archives E3/245. J. Harrison to the Secretary
> 13.viii.36).

When a fascist revival occurred in London in the
1970s, the level of support for it in Battersea was
again much lower than in other areas of inner London,
particularly in comparison to the East End and Dockland.
This is remarkable because there was a much higher
proportion of black people in Battersea than in either
Bethnal Green or Bermondsey and the issue of 'immigration'
and 'race', which comprised the main plank in the National
Front's (NF) platform should have been more real in
south London than in these other areas.

The lack of political support for the neo-Nazi NF
was reflected in both local and general elections.
Whereas in the two general elections of 1974 the NF
obtained an average of around 6-8 per cent of the poll
in north and east London and 10 per cent in Hackney
South and Shoreditch, in Battersea the NF was too weak
to put up candidates in both seats simultaneously.
In the February election they fought Battersea South
gaining 2.3 per cent of the poll and in the October
they managed 4.5 per cent in Battersea North. The
latter figure lost the candidate his deposit but was
the high point for local fascism in the seventies;
in the 1979 General Election when both seats were fought
by the NF they only received 2.8 per cent of the vote
in Battersea North and a mere 1.8 per cent in the South
constituency. Although in the quality of local life
the visible and felt deterioration set the conditions
for an extremist political protest, Battersea lacked
the local political tradition that might have given
it substance. The extreme right like the extreme
left was rejected by Battersea voters. Battersea
had developed a spirit of tolerance and an inclusive
boundary system as a part of its unique political culture.
This may confound the liberal pessimists who associate
a cosmopolitan outlook and tolerance of minorities
with high levels of income and education. Despite
the evidence to the contrary from interwar Europe,
it is still popularly assumed that middle class districts
and university enclaves are the home of mutual respect
and toleration, while working class districts are the

normal habitat of 'primordial feelings' like 'racism'.
The London working class is popularly pictured in an
East End 'Alf Garnett' mould made up of royalism, xeno-
phobia, jingoism and general bigotry, and London working
class areas are assumed to be the natural breeding
ground for reaction.   The inference drawn is that
without middle class leadership, working class politics
would quickly degenerate to the level of Mosley's Bethnal
Green in the 1930s or the NF's Hoxton stronghold in
the mid 1970s.

  Xenophobic radical right politics with an extra parliamentary orientation, are an important tradition in
parts of north and east London, but this tradition
has no roots and no appeal in areas like Battersea
which have a different and distinct leftist political
tradition.   Battersea people who are today aware that
at one time 'we elected an Indian MP' also know that
his election had no devastating effects on their way
of life.   Such knowledge is undoubtedly a factor in
removing some of the fear which finds expression in
prejudice.   More fundamentally it would seem that
an internationalist outlook and political and racial
tolerance can be included within the Battersea tradition
because that tradition has such strong local roots.
Local stands on moral principle can be taken even against
the tide of national opinion because the local citizenry
is so secure in its traditional political alignment
that it is not vulnerable to rabble rousers seeking
to exploit the insecurity and fears of the electorate.
In these terms the Battersea electorate has shown itself
to be sophisticated, self possessed and confident of
its local identity for nearly a century.

POLITICAL TERRITORY AND 'BATTERSEANESS'

Since local identity or 'Batterseaness' was very much
linked to a working class and leftist political tradition,
it is not surprising that those who neither regarded
themselves as working class nor subscribed to radical
or leftist politics should hold themselves aloof from
such an identity.   In fact 'Batterseaness' spread
through the borough southwards along with population
movements and residential change.   We can date the
change by a number of social indicators but the most
striking guide is the slow expansion of the political
territory of the Progressive Labour formation in municipal
elections.

  The Battersea population is described elsewhere in
this volume but it is useful to reiterate a number
of points here.   Firstly, population decline began
after 1901, accelerated after 1939 and peaked during
the 1960s.   The relatively stable pre-1939 population
was also homogeneous with regard to origin: from the

1870s to 1951, over 97 per cent of Battersea residents were born in the British Isles; and in 1911 and 1931 respectively, 95 and 96 per cent were born in England. This means that until 1951 Battersea was 3-5 per cent 'more English' than the metropolis as a whole. It also tended to be more local: in both 1911 and 1951 70 per cent of the population was born in London. The foreign born population is a recent addition which grew from 3 per cent in 1951 to 8 per cent in 1961 and 15 per cent in 1971. But it is class rather than national origin which is the major factor in social and political differentiation in Battersea and despite enormous changes in the characteristics of the voting population the basic trends in political behaviour in Battersea have not changed in a century. The continuity of party support on a territorial basis is both unusual and truly impressive.

When Booth described the Battersea population around 1890, one third were in poverty and these were concentrated among the working classes who huddled close to the river and the railway running through Clapham Junction. He found that the south of the borough was 'a superior area by the standards of Battersea as a whole' and that around Wandsworth Common 'servant keepers' existed (Booth 1902: 36). In general occupational terms the area was divided between artisans in the north, city clerks in the centre and middle class businessmen in the south. By 1930 only 8 per cent of Battersea remained in poverty and skilled artisans had begun to move into the residential districts further south where the large houses could be subdivided. In 1911 15 houses in Brussels Road had 15 families residing in them, but by 1939 there were 49 families in the same buildings. This population movement is reflected in the process of allocation whereby formerly staunchly 'anti-Battersea' wards became incorporated into the Battersea political alignment (Map 2.1), and is confirmed by the steady consolidation of the council's Labour majority after 1931 (Table 2.2).

People living in the south of the borough differentiated themselves from those to the north, and social outlook disinclined the population to identify with Battersea. Batterseaness as such grew slowly. Yet the change in outlook and the feeling of being part of Battersea was found to be very strong in the late 1970s, even though by then Battersea no longer existed for any practical purposes.

It was the borough's outlying areas in the south, defining themselves as New Wandsworth, Clapham or Balham, which were the power base of the political right (Map 2.1). But their anti-Battersea and Conservative stance was a respectable suburban tradition although it sometimes engaged in vituperative, anti-socialist polemic. It had nothing to do with fascism either in the 1930s or the 1970s.   Its main concerns were for respectability, patriotism, property prices and lower taxation.   The type of Conservative politician it adopted and elected shows its incorporation into the main stream of 'commuter Conservativism'.   Between 1918 and 1929 the MP for Battersea South was Viscount Curzon (1884-1964), an Eton and Oxford educated career naval officer and the son of the famous Viceroy of India.   Between 1931 and 1945 the MP was H. R. Selley, a privately educated estate developer and president of the Federation of Master Builders.   He was a local JP and LCC member 1925-37, and was eventually knighted.

At the level of municipal politics the Conservative designation was not adopted until after 1946.   The 'moderates' of the years up to 1907 were supported by the fiercely anti-Socialist London Municipal Society founded in 1894, which articulated the rate payer interest.   This grouping then evolved into the Municipal Reform Party which controlled the LCC from 1907 to 1934.   Its close links with Conservativism were shown by the fact that A. S. Benn, the 'MR' (i.e. Municipal Reform) councillor for St. John's Ward 1906-12, was the unsuccessful Conservative Party candidate against Burns in the general elections of 1906 and January 1910.   Moreover, the MR councillors moved out en bloc to become Conservatives in the late 1940s.

The loyalty of the electorate assured a continuity of political personnel on the right as much as the left.   For example, F. A. Abbott represented Broomwood Ward from 1909 to 1949, and its part successor Nightingale Ward from then until 1959;   K.S.D. Baker represented Broomwood from 1928 through to 1959.

The political territory of the right stayed loyal despite the fact that its representatives were almost permanently in a minority on the council.   Bolingbroke and Broomwood Wards were never lost by Moderates or Municipal Reformers before 1945 and even in the Labour landslide of 1945 Broomwood remained conservative. After 1949, when Battersea's nine wards were subdivided into 16, the political territorial divide hardly changed. The Conservatives held onto their traditional southern power base in Thornton, Broomwood and Nightingale Wards from 1949 until 1962.   Furthermore, postwar gentrification in Archer's old neighbourhood just across the river from Chelsea turned Park Ward into a Tory stronghold. The rejection of leftist politics continued in the southern, Balham area, even under the new London Borough of Wandsworth: Nightingale voters have never elected a leftist politician in nearly a century and Broomwood, when it acted out of character and rejected Conservativism in 1962, still kept itself apart from 'Batterseaness' by voting Liberal, not Labour.

The parliamentary constituencies also reflect this north south territorial division and indicate the slow invasion of the south by northern Battersea oriented migrants (Map 2.2). In the Edwardian age it was necessary to moderate political opinions at the local rather than the Westminster level because of the greater preponderance of right wing voters at the municipal level. We can also see that Battersea North constituency during the years 1918-49 was most centred on the working class heartland of the Battersea tradition. This helps explain the adoption and election of Saklatvala. On the other hand South Battersea's slow emergence from a Tory stronghold into a marginal seat in the late 1920s and the maintenance of its marginal character right down to the 1980s is explained by its steady geographical movement southwards into the retreating Tory strongholds along with population movements. Thus, by the 1970s the greater part of Battersea South was no longer really in old Battersea but was centred on Wandsworth proper.

Political traditions on both sides of the territorial divide continued despite enormous changes in the size and structure of the electorate. In 1901 only 26 per cent of the adult population could vote in local elections. Franchise changes meant that 63 per cent of adults were on the local voter's roll in 1921, 69 per cent in 1931, and fully 97 per cent by the 1970s. In real figures for the small LARA area discussed in later chapters there were 407 voters in 1901 and 1,722 by 1931. Despite these increases and the enfranchisement of new categories such as women, lodgers, 18-21 year olds, and new immigrants, the old alignments remained. No new political parties catering for new interest groups emerged on the local scene and, as we have seen, extremist parties were soundly rejected.

A unique example of how the strength of political tradition overlays interests based on age or sex occurred in Battersea in 1929. In that year the so called 'flapper vote' enfranchised women aged 21 to 30 years who had been overlooked by the grant of female suffrage in 1918. In February, before these young women joined the register of electors, the parliamentary constituency of South Battersea had a by-election because the sitting Conservative, Viscount Curzon, succeeded to the title of Earl Howe and joined the House of Lords. Later that year a general election fought by the same parties and candidates on a new roll took place. A comparison of the two results shows the Battersea electorate increased by over 12,000 or 27 per cent, and that women made up 43 per cent of the electorate in the first election and 55 per cent in the second (Table 2.3).

The actual results are revealing because the second contest almost replicates the first. All the changes connected with the enfranchisement of a cohort of thousands

of young women had virtually no impact on the result.
There was a slight swing to the Liberals but the slim
Labour majority remained.   Presumably the political
allegiance of this generation of young women was rooted
in the political traditions of their households on
one or other side of a well-differentiated social and
political boundary.

THE LOSS OF LOCAL IDENTITY AND THE
DECLINE OF POLITICAL AFFECT

Batterseaness had most meaning when the Battersea 'city
state' was a unique and effective political unit.
A local identity flourished in the period before 1930,
and particularly during the Edwardian age, on all three
governmental levels - Westminster, County Hall and
at the Town Hall.   The structural and political factors
already discussed affected it, but the role, or rather
the lack of role, of the Labour Party was also operative.

The London Labour Party (LLP) was formed in 1914.
Until that time the Labour movement in London was a
diverse collection of separate borough movements' of
which one of the strongest was undoubtedly Battersea's
(Rhodes 1972a: 19).   These borough movements were
finally united through the initiative of the London
Trades Council and 1919 saw the first elections fought
by the new LLP.   Herbert Morrison, its Secretary from
1915 in tandem with its Chief Whip, Isaac Hayward,
built up the LLP into a powerful but tightly authoritarian
party, the London County Council.   Its influence on
the local Labour party combined with the bureaucratic
centralism of Transport House at the national level
tended to restrict local initiative and diversity -
especially after 1934 when the LLP gained control
of the LCC, and after 1940 when Labour eyes were focussed
on Westminster.   Labour, particularly in the person
of leaders such as Atlee and Morrison, began to define
itself as a party of power rather than opposition,
of action rather than idealism.

This new attitude led to a shift in its focus from
micro to macro-politics and so to a decline in interest
at the grassroots or borough level.   This decline
was accelerated with the abolition of the local Poor
Law Boards in 1929, when the brunt of class warfare
and class politics moved to the national sphere.
The national parties began to lose interest in and
control over local councils and the once powerful local
loyalties and political cultures to lose their power
to affect crucial political issues.   The general lowering
of morale and lack of local efficacy was reflected
in less enthusiastic voter registration and poor election
turnout in the major urban centres.

When the vote was a hard won right, abstention was

low and political interest high.   In 1901 Battersea
Council had even appointed a Special Registration Officer
to help increase the numbers voting.   During the golden
age of Battersea, 1900-10, voter turnout in the four
general elections of the period reached an average
of 82.8 per cent - 1.2 per cent above the national
average.   This special political enthusiasm was quite
gone by the 1970s.   In the four elections between
1970 and 1979, average turnout in Battersea North was
only 64.7 per cent - 10.3 per cent below the national
norm.   Even in Battersea South, a marginal constituency
where voter interest is usually high, the turnout was
7 per cent below the national average.   This decline
in political involvement among Battersea North citizens
only became apparent in the 1950s: the deviation from
the national norm was only 2.4 per cent in 1951.
In Battersea South the voting decline began later still:
in 1959 turnout was still 0.2 per cent above average.
This national electoral picture was reflected on the
local government scene.   The small local electorate
at the municipal elections of the years 1900-09 averaged
a 45 per cent turnout while the last four elections
for Battersea Council after 1956 averaged only 30 per
cent.

The end of local political traditions after 1945
saw the rise of Labour politicians who saw themselves
as national politicians, important because of who they
knew and how they spoke.   Lacking local backing or
standing they had little to do with their constituencies
or constituents and certainly did not control local
communities.   For a by-election in 1946, Battersea
North adopted such a politician at the behest of Transport
House.   He was elected and remained in this safe seat
at every election down to and including 1979.   He
was Douglas Jay, a Hampstead resident and classic new
style Labour politician.   The very antithesis of a
Burns or even a Sanders, his background in Winchester
and New College, Oxford, was similar to that of his
friend and future party leader, Hugh Gaitskell.   Jay
had been a wartime civil servant and financial journalist
on The Times, Economist and Daily Herald, and was obviously
destined for high office and the inevitable directorship
of a multi-national company, in this case Courtaulds.
His was a career and a life very much divorced from
'the mean streets of South London'.

In his political autobiography, the Battersea which
Jay represented in Parliament for nearly forty years
merits three pages.   It receives a patronising slap
on the back for 'the genuine local community spirit
that prevails in Battersea'.   Jay also counts himself
fortunate in the lack of 'extremists, cranks and theorists'
in his constituency caucus, defining their absence
as political quiescence (Jay 1980: 157-8).   Describing
the working relationship with his local area party

and his formula for gaining 'autonomy on national issues', he writes of the local party's desire for 'support not interference' in its struggles with government departments, and his willingness to act solely as a listener at General Management Committee meetings. Thus his welfare work in Battersea was limited to an occasional 'surgery' and the follow up of letters of complaint from constituents. Only once did Jay become involved in a local issue which affected the ordinary life of large numbers of his constituents and that was when he worked against the planned London inner ringway that threatened to devastate parts of Battersea in 1967-8.

Jay's autobiography reveals that he was less a politician than a public servant; politics was for him a gentlemanly profession, not an arena. We may imagine how Edwardian Battersea folk would have reacted to an elected mandarin so very far removed from their political tradition. As the Maud Committee on local government discovered, these new style representatives create situations in which voter turnout (which is the mark of the strength of local democracy) progressively declines, where 'voters are unaware of the powers and responsibilities of various authorities', and where 72 per cent of London's elected councillors could declare that they considered the public indifferent to local government (Moss and Parker 1967: 82).

In the interests of 'efficiency' and their own careerist ambitions, the same elected mandarins create new maps and levels of local government with larger boroughs, larger counties and, despite Jay's personal opposition, even European communities. On this basis, when London's administrative structure was reorganised in 1964, Battersea was destroyed simply because, with only 106,000 inhabitants, it was considered too small - in spite of the fact that these same politicians advocated sovereign independence and United Nations membership for dependencies with similar sized populations. On the other hand the old Metropolitan Borough of Wandsworth with 347,000 people was considered too large and too awkward in shape for the slick era of London's government. It was impossible to achieve a balance by simply adding part of Wandsworth to Battersea because Wandsworth's municipal buildings were in adjacent territory and the move would have lost Wandsworth the equipment of public administration which was vital for the business of a vast London borough.

In the end the eastern parts of Wandsworth, Clapham and Streatham were placed in the new Lambeth borough, and Battersea was joined with the rest of Wandsworth to make a new and totally artificial unit with no ties or traditions in common and few natural geographic boundaries; Battersea had no more to do with its new partners of Putney or Tooting than with Hammersmith or Dulwich. Nevertheless, the lowering of morale and the sense of loss felt in inner city areas like Battersea apparently came as a surprise to the new ruling elite. Only 'areas that were formerly in the County of London scarcely seem to have been affected by the reforms' - an observation which created some temporary enthusiasm in the suburbs (ibid. p.81).

The growth of the size, functions and remoteness of local government in the second half of the twentieth century is plain. In terms of budget and employment particularly it became big business. Ordinary citizens were increasingly removed from council planners and officials with careerist priorities. Council officials did not live locally and were not known locally, and their offices were unresponsive to local residents' needs and demands. Even when structures such as Housing Action Areas were designated, the problems of a dominant bureaucracy remained, actually causing divisions in some neighbourhoods. In 1975, in the LARA area described later in this book, Wandsworth's housing policy created resentments among neighbours and tensions between elderly white people and black families.

Yet it was the planning blight which the council created which led to the development of a new sense of identity in the neighbourhood. New lines of 'us' and them' were drawn, no longer along class or ethnic boundaries, but between powerless local residents and their almost equally impotent ward councillors, and the faceless but powerful bureaucrats. Popular participation in new forms of political structure became acceptable media for citizen action because local government was no longer responsive to residents' wishes. Now the only people who had political power or affect were people who had connections with the technocratic decision making sphere.

The situation exemplified in LARA meant that ordinary working class people needed the better educated, middle class owner occupiers among them to work with them if they wished to accomplish change. By the 1970s ordinary folk had lost the networks of access and information they had had in a less complex and more caring Edwardian Battersea. Seeking welfare they no longer confronted Archer's face to face approach on Wednesday afternoons but impersonal offices run by socially distant bureaucrats with the aid of complicated forms and procedures. Self help among working people gave way to reliance on the impersonal bureaucracy of the monolithic welfare state.

At the same time the new political boundaries and demographic change meant that suburban, bourgeois interests began to prevail, both in the new Borough of Wandsworth, and in the vast Greater London Council. Burn's solution of municipal socialism gave way to the state socialism which he had forecast would increase the powerlessness of poor people. Their alienation, loss of confidence, and lack of involvement in deciding their own destiny all followed the attrition of Battersea's active political tradition. The survey on 'Living in the City' which forms the contemporary core of this volume shows ordinary working class people to be almost totally divorced from political work and the activities of community and leftist groups. Ironically, it is now an industrial worker who is a member of the Conservative Club and active in politics, while the leftist tradition, which continues through organisations such as community action groups and the anti-Nazi League, is taken over by young newcomers from the provinces lacking local kinship and social ties in the area. The only exception to this pattern is the LARA residents' association, - but even here working class people, both black and white, are under represented at the committee level.

Since the 1930s dualities between the centre and the local community, and between the local party and the central party have arisen. Politics is now run by elites without roots in the periphery, and local governments are independent of their environments. The contrast between this and the Battersea tradition could not be sharper. The two big parties may have welcomed the new political quiescence it brought, but unhappily it has also contributed to social disintegration through a loss of identity at the grassroots. These losses are essential factors in the syndrome of inner city disadvantage because healthy communities need vibrant political traditions. People who care about the quality of life in inner city areas may learn from the Battersea case that local identity has been one of its most valuable social resources.

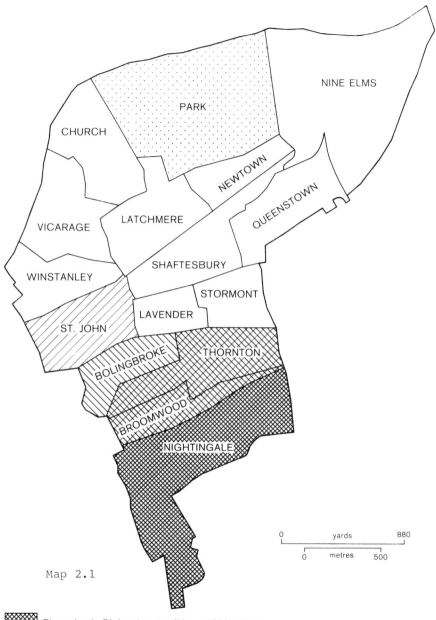

NINE ELMS

PARK

CHURCH

NEWTOWN

VICARAGE

LATCHMERE

QUEENSTOWN

WINSTANLEY

SHAFTESBURY

STORMONT

ST. JOHN

LAVENDER

BOLINGBROKE

THORNTON

BROOMWOOD

NIGHTINGALE

0   yards   880

0   metres   500

Map 2.1

Elected only Right-wing candidates 1900 - 1964

Elected only Right-wing candidates 1900 - 1964 with the exception of 1945

Elected only Right-wing candidates 1900 - 1945

Elected only Right-wing candidates until 1937 with the exception of 1919

Elected only Right-wing candidates 1949 - 1964

45

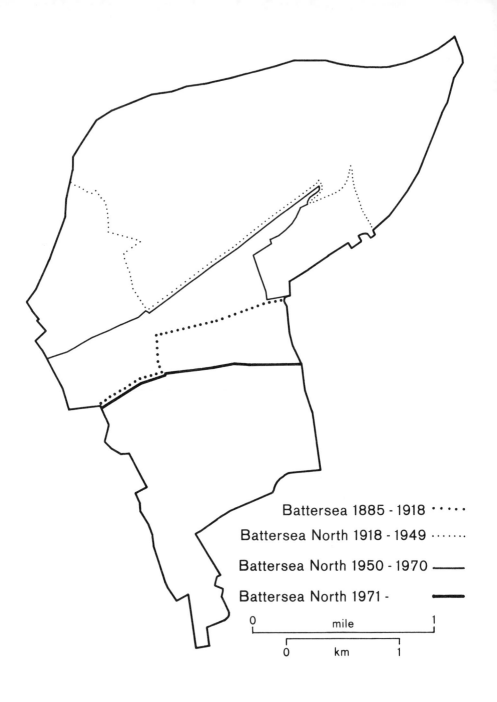

Battersea 1885 - 1918 ·····

Battersea North 1918 - 1949 ·······

Battersea North 1950 - 1970 ——

Battersea North 1971 - ——

0   mile   1

0   km   1

Map 2.2

TABLE 2.1

THE COMMUNIST VOTE IN GENERAL ELECTIONS IN BATTERSEA
NORTH CONSTITUENCY

Year		Votes	Percentage	
1922		11,311	50.5	
1923		12,341	49.6	
1924		15,096	50.9	
1929		6,554	18.6	
1931		3,021	9.0	
1950		655	1.8	
1964		471	2.0	
1966		650	2.3	
1970		179	1.0	
1974	(Feb.)	208	0.7	(CPE)
1974	(Oct.)	102	0.4	(CPE)
1979		181	0.6	

TABLE 2.2

PARTY AFFILIATION OF LOCAL GOVERNMENT COUNCILLORS ELECTED
BY METROPOLITAN BOROUGH OF BATTERSEA

		Left		Right
1900	37	Progressive (P)*	17	Municipal Alliance (MA)
1903	38	P*	16	MA
1906	31	P*	11	Moderates and MR
			12	Conservative Reform
1909	2	P	*52	Municipal Reform (MR)
1912	30	P*	24	MR
1919	41	Labour (L)*	11	MR
	2	Democratic Socialists		
1922	33	L*	21	MR
1925	29	L*	25	MR
1928	33	L*	21	MR
1931	23	L	*31	MR
1934	34	L*	18	MR
1937	37	L*	15	MR
1945	46	L*	6	MR
1949	34	L*	21	Conservative (C)
1953	37	L*	18	C
1956	37	L*	18	C
1959	34	L*	21	C
1962	40	L*	12	C
			3	Liberal

Governing Group *

TABLE 2.3

PARLIAMENTARY ELECTION RESULTS
IN BATTERSEA SOUTH, 1929

Party	By-election	General Election
Labour	45.5%	43.9%
Conservative	43.4%	42.8%
Liberal	11.1%	13.3%
Labour majority	576 votes	418 votes
Electorate	44,786	57,018

NORTH AND SOUTH BATTERSEA MEMBERS OF PARLIAMENT (1885-1979)

Election	Constituency		Party	Name
1885	Battersea		Liberal	O. V. Morgan
1886	"		Liberal	O. V. Morgan
1892	"		Ind. Labour (L/Lab)	J. Burns
1895	"		L/Lab	J. Burns
1900	"		L/Lab	J. Burns
1906	"		L/Lab	Rt. Hon. J. Burns
1910 (J)	"		L/Lab	Rt. Hon. J. Burns
1910 (D)	"		L/Lab	Rt. Hon. J. Burns
1918	Battersea	N	Coalition Liberal	R. Morris
	"	S	Coalition Conservative	Viscount Curzon
1922	"	N	Labour	S. Saklatvala
	"	S	Conservative	Viscount Curzon
1923	"	N	Liberal	H. C. Hogbin
	"	S	Conservative	Viscount Curzon
1924	"	N	Communist	S. Saklatvala
	"	S	Conservative	Viscount Curzon
1929 By	"	S	Labour	W. Bennett
1929	"	N	Labour	W. S. Sanders
	"	S	Labour	W. Bennett
1931	"	N	Conservative	A. Marsden
	"	S	Conservative	H. R. Selley
1935	"	N	Labour	W. S. Sanders
	"	S	Conservative	Sir H. R. Selley
1940 By	"	N	Labour	F.C.R. Douglas
1945	"	N	Labour	F.C.R. Douglas
	"	S	Labour/Co-op	Mrs C.S. Ganley
1946 By	"	N	Labour	D.P.T. Jay
1950	"	N	Labour	D.P.T. Jay
	"	S	Labour	Mrs C.S. Ganley
1951	"	N	Labour	D.P.T. Jay
	"	S	Conservative	E. Partridge
1955	"	N	Labour	D.P.T. Jay
	"	S	Conservative	E. Partridge
1959	"	N	Labour	Rt. Hon. D.P.T. Jay
	"	S	Conservative	E. Partridge
1964	"	N	Labour	Rt. Hon. D.P.T. Jay
	"	S	Labour	E. G. Perry
1966	"	N	Labour	Rt. Hon. D.P.T. Jay
	"	S	Labour	E. G. Perry
1970	"	N	Labour	Rt. Hon. D.P.T. Jay
	"	S	Labour	E. G. Perry
1974 (F)	"	N	Labour	Rt. Hon. D.P.T. Jay
	"	S	Labour	E. G. Perry
1974 (O)	"	N	Labour	Rt. Hon. D.P.T. Jay
	"	S	Labour	E. G. Perry
1979	"	N	Labour	Rt. Hon. D.P.T. Jay
	"	S	Labour	A. Dubs

Chapter Three expands the historical context with a profile of economic and social developments in Battersea since 1871, and it introduces the LARA neighbourhood which is the ethnographic focus of the second half of this book. Although LARA's separate identity within south Battersea is a product of organising for housing action in the 1970s, the area was physically complete a hundred years ago and can be traced through historical records, the national census, and the street surveys of Charles Booth (1890-1) and Llewellyn -Smith (1929-30).

These developments underline the differences between north and south Battersea which the previous chapter indicated. They were greatest when LARA (in south Battersea) was constructed. LARA's beginning was also its status high point. In 1871 it was a well-to-do servant keeping district - although never really wealthy by the standards of the time. In 1890 it was still comfortably off, but servent keeping had declined and some of the larger houses were shared by more than one household. By 1930 multi-occupancy was common, the majority of residents were enumerated as 'skilled workers' and the sharp social distinctions between south and north Battersea had begun to fade. Since World War II there was increasingly less formal evidence of social or economic difference between the two halves of the old borough.

Like Battersea as a whole, the LARA area has always been open to outsiders. At the end of the nineteenth century it had a small but varied proportion of foreign born residents, and 'New Commonwealth' immigration in the third quarter of the twentieth has expanded its cosmopolitan element. At no time in its history has the area been homogeneous or narrowly associated with a single migrant group or status category.

3 Development of a neighbourhood

IAN BUCHANAN

THE BATTERSEA CONTEXT

The Battersea neighbourhood which is the focus of the ethnographic survey reported in the second half of this book is called LARA - after the Louvaine Area Residents Association which gave it definition. As a named area it came into being in the early 1970s when local residents organised to resist the compulsory purchase implied in a letter from Wandsworth Council (see Chapter 4). The social identity of the LARA area dates only from this point, but it is readily distinguished as a geographical unit (Wallman 1978). The name LARA refers here to the collection of streets which became the Louvaine Housing Action Area in 1975.

The LARA area has always been an integral part of Battersea and it is treated in that context throughout this chapter. It was completed in the last quarter of the nineteenth century, coinciding with the formation of Battersea Metropolitan Borough and the culmination of population growth in Battersea as a whole. Battersea Metropolitan Borough came into existence along with 28 others when the Administrative County of London was reorganised by an Act of 1899. These political boundaries remained intact until the London Government Act of 1963.

Battersea entered the twentieth century with a stable population, which declined at an accelerating rate after 1921. The Registrar General's population estimate of 142,000 for 1938 represents the low point of interwar decline. It was caused by slum clearance programmes and the extension of outer suburbia; the Second World War accelerated the downward trend. Although peace and safety brought thousands back to the cities after it ended in 1945, the Battersea population tailed off by 1951, still about 18 per cent less than the 1938 estimate. The steady loss resumed through the 1950s and accelerated during the heyday of urban redevelopment in the 1960s. Population decline itself has promoted the current urban malaise (Dennis 1978: 89). The loss of population has been specific - proportionately more of the middle classes and, more recently, skilled workers have tended to leave the city - but has not alleviated pressure on the housing stock because smaller family sizes and earlier marriage have increased the demand for separate units.

The LARA area illustrates these trends. Within its boundaries there is a mixture of dwelling types. Some houses might have been custom built for the twentieth century nuclear family, but the majority are too large for most contemporary families on contemporary incomes because they were constructed as town houses for the servant keeping classes. As properties there was nowhere they could go but downhill.

This contrasts strongly with much of north Battersea where housing was purpose built for the working classes. It was high density, low cost and low status from the outset. There was less scope for social change and the main change has been the decay, destruction and replacement of the original housing stock by high rise developments. In LARA as in much of south Battersea however, time has had only a limited impact on the physical environment but has seen enormous changes in the social structure. Some of the older residents claim to recall households in the area with coaches and coachmen. On the evidence of the 1871 census these tales are extravagant, a transfer of recollections from nearby Wandsworth Common perhaps but they nevertheless suggest the 'golden beginning' of LARA.

The area's residents association in the 1970s was an articulate and polemical group. Its spokespersons made the case that they were a community with clearly defined physical boundaries, suffering from 'housing stress', but with sufficient cohesion to benefit from an attempt to refurbish 'the community' according to the provision of the Housing Action legislation. Members of the residents association described the neighbourhood with justification, as a classic victim of urban decline: 'The area suffered the normal flight of these (the professional and middle) classes to the outer suburbs and throughout the twenties, thirties and early forties a gradual process of decay began...(more-over)... since the fifties our area has been blasted by wave after wave of planning blight. It has been the victim of what seems to many residents as purblind planning, decisions made about the future of the area with no consultation and the legal minimum of notice. It has been this attitude which has produced the worst blight - in peoples minds; the feeling of powerlessness when dealing with authority' (Louvaine Action Plan, para. 2.1).

53

In this self appraisal LARA placed itself at a turning point in the development of the area, which it interpreted as the culmination of years of social change. The purpose of this chapter is to examine the process of change in more detail and to shed light on the emergence of one small, late twentieth century, inner city area.

ORIGINAL LARA

A walk around the LARA area reveals the well defined natural boundaries and a surprising variety of housing. The area lies between the Southern Region main line in the north, Clapham Junction sheds and yards in the east, a main thoroughfare in the south, and the new East Hill and Usk Road redevelopment scheme in the west (Map 3.1). Until recently late Victorian working class terraces (Usk Road) lay to the west; they were always inferior to and easily distinguished from the area which is* now LARA. The houses on the edge of the area are diverse: there are large three and more storied Victorian terraces on the main road, and smaller originally less imposing terraces on Harbut Road and Plough Road. The housing in its interior varies from extremely pleasant villas on St. John's Hill Grove to straight forward terraces on Cologne Road, and more large late Victorian semi-detached and terraced family houses in Brussels, Oberstein and Louvaine Roads. This mixture reflects the piecemeal construction of the area in the second half of the nineteenth century.

The first edition of the Ordinance Survey 25 inch sheet covering the district (see Map 3.2) shows that in 1866, when the area was surveyed, Harbut Road did not exist and Plough Road was the site of a few cottages, not of the buildings which stand today. Both sides of St. John's Hill Grove (then The Grove) were completed as far as the path through to Cologne Road, Louvaine Road was complete and only nine houses remained to be constructed on Oberstein Road. However, only half a dozen houses were built on Cologne Road and none on the east side of Brussels Road. The survey was clearly made during a period of expansion. The rest of Brussels Road was listed in a street directory the following year and when the decennial census was taken in 1871, Oberstein Road was also complete, 22 more houses had been added in Cologne Road and 4 were under construction (Metallurgicon Local Directory 1867: 82-7). At this time the area now covered by Harbut Road was a market garden, but this rural appendage survived for less than a decade: Board of Works Building Notices and Plans for 1880-1 listed five developments totalling 24 houses in Harbut Road. By 1896, the date of the second edition O.S. 25 inch sheet, the area as we know it today was complete.

Dating the area throws up sources which can also be used to establish the social class, household structure and origins of its first population and hence the initial pedigree of the area. For this purpose the 1871 census is an ideal baseline for social change in the area. It is the most recent census open to public scrutiny and cannot be matched in richness of data until the 1974 and 1978 LARA surveys. Indeed in some respects it is richer still because it is not constrained by the present need to preserve confidentiality.

In 1871 there were 158 households in the area and a total population of 819. It had a demographic structure which is unlikely to be found anywhere in twentieth century London. High mortality and high birthrates in combination accounted for the fact that only a small proportion of the population (11 per cent) was aged 50 and over. This skewed age structure was not peculiar to LARA: only 10 per cent of people in Battersea Registration Sub-district (an area similar to the Metropolitan Borough) and 13 per cent of the population of London as a whole was aged over 50 years. At the other end of the scale 44 per cent of LARA, 49 per cent of Battersea and 43 per cent of the London population were under the age of 20.

In 1871 the demographic structure of the area was typical of Battersea and the rest of Victorian London, except in the extent to which women outnumbered men: 58 per cent of its population was female compared to 51 per cent in Battersea and 53 per cent in London. The fact that there were at that time more female residents aged 10-19 and 20-29 than aged 0-9 reflects an unusually large number of domestic servants: there were 125 in the LARA area of whom 122 were female. Excluding these, the sex ratio of the population was the same as for Battersea. Keeping servants was not necessarily a sign of conspicuous wealth. Throughout mid Victorian England it was a major source of employment and the servant employing classes stretched well down the social ladder. LARA certainly was not a wealthy area: 36 per cent of households did not have servants and 49 per cent had only one servant, at a time when the downstairs staff of the really wealthy classes were numerous enough to make up a strict hierarchy. The occupation of most servants in the area was described in the census simply as 'domestic/general servant' or 'nursemaid' - the latter term applying to teenage girls engaged at low cost to lighten the burdens of motherhood. Only the establishment of Reverend Israel Soule, the Baptist Minister, who occupied a house on Plough Lane, had a sizeable complement of servants. He kept a cook, a housemaid, a lady's maid and a footman. In other households with more than one servant, separate positions were indicated, usually housemaid or cook, although Mr Witton of 9 Cologne Road kept a butler

55

in addition to his general servant.

On the evidence of servant keeping in 1871 LARA was a well-to-do area but certainly not a wealthy one, and the pattern of domestic service varied from street to street. Three quarters of all households in Cologne Road, Oberstein Road, Louvaine Road and Brussels Road had one servant or more, so these streets were the most prosperous and respectable part of the area at that time. On the other hand, most of the households in Plough Road and half of households in The Grove and St. John's Hill had no servants at all. In The Grove furthermore it was younger servants whose inexperience would command the lowest wages who predominated: fourteen out of the nineteen servants in The Grove were under 20 compared with less than half in each of the other streets. The overall pattern reflects the physical capacity of the buildings as much as their respectability: the smaller buildings in The Grove had no room for more than one servant. (Harbut Road which contained many of the smallest units least suitable for keeping domestic servants, had not been built at this time.) It was also related to the use to which buildings were put: St. John's Hill was a commercial street and a third of the householders were shopkeepers who tended to emply shop assistants rather than to keep domestic servants.

The social standing of the neighbourhood in 1871 is also shown by the characteristics of heads of household. Over three quarters of them were men and the majority were married. Most women heads of household on the other hand were widowed and half of them lived in two streets, Oberstein Road and Louvaine Road. Indeed, over a third of the households in these two streets were headed by women. Out of a total of nineteen, sixteen lived off private means, two kept lodging houses and the last was a school mistress. In the area as a whole, women heads of household fell into four occupational categories; those not belonging to the three already mentioned were laundresses. Investment was by far the most important source of income for women heading households: three quarters of them returned an occupation consistent with the life of a rentier. Their incomes derived from a variety of sources, ranging through rentals on houses, annuities, incomes from consols and dividends, to less specific terms like 'widow', 'independent' or 'supported by an absent husband' which nevertheless denoted an independent income. It seems that LARA began as the kind of area where a lady with a fixed income might choose to settle (Table 3.1).

In addition to the 25 women rentiers who were heads of household, fourteen men had rentier incomes. Together they account for a quarter of all heads of household and make up the largest 'occupational' category. The men drew their incomes from similar investments to the women, although the more specific terms differed. Indeed, we are indebted to Mr Grosse of 7 Cologne Road for listing his occupation as 'retired greengrocer' because he corrected an inflated impression of the area gained through his neighbour, Mark de Salamas, of 6 Cologne Road, who returned himself as 'a Count'. No doubt the latter was an aristocrat, but one suspects that he may have fallen on comparatively hard times. A more realistic impression of LARA's social status is given by the evidence that after rentiers, the numerically most important occupations of heads of household were shopkeepers (12 per cent) and clerks (11 per cent). Three quarters of the shopkeepers were found in St. John's Hill, mainly living on the premises. Clerks were spread more evenly throughout the area, but five out of the eighteen were found in The Grove. Together with a tailor's foreman, a house carpenter and a labourer, this distribution confirms the impression that The Grove ranked a little lower in the social scale than the streets of larger houses in the area (Table 3.1).

The 1871 census was taken at LARA's highest status point. The census provides no more information specific to LARA until small area statistics were introduced after 1961, but two massive social surveys approximately forty years apart help us span the period very adequately. Around 1890 Charles Booth carried out much of the research for what became The Life and Labour of the People in London (Booth 1902-3) and in 1930 Hubert Llewellyn Smith directed a replication of Booth's work in The New Survey of London Life and Labour (1933-5).

THE BEGINNINGS OF CHANGE

Booth's Life and Labour of the People in London was based on street by street investigations which he reported as general descriptions and classifications of small areas. LARA fell within the area which stretched from the railway in the east (where it passes under the bridge on St. John's Hill) to Alma Road in the west, and was bounded by the railway in the north (behind Harbut Road) and Wandsworth Common in the south. LARA covered about a fifth of the total area. Booth wrote of it that, 'Clerks and others engaged in (the) City form (the) majority. Near Clapham Junction the houses are large and sometimes occupied by two or three families. Nearer Wandsworth houses are smaller, and occupied by one family. Near Wandsworth Common many keep servants.' (Booth, Vol.ii: 44). Since Wandsworth Common lies some way to the south of LARA, it is possible that the instance of households supporting a domestic staff may have decreased between 1871 and 1890. The inference is supported by the fact that the 1870s and

1880s were decades when middle class incomes were precarious and by other entries in the survey notebooks (Booth Papers Group B, B.62).

We should note that Booth's use of terms like 'interviewer' and 'house to house visitation' refer to methods of enquiry somewhat different from those in use today. The Booth surveys were made at two levels - the family and the street. The family level, because it was labour intensive and extremely time consuming, was used only during the early stages of the project (for east London initially, then central London and, significantly, Battersea), but it provides the better source. Although it was a house-to-house investigation, it is unlikely that the householders even knew that it was happening because they were not approached directly. Information was taken out of interviews with School Board Officers - intermediaries who had access to families and could provide basic information on occupation, social class,' family size, housing and other basic elements in their everyday lives. Great care was taken to avoid intruding into peoples privacy or interfering with the operation of the School Boards:

> 'With the insides of the houses and their inmates
> there was no attempt to meddle. To have done
> so would have been an unwarrantable impertinence;
> and, besides, a contravention of our understanding
> with the School Board, who object, very rightly,
> to any abuse of the delicate machinery with which
> they work. Nor, for the same reason, did we ask
> the visitors to obtain information specially for
> us. We dealt solely with that which comes to
> them in a natural way in the discharge of their
> duties.' (Booth, Vol.i: 25).

School Board Officers were nevertheless invaluable informants because their day to day work demanded that they keep in close touch with the population. They had to visit each house in their area and collect details of every family with children of school age. This 'scheduling' began two to three years before the children reached school age and was to be repeated annually. It limited Booth's coverage to families with children attending or about to attend schools which were the responsibility of the School Board so excluded the childless and the elderly as well as those whose children did not attend the prescribed institutions. Two sets of children did not attend state schools: street urchins who did not attend any establishment and children who were privately educated (ibid: pp. 4-5). From what we know about the LARA area in the late nineteenth century, it is safe to assume that only the better off were omitted from the notebooks which cover the area.

Booth classified the population according to eight

social classes and 39 employment categories. The
most significant element in the schedules for LARA
is the absence of anyone in social classes A-D: those
in poverty. Although the schedules pertain to the
least well off the households surveyed were all relatively prosperous and some of them were actually ascribed
to social classes G and H: the highest social classes.
Brussels Road, Louvaine Road and Oberstein Road were
too prosperous to be scheduled at all; their populations
were not differentiated and were ascribed to classes
G/H, G and G respectively. LARA very much appears
as an island surrounded by the railway and Usk Road.
Harbut Road was the least prosperous street but the
contrast between it and the rest of the area was not
as striking as that with Usk Road which ran parallel
with Harbut Road to the west. In this street three
'very poor families' and seventeen 'poor families'
were enumerated (Table 3.2).

Booth's notebooks suggest that servant keeping had
declined since few families were put in social class
H, the main servant owning class (ibid. p.297). Even
in the unscheduled streets it was only in Brussels
Road that there was any suggestion that servants were
common. They were spread wider than this but Booth's
observation on St. John's Hill Grove holds the key:
servants in that street were few and in the keep of
elderly residents.

Change in the character of LARA in the decades after
1871 also involved an increase in the numbers of skilled
workers - in Booth's terms: 'high class labour/the
comfortably off': the proportion of artizans had doubled
by 1890. In the same period professionals and, more
noticeably, rentiers had dwindled. But these changes
are hardly signs of a precipitate social decline:
the evidence for 1890 excludes the wealthiest inhabitants
because they were 'unscheduled' and the expansion of
the area after 1871 extended it to include Harbut Road
which was never intended to be quite the same class
of property as, for example, Brussels Road (Table 3.3).

Although its initial glories were gone, LARA remained
a superior area by the standards of Battersea as a
whole. It had lost some of its higher status residents
when the wealthiest classes moved southward away from
the more central areas, but in 1890 the poorer sections
of the Battersea working class were still confined
to the area closest to the river. The railway line
through Clapham Junction which passed behind Harbut
Road divided poverty or its potential from gentility
or its possibility (ibid. Vol.xiv: 192-4). The long
projecting split of Battersea which ran south of the
railway nearly as far as Tooting shared the advantages
of both Clapham and Wandsworth Commons and was inhabited
chiefly by business men and clerks considerably above

the position of artisans.   LARA formed the northerly
boundary of this district.   But as Booth pointed out,
the area was not typical of Battersea:

> '...on the whole socially, the most characteristic
> part of Battersea is that lying between the railway
> and the river.   Its general aspect is not unfamiliar
> to most travellers, for it is the view seen on the
> north from Clapham Junction - a wilderness of houses
> chiefly of two stories, with church spires, a
> fringe of factory chimneys, and the conspicuous
> masses of the Board Schools rising high above the
> dead level of the roofs' (ibid. p.291).

By the time the New Survey of London Life and Labour
was carried out in 1930, the main social divide had
been pushed out much further from the centre of the
Metropolis and LARA was no longer in a conspicuously
superior part of south London.   At the same time however,
the class structure and its implications had changed
considerably. •   Although it was not possible to replicate
Booth's original analysis in the New Survey, its two
lowest categories, the 'degraded or semi-criminal population' and those living below the poverty line, provide
a point of comparison with Booth.   On this basis,
neither in 1890 nor 1930 was any of the population
of LARA at or below the poverty line, and in Battersea
as a whole the proportion of the population living
in poverty fell from one third in 1890 to 8 per cent
in 1930.   Above the poverty level the match of categories
in the two surveys was very inexact.   In the years
between the two surveys economic growth and demographic
changes had substantially increased the population
which was free from poverty.   In 1890 those above
the poverty line were 'the wealthy', 'the well-to-do'
and 'the comfortably off' while in 1930 they were 'the
middle class and wealthy', 'skilled workers' and the
mass of 'unskilled labourers'.   Not all skilled workers
were 'comfortably off' in 1890 but virtually all the
unskilled would have been below the poverty line at
that date.

On this evidence also, the changes in the social
composition of LARA between 1890 and 1930 did not entail
a decline into poverty.   According to the New Survey
of London poverty maps the population of LARA consisted
mainly of skilled workers and others with similar income.
The same impression is given by the house sample survey,
even though its coverage was limited.   Over Battersea
as a whole all the households in every fiftieth building
were asked questions on the ages of each occupant;
their relationship to the household head;   the birthplace
of adults;   the occupations, place of work, cost of
travel to work and earnings of each employed person;
and of rents paid and accommodation received.   In
the LARA area the sample covered seven addresses, including
48 persons in 15 households.   Details of these 15

households are reproduced in the Appendix to this chapter.

We know that two households refused to answer the
New Survey questionnaire and can calculate that others
were not counted. Electoral registers over the period
1929-31 reveal that there was a fourth household at
13 Brussels Road containing two adults, Alfred and
Agnes Room, presumably man and wife; and at 13 St.
John's Hill Grove there appears to have been at least
one and possibly two extra households: besides the
Jacksons who appear in the New Survey, the electoral
registers list Emma and William Scarff (again probably
man and wife) and Mabel Chadwick. Mabel Chadwick
may have constituted a separate household or been a
member of the Scarff household as a relative or lodger.
The New Survey waste cards (i.e. refusals) provide
one direct connection with contemporary LARA: Mr Wallstab,
the occupant of number 19 Harbut Road, a 40 year old
glass blower, married with a wife two years his junior,
refused to answer the questionnaire in 1930. Contemporary
residents in the area know that his wife Ida, who was
born in Germany outlived him and continued to occupy
19 Harbut Road until her death in the mid 1970s.

Wallstab's occupation was typical of others surveyed
in 1930: the range included a lighterman, a watchman,
an iron erector, a barge builder, two printers, a signalman, a railway fireman, a grocery assistant, a chemist's
assistant, a bus driver, a newsagent, a butcher, a
grocery manager, a clerk and a travelling salesman.
Almost all of the occupations fall within the category
'skilled workers and others of similar grades of income'.
Of the 12 households headed by men in employment, 10
earned between 60 and 75 shillings per week, a range
at or above the median adult male earnings for the
whole of the London House Sample Survey (N.S.O.L. Vol.vi:
70). The two exceptions were Mr Payne of 130 Harbut
Road who was an iron erector in casual employment earning
54 shillings per week and, at the other extreme, Mr
Freakes, a printer earning the exceptional wage of
130 shillings per week. None of these households
was in any obvious financial difficulty. Of the three
remaining households, one was headed by an unemployed
cellarman, and two by old age pensioners. Of these
two, Miss Snowden can have had little difficulty on
her 10 shillings old age pension and 15 shillings retirement pension, but Mr Clary could not have managed on
10 shillings old age pension with a rent of 12 shillings
per week had his wife not supplemented their earnings
by casual employment to the extent of 20 shillings
per week. Londor, the out of work cellarman, must
have had difficulty balancing his budget with weekly
earnings of 24 shillings and a rent of 22 shillings
and sixpence to pay, although he did receive 6 shillings
from a sublet. In this position his sister's income

was crucial to the domestic economy. At 35 shillings a week it would have been sufficient to keep the wolf from the door - always supposing, as the New Survey did, that all earnings entering the household were aggregated into joint income - an assumption no more realistic then than it is now.

The New Survey also illuminates another changing aspect of city life; the type and level of house occupation. In 1871, most of the LARA properties were occupied by only one household, although many of these households had servants; where a building housed more than one household the second was usually a single lodger or boarder. By 1890 there appears to have been a change, because although the Booth notebooks do not specify multiple occupancy, there were 40 'scheduled' addresses in the area at which more than one family with school aged children was returned. Twenty of these were in Harbut and Plough Roads which had not been built in 1871, and of the remainder, 17 were in Cologne Road. Change appears to be concentrated in that street because there was no information on the unscheduled areas (Louvaine, Oberstein and Brussels Roads). It is more significant that there was only one multi-occupancy in the family sized 'villas' of St. John's Hill Grove on which the notebooks were fairly full. Multi-family occupancy had begun in the larger properties which had been deserted by the servant keeping classes. As family sizes declined, it became feasible for more than one family to share a house. Multi-occupancy in this case represents an environmental gain for the new population over the options available in north Battersea. It was far from the bottom of the housing market; LARA was still a distinctly superior area in 1890.

By 1930 the change in the pattern of house occupation was complete. Among the houses surveyed within the area, only number 50 St. John's Hill Grove was occupied by one family, and that family had a single lodger. The other six houses all contained at least two families each. This was the pattern for the whole of Battersea: only 177 of 847 working class families in the Household Sample survey were sole occupiers of a house. Fourteen lived in blocks of flats, 356 lived in houses divided by the landlord and 300 lived in sublets of various kinds (ibid. p.441). Subletting seems to have been an important source of income for many families.

Once established, multi-occupancy continued and continues in LARA. It is the most rational method of utilising large dwelling houses. In the interwar years the middle classes 'fled' to suburban housing and the division of properties into several dwelling units became more and more common.

It may be that mixed housing has contributed to the fact that LARA has never been a blighted area. Certainly it worked in the area's favour in the 1970s. The irony is that some of the most modest houses of the 1870s (St. John's Hill Grove) are an important resource today. They contain a core of owner occupiers who were unwilling to surrender their autonomy to threats of compulsory purchase, and were active instigators in the residents' association.

THE POSTWAR YEARS

A social characteristic of present day Battersea that has not yet been considered historically is its sizeable immigrant population. Although large scale immigration is a postwar phenomenon, Battersea has never been without foreign born residents, and as London has always been the centre of internal migration as well as immigration, the historical dimension still helps put the present in perspective.

At first sight the birthplaces of the LARA population in 1871 do not seem to have been very diverse. Although LARA and indeed Battersea were newly built there was a ready made population for it in the metropolis. Despite Booth's claim that proximity to the Southern Railway's main London junction at Clapham Common attracted migrants to Battersea from the south west, it was not particularly attractive to new arrivals (Booth, Vol.i: 292). In 1871 when LARA was still under construction 12 per cent of the population was born in Battersea or New Wandsworth, 59 per cent in the Metropolitan Counties (Surrey, Kent and Middlesex), and only 4 per cent outside the British Isles. A third of the population was born in non Metropolitan Counties throughout the kingdom.

Although LARA had collected much of its population locally, it was more cosmopolitan than London and Metropolitan Surrey at that time: 2.7 per cent of London's population and 1.4 per cent of Metropolitan Surrey's was born outside the British Isles. A large proportion of the population of London (69 per cent) and Metropolitan Surrey (72 per cent) were born in the Metropolitan Counties.

At a time when the Irish were popularly equated with the lower urban strata it is significant that the proportion of Irish born in the comfortably off LARA area (1.1 per cent) was less than half that in Metropolitan Surrey (2.4 per cent) or London (2.8 per cent).

A closer look at the foreign born population enhances the cosmopolitan impression. Ten of the residents born abroad were foreign subjects or naturalised British subjects.   These were: a Swedish commercial clerk, male aged 29;   a French cook, male aged 38;   an Austrian teacher, female aged 28;   a Prussian tailor's foreman and his wife, aged 40 and 38;   an Italian translator, male aged 41;   the American wife of an American agent (mercantile not espionage), aged 42;   a general servant from Holstein, female aged 23;   and two French domestic servants, with separate employers, and apparently not related to each other, both female, aged 21 and 64. These individuals were distributed throughout the area; there was a foreign subject in every street except Louvaine Road and Plough Lane.

The remainder of the foreign born population were British subjects, probably born while their parents were working abroad.   Although this group can hardly be equated with the national populations of their countries of birth, neither can they comfortably be classified along with the indigenous British.   Their place of birth suggests an experience of other life styles and adds to the cosmopolitan element in the population. Differences in the birthplaces of siblings are interesting in this respect because they provide evidence of their parents' travels.

The household of Mark de Salamas, the Count of No.6 Cologne Road, combines this variety of experience. He was a British subject, born in Greece, married to a woman born in Walington in Somerset.   They had two children: a son, Mark, aged two who was born in London and a daughter, Dora, aged one who was born in France. They also kept a French born servant.   Count de Salamas was a wanderer and London was no more a permanent home to him than it is to many today.   He married an English girl and their first child arrived while they lived in London.   Within a year their second was delivered, this time on French soil, but by the time of the English census, during that child's second year, he and his family were back in south London.

If we consider that everyone in a household containing one or more members born abroad, is likely to have horizons extending beyond Britain, the number of people with cosmopolitan experience extends beyond individuals born abroad to include their relatives and servants and the relatives and servants of anyone who had children born abroad.   By these measures the cosmopolitan element includes the entire de Salamas household on the one hand and all the Siese children on the other.   William Siese, the Prussian born tailor's foreman of number 10 The Grove, married a fellow country woman, Rosalie. They had ten children aged between 13 years and one month all of whom were born in London, the last six in Battersea.

The process of aggregation boosts the cosmopolitan

element at each stage.   Thus, while the foreign born
who were also foreign subjects or naturalised British
subjects accounted for only 1.2 per cent of the total
population of the LARA area their co-residential kin
raise the proportion to 4.4 per cent and other members
of their households to 5.9 per cent.   Only 4.2 per
cent of the population was foreign born but 14 per
cent lived in households containing at least one foreign
born person.   The last figure is the most spectacular,
but the most significant is the 4.4 per cent of the
population who were foreign born non British citizens
or their kin.   This is a relatively large proportion
in an area which did not contain a concentration of
refugees.

These observations cannot be used to define a trend
or to anticipate the future.   There were foreign born
residents and non Londoners in the LARA area in 1871,
but neither category was large.   The position did
not change markedly until the second half of this century:
up to 1951 the proportion of Battersea's population
born in the British Isles never fell below 97 per cent
and the vast majority of those were English.   This
was similar to the proportions of English born in London
as a whole, although Battersea was slightly more 'English'
than the Metropolis at that time.   The proportion
of London born residents in Battersea also varied little:
it was 70 per cent in 1911 and in 1951, and 75 per
cent in 1931.

The proportion of Battersea people born outside the
British Isles began to rise after the Second World
War.   The slight increase shown in 1951 reflects the
fact that the previous census was taken in 1931 before
Nazism displaced large numbers of people and precipitated
Europe into War.   By remaining unconquered Britain
received her share of European refugees.   But by 1961
the British born population had fallen from 97 per
cent to 92 per cent of the whole, and the English born
to 85 per cent;   and in 1971 to 85 per cent and 78
per cent respectively.   These changes were due mainly,
though not entirely, to immigration from the New Commonwealth: New Commonwealth born residents accounted
for 5 per cent of the Battersea population in 1951,
4¾ per cent by 1961, and almost 9½ per cent by 1971.
However, after a temporary decline the 'other foreign
born' population made a similar advance, from 2 per
cent to 5 per cent of the total population between
1961 and 1971.

So in the early 1970s about 15 per cent of Battersea's
population was born outside the British Isles and almost
two thirds of these immigrants were New Commonwealth
born.   But any assumption that this was a homogeneous
non white influx would be misplaced.   The Irish born
alone make up 4 per cent of the total population and
although the vast majority of New Commonwealth immigrants

in Battersea are black rather than brown, a sizeable proportion of the former are African rather than West Indian (over a quarter in 1971). This heterogeneity is missed if immigration is regarded simply in terms of colour.

The LARA area conformed fairly closely to the Battersea pattern in 1961 when 91 per cent of its population was born in the British Isles and 2 per cent in foreign countries. Only the proportion of New Commonwealth born (7 per cent compared with approximately 5 per cent) and the complete absence of Old Commonwealth born put it out of line with the borough. But by 1971 almost a quarter of the LARA area population was born in the New Commonwealth compared with 10 per cent in Battersea, and the British born had declined proportionately to less than two thirds of the total - this at a time when 85 per cent of Battersea residents were British born. The internal balance of the foreign born element in LARA was however, similar to Battersea's: as well as the 24 per cent New Commonwealth born there were 10 per cent other foreign and 4½ per cent Irish born. Like Battersea too, almost all the New Commonwealth born in LARA were African or West Indian, and Africans accounted for just over a third of their combined total.

CONTEMPORARY LARA

By 1961 the trend towards change in the social status of LARA had consolidated so that skilled workers were the main occupational group. By 1971 the social structure of the area corresponded to that of Battersea as a whole except that the small unskilled group was around twice as important (Morrey 1976, Vol. ii: 120). The main change between 1961 and the 1970s was the reduction in 'skilled workers' and 'workers on their own account' but this was no more marked than in Battersea as a whole. Overall, the balance of status groups found in the old Metropolitan Borough is reflected in the LARA area.

The various indicators of change in the social status of the area are not strictly comparable. The trend is clear when information from Booth's notebooks and the New Survey of London House Sample Survey is arranged in categories which match socio-economic groups (SEG's) used in the 1971 Census (Table 3.4), but the comparison is impressionistic. Booth's material is highly selective and the New Survey sample was very small. Perhaps more important, (SEGs are dubious indicators when used retrospectively, because of changes in job content: for example, a clerk in 1890 probably performed more demanding tasks than a clerk in the mid twentieth century. Since many civil servants described themselves as 'clerks' and the term 'managing clerk' was common in 1890, it is likely that many of the tasks then performed by clerks would be 'managerial' today.

It is interesting to look at changes in LARA in the context of Battersea as a whole and in the way Battersea people saw themselves. In the latter years of the nineteenth century when LARA was newly constructed, the population seems not to have identified itself with Battersea although the area lay within Battersea Registration District and what became Battersea Metropolitan Borough. Its dwellings were superior and its people preferred to identify with the more salubrious surroundings of Wandsworth Common. At the end of the 19th century the area to the south of Clapham Junction Station, which included what was to become LARA, was known as 'New Wandsworth' in local directories. Working class north Battersea was little more than a dormitory settlement whose population travelled away to work and for recreation. In 1890 there was only one Music Hall in Battersea and there was still only one in 1930, although by this time the popularity of music halls was waning and the film industry was about to enter its golden years. There were already five cinemas in Battersea (Booth, Vol. i: 294; N.S.O.L., Vol. vi: 440).

The popularity of local entertainment reflects the amount of time people spend near home, but their acceptance of a particular local label is a sounder guide to the area they identify with. On this point it is significant that LARA residents identified with Battersea in 1978 almost a decade and a half after the administrative demise of Battersea, despite the fact that they must have shed the mantle of New Wandsworth before considering themselves Battersea folk. Some inkling of the process was given in a recent article in the local resident's association newsletter (LARA Echo No. 39, Dec. 1978). The author, a Battersea man, worked as an electrician in the district and moved into the area during the last war. He was most surprised, as a local to find that his postal address was New Wandsworth because he had always associated SW11 with Battersea.

It seems likely that 'Batterseaness' came to LARA as the population changed and that it remains a recognisable referent for the population, young and old, because many of them originated north of the Junction. There was no reason why the population should have moved into LARA mainly from the north - i.e. from Battersea - because the area lies in the extreme west of Battersea, within walking distance of Wandsworth. Nevertheless, the vast majority of people not born in LARA had previously lived in other parts of Battersea. In the 1978 survey 60 per cent of all respondents reported living in Battersea before moving to their surveyed address. Of the 40 per cent of all respondents aged 50 or over, 76 per cent had lived in Battersea for 20 years or more and nearly half of these were born in Battersea. Three quarters of them also made their last move within Battersea. The attachment to Battersea is emphasized by the number of people who, when asked where they lived previously or where they were born, responded with the name of a Battersea street as though its location were self-evident. 22 respondents, or 5 per cent of the total, volunteered this kind of information. The fact that a good handful of them were under 35 suggests that local identity is not exclusive to the elderly. Nor is there any reason why it should be the preserve of the indigenous population. Attachment to the shops and amenities of Battersea may come quickly to immigrant groups, particularly when their children are growing up on the local streets. Ethnic variations in the management of livelihood were either not present or not recorded in the past but are important indicators of whether postwar immigration has been a significant influence on the character of LARA over the past century, or whether the newcomers have fallen into already established patterns.

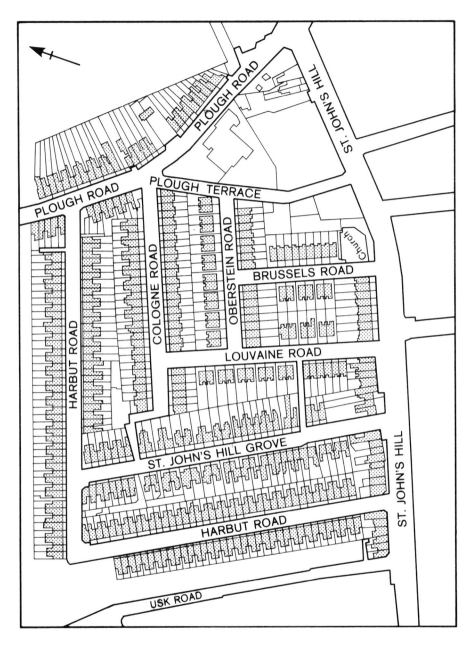

Map 3.1

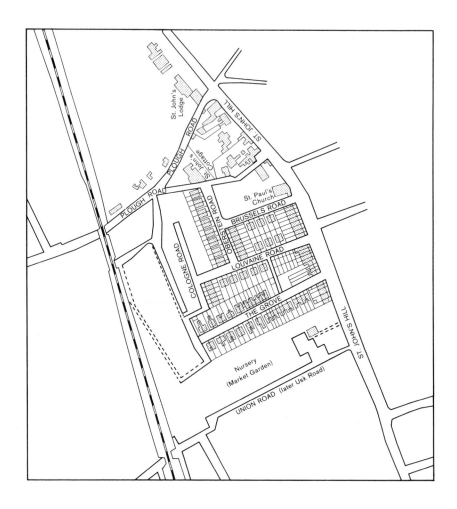

Map 3.2

70

TABLE 3.1

1871 CENSUS ENUMERATORS' DATA: PRESENT LARA AREA
OCCUPATIONS/RANK OF HEADS OF HOUSEHOLD

WOMEN

	Brussels Road	Oberstein Road	Louvaine Road	Cologne Road	The Grove	Plough Lane	St.John's Hill	Total
Rentiers	2	9	4		4		6	25
Lodging Keepers		1	1				2	4
School Teachers		1	1					2
Supported by Absent Husbands			1		1			2
Laundresses						1		1
Shopkeepers							1	1
TOTALS	2	11	7	0	5	1	9	35

MEN

	Brussels Road	Oberstein Road	Louvaine Road	Cologne Road	The Grove	Plough Lane	St.John's Hill	Total
Rentiers	1	3	1	4	1	2	2	14
Clergymen	1	1		1		1	1	5
Solicitors/ Barristers			2				1	3
Bankers		1						1
Manufacturers	3	1		2	1			7
School Masters			1		2			3
Surveyors	1	2			1			4
Accountants					2		1	3
Undertakers	1							1
Literary/Artistic	1				3			4
Agents & Brokers				1	1		2	4
Shopkeepers/ Merchants			1		1	2	13	17
Salesmen/Travellers		2	1	1	3			7
Specd. White Collar		6		1	3			10

TABLE 3.1 (Cont'd)

	Brussels Road	Oberstein Road	Louvaine Road	Cologne Road	The Grove	Plough Lane	St.John's Hill	Total
			MEN					
Clerks	1	3	3	1	5		4	17
Engineers				1	1			2
Builders			1					1
Cooks	1							1
Foremen				1	1			2
Building Artisans, etc.					1		3	4
Policemen						1		1
Cab Drivers/ Proprietors						1	1	2
Nursery Seedsmen							1	1
Skilled Factory Workers							1	1
(Shop) Assistants			2		1		1	4
Misc. Wage Earners						1	2	3
Labourers					1			1
TOTAL	10	19	12	13	28	8	33	123

TABLE 3.2

SOCIAL CLASSIFICATION OF THE 'SCHEDULED' POPULATION OF
THE PRESENT LARA AREA FROM CHARLES BOOTH'S NOTEBOOKS

	A	B	C	D	E	F	G	H
Harbut Road					9	29	1	
St. John's Hill Grove					2	2	4	
Cologne Road						10		
Plough Road					1	10	4	3
St. John's Hill					4	13	10	1
Brussels, Louvaine & Oberstein Roads					Unscheduled			

| Contrast: Usk Rd.,
S. of R'way
i.e. W. of LARA | 0 | 3 | 8 | 9 | 39 | 4 | 1 | |

KEY TO CHARLES BOOTH'S SOCIAL CLASSIFICATIONS

CLASS

A. The lowest class of occasional labourers, loafers and
    semi criminals.

B. Casual earners - very poor.

C. Intermittent earners.   )
) the poor
D. Small regular earners. 18-20s. p.w.)

E. Regular standard earners - above the line of poverty.

F. High class labour.

G. Lower middle class.

H. Upper middle class.) the servant keeping classes

TABLE 3.3

THE OCCUPATION OF MALE HEADS OF HOUSEHOLDS IN LARA IN 1871
AND 1890 ACCORDING TO BOOTH'S EMPLOYMENT CATEGORIES

BOOTH'S CATEGORY	1871	1890
1. Lowest class	0	0
2. Labour uncertain from day to day	0	0
3. Labour irregular from month to month or according to season	0	0
4. Labour, regular employ. Low pay not over 21/- per week	0	0
5. Labour, regular employ. 22/- to 30/-	0	0
6. Labour better class, over 30/- (if in work)	1	0
7. Artizans. Building Trades	4	2
8. Artizans. Furniture, ships etc.	0	5
9. Artizans. Machinery, tools and metals	3	1
10. Artizans. Printing/Watches, etc./Furs, etc./ Sundry manus.	0	10
11. Artizans. Dress	0	1
12. Artizans. Food drinks and stimulants manufacture	1	0
13. Railways	0	3
14. Road passenger conveyance. (Bus, cab and tram service)	2	0
15. Dealer's artizans	4	2
16. Soldiers, police, firemen and subordinate wage earning officials	1	3
17. Seamen	0	0
18. Other wage earners	3	4
19. Home industries/small industries	1	0
20. Small employers, (with less than 10 employees)	1	3
21. Larger employers, (with more than 10 employees)	7	0
22. Street and poorer classes	0	0
23. Small dealers	0	0
24. Shopkeepers and dealers, (without employees).	16	12
25. Shopkeepers and dealers, (with assistants)		
26. Refreshments. Coffee and boarding houses	1	0
27. Refreshments. Licensed houses	0	1
28. Salaried etc. Clerks and agents	38	27
29. Professional. (Subordinate class)	17	5
30. Professional. (Upper)	9	1
31. Ill or no occupation	0	0
32. Independent persons	14	1
TOTALS	123	81

TABLE 3.4

PERCENTAGE DISTRIBUTION OF THE LARA LABOUR FORCE BY SEGs
AT VARIOUS DATES

Socio Economic Groups	1890	1930	1961	1971	1974	1978
Employers and Managers (Groups 1, 2 and 13)	16	6	0	5	11	9
Professional Workers (Groups 3 and 4)	7	0	3	3	3	6
Skilled Workers and Workers on Own Account (Non Professional) (Groups 8, 9, 12 and 14)	27	38	51	30	27	30
Non Manual Workers (Groups 5 and 6)	48	44	17	20	27	28
Personal Service Workers Semi skilled Manual and Agricultural Workers (Groups 7, 10 and 15)	0	6	11	20	17	20
Unskilled Manual Workers, Armed Forces & Inadequately Described Occupations (Groups 11, 16 and 17)	0	6	18	23	16	6
OTHERS	1	-	-	-	-	-

NOTES: 1930, 1961, 1971, 1974 and 1978, Economically Active
Males; 1890 Selected Male Head of Household.

The 1890 data was not part of a structured sample, 1930 was
derived from a 2% sample, and 1961 and 1971 were 10% samples
from the full censuses (and relate to the core area), and
1974 and 1978 were 100% surveys.

75

Appendix to Chapter 3

NEW SURVEY OF LONDON, HOUSE SAMPLE SURVEY (1930)
ENTRIES FOR THE 15 LARA AREA HOUSEHOLDS SURVEYED

Source: British Library of
          Political and Economic Science,
          manuscript collection, N.S.O.L. Survey
          boxes 3 and 4.

93 Harbut Road

Mr Stembridge Aged 30. Born in Islington. A printer at
 St. Luke's Works, Old St. E.C. Earnings: 70/-
 in a 48 hour week, less 1/4d National Insurance
 and 4/- transport cost.

Wife Aged 28. At home. Born in Camberwell. Sons Aged 5 and 7.

Rent 10/- p.w. for 1 bedroom, kitchen and the use of garden.

93 Harbut Road

Mr Miller Aged 40. Born in London. A newsagent at
 Wyman's in Fetter Lane. Earnings: 60/-
 in a 48 hour week, less 1/4d National Insurance
 and 4/- transport cost.

Wife Aged 40. At home. Born in London. Sons Aged 6 and 8.

Rent 10/10d p.w. for 1 bedroom, 1 parlour, kitchen and
 1 small yard.

93 Harbut Road

Mr Patterson Aged 30. Born in Battersea. An LCC driver
 at Chiswick. Earnings: 61/8d in a 48 hour
 week, less 1/4d National Insurance. No
 transport cost.

Wife Aged 31. Born in Battersea. A machinist at
 Ironclad Mantles, Garratt Lane. Earnings: 20/- in
 a 40 hour week, less 1/- National Insurance.

Rent 16/- p.w. for 1 bedroom, parlour, kitchen and scullery.

130 Harbut Road

Mr Payne   Aged 30. Born in London. An iron erector
                in casual employment. Earnings: 54/- in
                a 47 hour week. Weekly transport cost nil.
                No National Insurance deductions.

Wife   Aged 29. At home. Born in London. Sons Aged 2 and 4.

Rent   12/- p.w. for 2 bedrooms, parlour, scullery and use
        of garden.

130 Harbut Road

Mr Chamberlain Aged 54. Born in London. A barge builder
                for General Lighterage in Roote Lane. City.
                Earnings: 70/- in a 48 hour week, less 1/4d
                National Insurance and 2/6d transport cost.

Wife   Aged 53. At home. Born in London.

Son   Aged 22. Born in London. A lighterman for General
        Lighterage. Earnings: 30/- in a 48 hour week, less
        1/4d National Insurance and 2/6d transport cost.

Daughter Aged 17. A typist for Freeman of Lavender Hill.
        Earnings: 17/- in a 44 hour week, less 9d National
        Insurance. No transport cost.

Rent   24/4d for 2 bedrooms, parlour, kitchen and scullery
        + large garden.

        Possibly 12/- from a Lodger)

13 Brussels Road

<u>Mr Clary</u>	Aged 72. Born in Bury St. Edmonds. A retired tailor. Retirement pension of 10/- p.w.
<u>Wife</u>	Aged 38. Born in Staffs. In casual employment. Earnings: 20s in a 24 hour week, less 1/- National Insurance.
<u>Rent</u>	12/- p.w. for 1 bedroom, parlour and use of bath.

13 Brussels Road

<u>Mr Freakes</u>	Aged 52. Born in Guildford, Surrey. A printer at Templer Co. St. John St. Battersea. Earnings: 130/- in a 48 hour week, less 1/4d National Insurance. No transport cost.
<u>Wife</u>	Aged 42. At home. Born in Redcar, Yorks.
<u>Rent</u>	11/- p.w. for 1 bedroom, parlour, scullery and garden.

13 Brussels Road

<u>Mr Back</u>	Aged 32. Born in Exeter. A fireman employed by Southern Railway at Nine Elms. Earnings: 73/- in a 48 hour week, less 1/4d National Insurance and 4/- transport cost.
<u>Wife</u>	Aged 30. At home. Born in Exeter. <u>Son</u> Aged 7.
<u>Rent</u>	15/- p.w. for 1 bedroom, parlour, kitchen.

132 St. John's Hill

Mr Hiscox   Aged 45. Born in Wandsworth. A butcher,
                   employed by Youngman of High St. Peckham.
                   Earnings: 75/- in a 71 hour week, less 1/4d
                   National Insurance and 4/- transport cost.

Wife   Aged 37. At home. Born in Fulham. Daughter Aged 7.

Rent   8/- p.w. for 1 bedroom, parlour, kitchen/scullery
          and use of garden.

132 St. John's Hill

Mr Londor   Aged 56. Born in Hoxton. A cellarman out of
                   work. Earnings: last week 24/-.

Wife   Aged 53. At home. Born in Fulham.

Sister   Aged 39. Born in Fulham. A barmaid, Northcote Hotel,
          Battersea. Earnings: 35/- for 32 hours, less 1/-
          National Insurance. No transport cost.

Rent   22/6d p.w. for 2 bedrooms, parlour, kitchen, scullery
          and use of garden.

132 St. John's Hill

Mr Snowden   Aged 67. Born in Lambeth. OAP. Earned 10/-
(Lodger)   last week. Retirement pension of 15/- p.w.

Rent   6/- for 1 room.
          Pays rent to Londor (downstairs).

13 St. John's Hill Grove

Mr Jackson   Aged 32. Born in Stoke on Trent. A signalman
                        and telegraphman for the Southern Railway at
                        Clapham Junction. Earnings: 60/- in a
                        48 hour week, less 1/4d National Insurance.
                        No transport cost.

Wife   Aged 33. At home. Born in Battersea. Son Aged 2.

Rent   12/- p.w. for 1 bedroom, parlour and kitchen.

50 St. John's Hill Grove

Mr Dobbinson   Aged 52. Born in London. A watchman at a
                        Chemical Works in Carshalton. Earnings: 60/
                        in a 48 hour week, less 1/4d National Insurance
                        and 8/- transport cost.

Wife   Aged 53. Born in London.

Son   Aged 25. Born in London. Works in the Fruit Dept. at
          Lyons, Cadby Hall. Earnings: 60/- in a 48 hour week,
          less 1/4d National Insurance and 3/- transport cost.

Sister   Aged 29. Born in London. A typist for a Travel House
          on Drury Lane. Earnings: 50/- in a 44 hour week,
          less 1/- National Insurance and 4/- transport cost.

Lodger   Aged 28. Born in London. A collector for Liverpool
          Victoria (Ins. Co.) in Finsbury. Earnings: 40/- in a
          40 hour week, less 1/- National Insurance and 3/6d
          transport cost. (Paying 5/- p.w.)

Rent   23/- p.w. for 3 bedrooms, parlour (sleeping),
          kitchen (sleeping), scullery, pantry and bath
          and small garden.

23 Cologne Road

Mr Miller   Aged 55. Born in High Barnet. A grocery
                   manager for Lister & Co., Old Kent Road.
                   Earnings: 68/- in a 48 hour week, less 1/4d
                   National Insurance and 4/6d transport cost.

Wife   Aged 60. At home. Born in Battersea.

Son   Aged 23. Employed by Boots (the Chemist) in Askew Road.
          Earnings: 50/- in a 46 hour week, less 1/4d National
          Insurance and 12/- transport cost.

Son   Aged 19. A clerk for Horniman's in Shepherd's Bush.
          Earnings: 40/- in a 44 hour week, less 1/3d National
          Insurance and 12/- transport cost.

Lodger   Aged 33. Born in Lambeth. Unemployed. Contributes
          20/- weekly.

Lodger's Son   Aged 13.

Rent   28/6d p.w. for 4 bedrooms, parlour (sleeping), kitchen
          scullery, pantry, bath and small garden.

23 Cologne Road (Middle Class)

Mr Manning   Aged 46. Born in South Wales. A traveller,
                   employed by Neatby (draper) of Wandsworth.
                   Earnings: 60/- in a 40 hour week, less 1/4d
                   National Insurance and 4/- transport cost.

Wife   Aged 39. At home. Born in South Wales.

Rent   17/6d for a bed-sit with use of bath.

Chapter Four is the first of the 'livelihood' chapters. It tells the story of the neighbourhood's battle for its housing. It describes the council's plans for the area and the blight caused by the uncertainty of those plans; the residents' fear of losing their neighbourhood to the bulldozer and their determination to have local views taken into account; and it documents the series of events and exchanges which eventually persuaded the Wandsworth Council to declare LARA a Housing Action Area.

Residents' involvement in the housing improvement programme had a series of direct effects on policy decisions concerning the area. These are spelt out in the course of the chapter.

The effect that their involvement has had on LARA's morale is less explicit but just as vital. It provides a nice illustration of the feedback from participation in local affairs to the sense of local identity which is both cause and effect of local involvement. This chapter's description of the waxing and waning of local identity echoes the processes described for Battersea as a whole in Chapter 2. It ends with a summary of the factors which contributed most obviously to the neighbourhood's achievement. Although there can be no single recipe for successful local action, it may be that there are general lessons to be learned from the analysis of one period of participation in one small local area. Certainly the LARA story demonstrates that the most material business of livelihood inevitably depends on other than material resources. Housing action is here shown to be as much a matter of information and identity as of building blocks and government funds.

4 Livelihood I:Housing and housing action
MAI WANN

HOUSING ACTION AREAS

The government white paper 'Better Homes - The Next Priorities' (June 1973) officially acknowledged problems arising from the comprehensive redevelopment of large city areas. This 'redevelopment' which involved massive demolition and left communities disrupted and vast areas derelict and devastated for very long periods of time had already been criticised on social grounds by academics during the 1960s. But their criticisms were apparently given consideration by government officials only when they implied a decrease in expenditure on housing. The heavy financial burden that redevelopment imposed on the state was then weighed against the cost of repairing old houses and providing the basic amenities where lacking. This alternative was found preferable both by a Conservative government eager to cut down public expenditure and by critics of high rise accommodation and community disruption.

The new approach was to accomplish the improvement of houses in areas of concentrated housing problems, particularly those 'areas where very many houses are in bad condition but where nevertheless there is a heavy demand for accommodation' (ibid) - a description which applied to many inner city areas in London and elsewhere. The advantages of the new approach were threefold: firstly, people would continue to live in their familiar surroundings. Secondly, money would be saved by improving existing houses rather than demolishing them and building new estates which rarely housed more people than the houses demolished to make way for them. And thirdly, the government could bring a drastic reduction to expenditure on house building without it being noticeable. The new approach was presented only as a change in emphasis from new development to improvement of the existing stock, not as a reduction in the amount of new housing provided.

Implementing the new approach the government proposed to assist local authorities with their house improvement

programmes by the declaration of Housing Action Areas
(HAAs). These were defined as areas of social stress,
combining bad housing conditions and overcrowding with
a high rate of furnished tenancies, shared accommodation,
elderly people and large families. Local authorities
were to select such areas on the basis of a corporate
approach. Housing conditions were a central criterion
of stress but social conditions, 'in their widest sense'
were also an element in the selection of the special
areas (DoE Circular 14/75).

The declaration of any HAA by any local government
authority committed it to improving its physical stock
and accommodation management over the next five years,
and to look after the well being of residents in the
process. Increased financial assistance towards works
of improvement, repair and conversion and increased
compulsory purchase and improvement powers were made
available by the Housing Act, 1974 to help local authorities achieve the objective of improving accommodation.
Further provisions had to be made to implement the
basic and novel feature of HAAs which was 'the statutory
provision which makes the well being of the people
living in them one of the requirements for, and objects
of, declaration. This means involving people, and
groups, in the scale, nature, and timing of proposed
action programmes'. Because involving the residents
was a requirement of the legislation, each local authority
was advised to publicise its plans to establish a 'presence' in the area in the form of a local office to
accommodate the team which would manage the action
programme, and to set up steering committees to 'ensure
a regular flow of information about progress and problems
that may be encountered' (ibid).

This twofold objective of Housing Action Areas should
be taken into account in assessing the success of any
one of them. Even while housing improvement is being
measured, the extent of residents' participation and
involvement in the process should be added. The legislation itself recognised that social stress could be
relieved only through cooperation between the authority
and the residents, and through the continuous involvement
of the latter in decisions concerning their neighbourhood.

In the case at issue here, this ideological framework
was from the start considered acceptable and desirable
by all those closely involved; it was an explicit
theme in the negotiations of the Louvaine Area Residents
Association (LARA) throughout the Housing Action period.

THE LOUVAINE HOUSING ACTION AREA

The Louvaine Housing Action Area includes Brussels,
Cologne, Harbut, Louvaine and Oberstein Roads, part

of Plough Road and part of St. John's Hill and St. John's Hill Grove. It is bounded by the railways to the north and east, a busy road to the south and what was in early 1974 a demolition site to the west. The area lies entirely within the St. John Ward of the London Borough of Wandsworth. Apart from some derelict shops in Plough Road, a few business premises and a church on St. John's Hill, and a small feather factory in Cologne Road, the area is predominantly made up of streets of terraced houses.

Proposals to demolish the whole or part of this area were never executed. But coupled with a depression in the housing market from the beginning of 1973, even the discussion of them created uncertainty regarding the future of the neighbourhood which led to a number of houses being left empty. An additional number of houses had become derelict due to the decline in the private rented sector. All in all, at the beginning of 1974 the LARA area presented the visitor with a picture of desolation. Out of the 400 residential properties in the area, 53 were totally empty and a further 20 were only partly occupied. Many of the large four storied Victorian houses lacked all or some of the basic amenities and some were overcrowded; and the smaller, two storied terraces in Harbut Road, originally built to house the railway employees when Clapham Junction was developed, had seen little repair or improvement since.

The more attractive and slightly older semi-detached villas in St. John's Hill Grove had in the recent past provided an opportunity for private sector improvement, but the trend towards renewal that was evident in the private sector in the late 1960s declined following the statutory rent freeze, the depression in the housing market and the cancellation of a policy of grants in aid for the improvement and conversion of houses on the grounds that they had been used by developers to increase the value of their properties and hence the profit from sales - a practice considered contrary to the spirit of the legislation. As a result formerly rented houses remained empty and others that would be for sale were kept out of the market as they could not get the asking price.

Potential house buyers were also put off by the uncertainty created by the demolition plans. The Inner London Education Authority had put forward a proposal for the expansion of the Highview School situated on Plough Road. The plan if executed would require the demolition of part of Oberstein Road; the council had already bought a few houses for that purpose. Furthermore there had been a proposal to construct a motorway which would have required the demolition of another part of the area and would have rendered the rest of the land unsuitable for residential use. Although the proposal had been filed away, its possibility still loomed over the area.

But the policies and events which contributed to blighting the area, also helped to develop a vigorous community spirit. This found its expression in the residents' association, LARA which, just one year after its formation, could boast of several important achievements: the association had persuaded the council to declare the neighbourhood a Housing Action Area, had put in a successful application for an urban aid grant to convert St. Paul's Church into a community centre and nursery, had organised a series of 'clean up the area' campaigns and had conducted other social activities involving the majority of the residents.

THE EVENTS THAT LED TO THE CREATION OF LARA

The main events which provoked the creation of LARA took place in the beginning of 1974, when a routine town hall procedure offended some of the residents, reinforced their mistrust of the council and led them to take important steps towards deciding about the future of their neighbourhood.

On 11 February owners of houses in the Louvaine area received a circular letter from the council, requesting them to offer their properties for sale to the council. The letter did not specify why the council was interested in these houses, or what plans it had in mind, but since there had in the past been rumours about the demolition of houses in the area, residents were certain that this was now the council's intention.

On 14 February, referring to the above circular letter, sixty one owners of properties in St. John's Hill Grove and their dependents signed a letter to the chairman of the Housing Committee to say that they were 'unwilling to consider selling...properties to the council'. The same day another letter was written to the chairman of the Housing Committee stating opposition to any council plans for the compulsory purchase of houses in the Louvaine area. This letter was signed by ten tenants who had been long time residents in St. John's Hill Grove.

Not all residents reacted to the council's suggestion, some because they did not own the property they lived in and did not feel concerned, others because they did not think that they, as individuals, could oppose the council. There was also a number of people, both tenants and owner occupiers, who had seen their district deteriorate and wanted to move out and for whom the wholesale demolition of the area implied being rehoused

elsewhere at the council's expense. The initiative
to oppose the council's plans was taken mainly by owner
occupiers who of all categories of resident, were most
eager to stay and improve the environment of their
neighbourhood. Following their precipitated action,
they started a campaign of information and persuasion
in order to gain more residents' support for it.
The proposals and possible alternatives to them were
discussed and, as a result, an increasing number of
residents began seriously to consider opposing the
council. It was fortunate that their opposition came
to a head before the council had prepared any specific
plans for the Louvaine area and it was still possible
for the residents to express their views. LARA was
formed for this purpose and a local newspaper reported
the event:

> 'Home owners and tenants living in properties off
> St. John's Hill, Battersea have formed themselves
> into the Louvaine Area Residents Association to
> resist any attempt by the local authority to
> demolish homes in the area...Compulsory purchase
> rumours, strongly denied by Wandsworth Council,
> loom over Cologne, Louvaine, Brussels, Oberstein
> and Harbut Roads and St. John's Hill Grove'.
> (South Western Star 22.iii.74).

THE EVENTS LEADING UP TO THE DECLARATION
OF THE HOUSING ACTION AREA

Following the letter to the chairman of the Housing
Committee and with the support of more Louvaine residents,
a petition was drawn up opposing the compulsory purchase
and subsequent demolition of homes and other properties
in the area. On 4 April it was presented to the Housing
Committee bearing 300 signatures of residents of the
Louvaine area.

Meanwhile, officers of the council had not been completely idle. On 16 January a memorandum circulated
in the Departments of Housing, Finance, Public Health
and Valuations, asked senior officers to provide information about the Louvaine and Shelwood areas in view
of an urgent meeting to investigate the areas' potential.
The memorandum was entitled 'Louvaine Road and Shelwood
Road Areas', but it was explained that councillors
wanted priority to be given to the Louvaine area.

On 14 March a meeting took place between senior officers,
ward councillors for Louvaine, and one ward councillor
for Shelwood. Officers were instructed to intensify
the purchase of properties by private treaty and to
start rehabilitating the ones already in council ownership.
It was also decided to make compulsory purchase orders
only where qualitative improvements of accommodation
could not be achieved in any other way.

The decision to rehabilitate rather than to demolish was announced by J. Tilley, the St. John Ward councillor, at a public meeting attended by about sixty residents of Louvaine: 'The council had agreed that there would be no widespread demolition in the district, but that poor housing would be rehabilitated' (South London Press 26.iii.74). Representatives from Solon Housing Association were also present at the meeting. One of the architect's speaking on the association's behalf said he could improve the area with a council grant and spoke of the advantages of speed and simplicity that a small organisation had over the council, making it obvious that Solon was very interested in taking on such an area improvement project itself. All in all, keeping and improving the houses in the Louvaine area seemed more than a faint possibility by the end of March 1974. The time was ripe to decide how and by whom this would be achieved.

Reassured by their ward councillors that their homes would not be demolished and encouraged by their own success in achieving participation in the decision making process, members of LARA expressed the wish that the neighbourhood be declared a Housing Action Area. To this end, they did their own research into the housing conditions in the area, compared census figures with the rest of the Borough and built up a case for the declaration of an HAA in Louvaine. At the same time being concerned with improving the looks of their neighbourhood and their immediate environment, they started a 'clean up' campaign, getting the council to provide free skips at strategic points in the area and encouraging people to use them (South London Press 26.iii.74).

Effort was also directed towards gaining the support of St. John Ward councillors: J. Tilley was already convinced of the popularity of the improvement programme, and N. Morgan expressed his special interest in improving the housing conditions in Louvaine. In a letter to a council officer, he suggested that the council should set up a 'shop' to provide 'a comprehensive local service and focal point', and added that he was 'giving up on redevelopment'.

LARA at the same time cooperated with Solon Housing Association so that it could produce an action plan, a proposal for the improvement of the Louvaine area. Its report expressed the view that the comprehensive improvement of both the houses and the environment was the best and quickest solution to the severe problems of the Louvaine area. As this view coincided with the residents' wishes - LARA members had voted in a meeting on 29 April in favour of the improvement of the existing housing stock in their area - and since the council had not yet decided on any comprehensive plans for the area, Solon was invited by LARA to suggest how improvement could take place.

The basic idea was that Solon would acquire houses, then improve or convert them to provide modern dwellings for LARA area residents in need of rehousing. Declaring the area an HAA would reinforce their powers to acquire properties for rehabilitation, and would provide extra finance for the improvement of the environment. Furthermore, the need for public participation would be met by Solon's involvement since it already operated a tenant participation management scheme by which members of LARA would take part in decision making.

The project looked well thought out and feasible: Solon was enthusiastic and its relationship with LARA was good. But Wandsworth's Labour Council was generally unfavourably disposed towards Housing Associations. Political dogma - i.e. support for municipal enterprise on the one hand and mistrust of housing associations for their lack of elected representation on the other - could not allow handing over what would be Wandsworth's first HAA to a housing association, however friendly that particular association might be.

If Solon was to be kept out, the council had only one option: it must itself declare the HAA. So, on 31 March, before the Government's White Paper on HAAs was enacted, the Policy and Resources Committee approved of a report submitted by D. Nicholas, then chairman of the Housing Committee, which recommended: 'a) that, upon the new Housing Bill becoming law, the declaration of HAAs be proceeded with by the council; b) that the Louvaine Road area SW11 (St. John) be selected for declaration as the council's first HAA; and c) that a further report be submitted on the availability of resources to enable the council to achieve these aims'. (Agenda for Housing Committee Meeting, July 1974).

In September 1974, following the summer recess, a survey was organised to provide information about housing stress and the social composition of the area which would be required before the Secretary of State for the Environment could give his official approval of the proposed HAA. On 10 September a meeting took place between council officials and LARA representatives to begin the survey work. Wandsworth's Director of Housing expressed the wish to act in consultation with LARA, recognising the invaluable assistance LARA could provide by keeping the residents informed and securing their cooperation.

Following the survey and the writing of the declaration report, council officials called a meeting in St. Paul's Church to explain the Housing Action Area to the public:

according to the Department of the Environment's guidelines it was their duty to advertise the plan locally and to involve the residents in it. LARA for its part produced posters and did its best to inform residents that the meeting was to take place.

This close cooperation did not actually mean that there was mutual trust between the town hall and LARA. LARA was still, in the eyes of most government officers, a group of activists, similar to squatters and other trouble makers. But it was a group which had to be respected because it was supported by several councillors, and because its right to participate in decisions that concerned the neighbourhood were safeguarded by the Housing Act 1974 and government circulars that followed it. LARA on the other hand still remembered the council's bid to buy their properties without specific plans for them, and was suspicious of council officers' activity in general. It therefore acquired and kept the habit of keeping itself informed and ready to oppose any council plan it felt was not to the benefit of the area and its residents. Caution became in effect one of its most useful weapons during the months ahead. The other was the steering committee - also recommended by government's guidelines - which consisted of ward councillors and elected LARA representatives and which was the main decision making body for the HAA.

The immediate aim of Housing Action was common to both parties however, and cooperation was achieved once each had accepted the existence of the other. In March 1975, a tour of the LARA area by members of the Housing Committee ended in St. Paul's Church where residents had gathered to hear the declaration of the HAA from their councillors. 'We will be making a critical decision here tonight', Councillor Nicholas, chairman of the Housing Committee, is reported to have said, 'this area has had a troubled past and I hope from this time onwards these troubles will be over'. Councillor Tilley made a point of underlining the meeting's special importance: 'This is the first time in 75 years the Housing Committee has met in anything other than a town hall. We will be one of the first in the country to declare an HAA...'. The residents' representative expressed its significance from their point of view: 'These proposals represent the views of the people living in this area. We would like to think that because we live in this area our views matter.' (South Western Star 13.iii.75).

The Louvaine HAA was officially declared by the council meeting on 25 March, three months after the Housing Act came into full effect. LARA, at least on paper, had achieved its first aim.

THE BEGINNINGS OF THE HAA

Many obstacles still had to be overcome before the
achievement could be measured in any tangible way.
At that time, after a year of meetings, reports, and
councillors' promises, the residents' expectations
had risen but very little had been done to meet them.
On the day of declaration, there was no special staff
appointed, no area office designated, no plan of action
written out.   The beginning was not only slow, it
was full of bad surprises for everybody.   These were
mainly due to the chaotic working of the Housing Department: it tended to leap from one crisis to another
and to spend a considerable amount of uncoordinated
energy trying to smooth the effects of each.   They
can also be attributed to other minor but still important
features of town hall bureaucracy, such as interdepart-
mental competition and routine difficulties in the
way of implementing anything new, - features which
led in turn to a submissive acceptance of the status
quo and a general lack of will to break new ground.

In April 1975, a project leader was appointed to
work in the Louvaine HAA under the supervision of the
Housing Improvement Officer.   He was to set up a local
team which would, according to government recommendations,
manage the action programme from a local office.
LARA and the ward councillors wanted the local office
to be manned by officials capable of dealing with the
area's problems: i.e. qualified to give housing advice
and legal assistance in landlord-tenant conflict, to
serve public health notices, to provide building expertise
and meet the need for social work.   These demands
were indeed inspired by the government's recommendations:
'The resources of several local authority departments
- notably housing (including those officers dealing
with rent allowances and rent rebates), finance, environmental health, and social services, but also planning,
roads, education and others - will be needed if an
action programme is to be carried through successfully.
Some authorities have already found it useful to set
up area teams to coordinate and carry through action.
Such teams, involving officers of the various departments
of the housing authority and where necessary, of the
county council or of the other agencies should ideally
be based within the HAA'. (DoE Circular 13/75).

But the town hall structure did not allow the formation
of a multi-disciplinary team and no chief of department
would agree to 'lend' his officers to the housing improvement officer responsible for the HAA.   For senior
officers, most of whom saw the HAA as a new toy acquired
by a small section of the Housing Department, an area
office with one or two friendly officials to register
complaints and pass them on to the relevant departments

was more than sufficient.

In June 1975 the first Steering Committee meeting since the declaration of the HAA showed the effects of strict departmental boundaries and officers' 'empires'. The chief environmental health officer, who had been asked to provide the area office with one of his inspectors, announced that he had no intention of allowing any of his 'boys' to work in another department, and that this area would be treated just like any other area in the borough. He then walked out. Equally the Social Services Department could not spare any of its workers and neither could the Housing Aid centre. And even the grants administered by the same officer who was responsible for the HAA were to continue to be dealt with by the central office with no priority given to applications from the Louvaine area. At the same meeting the newly appointed project leader who had acted as a buffer for two months, lost his job after openly expressing the frustrations known to everyone involved: the council's dirty linen was not to be washed in public.

In the months that followed frustrations accumulated: decisions were being postponed until the appointment of a new project leader, which actually took six months, and the time was filled with collecting information and devising ways of deferring residents' questions without allowing their frustrations to grow out of control. Only one activity was rewarding: the Department of Development and Building Works had been busy rehabilitating council owned houses in the LARA area since the original decision not to demolish them was taken in 1974. By the summer of 1975 the fruit of their work had ripened, the first dwellings were ready for occupation and a show house was open for a weekend. The residents were impressed by the standard of the building work and the transformation of the old and damp houses they had grown to hate into nice flats with central heating, large bright kitchens, bathrooms, and each with its own front door. But even here there were frustrations: housing need had not yet been assessed, and as soon as the new houses were ready, problems of allocation arose - because demand exceeded supply, and because the ultimate responsibility for who is housed rests with the lettings officer who respected rules such as 'five years in London and one in the borough' and registration on the council's waiting list even when they came into conflict with actual housing need.

The first offers of accommodation were made in such a way as to satisfy the criteria used for the rest of the borough as well as those of special relevance to the HAA. Households who satisfied both sets of regulations were rehoused, to the disappointment of other tenants who, if common sense had prevailed, would have been rehoused first. Moreover, the units available were all family dwellings and not suitable for the large number of single elderly people who were in great need of rehousing and who wanted to remain in the area. Changing the architects' brief and convincing all the officers involved of the need to provide single person dwellings was a lengthy procedure and no old age pensioner was among those rehoused within the first year. It became significant that most elderly people were English, born and bred in Battersea, whereas a considerable number of families in need of rehousing were of West Indian and African origin. This further embittered the elderly members of the community, who felt they had been cheated of their rights by newcomers, and some 'racialist' resentment was generated among neighbours.

Complaints were made both to LARA and to the area office. LARA's position was very delicate: if it interfered with the letting of council property it risked being criticised for favouring its own members. The area office on the other hand had no power to change council rules and had the difficult task of trying to satisfy the council's general lettings criteria while at the same time offering accommodation to the worst housed. Almost every week in the first year of the HAA, new cases of families in housing stress worse than the ones already known came to light. As this information accumulated it became increasingly urgent to devise a new system of allocation which would give priority to the special requirements of the HAA without breaking council rules.

BRINGING ABOUT CHANGE

Because each chief of a different section within the local authority saw the sovereignty of his own section as most important and found it difficult to cooperate with the others it was necessary to find a decision making mechanism outside officers' jurisdiction. In this and other circumstances in which a change in policy was required, the Steering Committee, which included three councillors, proved extremely useful.

The question of how to allocate council accommodation was raised by LARA and discussed at the Steering Committee meeting. LARA held the view that newly converted properties should be offered to families according to their housing need, and that the qualification of five years' residence should be replaced by living in the HAA at the date of declaration. Housing need was generally defined in terms of overcrowding, lack of amenities and poor quality housing. Other reasons for rehousing a family could also apply, but only as a second priority.

The meeting reached the somewhat ambiguous conclusion that although criteria applying to the rest of the borough could not be ignored, exceptions should be made for HAA residents when there was good reason for them. This decision neither pleased the lettings officer or made the allocation system any fairer, but it did allow a measure of flexibility in the offering of accommodation in the area and enabled more residents to be rehoused.

Under the new system almost every case had to be judged on its own merits. LARA's view, supported by the area office, was that the aim of the HAA was to offer better accommodation to all residents who needed rehousing, especially as it was the 'government's wish that at whatever level of constraints on resources, action to help people living in sub-standard homes, especially in difficult areas, should be given priority even at the expense of other areas and services' (DoE Circular 13/75). It was therefore only a question of time before all households in need would receive an offer. The principle of priority rehousing for LARA area residents involved the area office staff in close cooperation with LARA; both were concerned to improve the housing conditions of people living within closely defined boundaries. Without this cooperation the area office, comprising as it did a small group of new staff, powerless within the local authority's hierarchy and working outside the town hall, would have been totally isolated and unable to achieve the aims of the HAA to any extent.

On another matter, the question of ways of spending the environmental grant, the Steering Committee structure allowed LARA to decide entirely on its own. This grant, offered by the Department of the Environment to all HAAs, involves a payment of £50 per privately owned house which should be spent on improving the general environment of the HAA. LARA, after considering different possibilities, decided to give financial assistance to owners who were willing to redecorate the facades of their houses.

PARTICIPATION IN THE PROCESS

This degree of public participation in decision making is not customary in council projects: minor decisions that do not require councillors' approval are usually made by senior officers and in any case not by groups of tenants or residents. Here, nevertheless it functioned very well. Judging each case on its merits allowed exceptions to be made and rules to be bent without it being necessary to bring any formal change of policy or even to establish a precedent for a similar decision in a future case. This rather anarchic procedure ensured some 'victories' for LARA, but did not generate a reconsideration of council policies. So, despite continuous exchange of views between councillors, officers and members of the public involving a regular feedback to the policy makers about the implementation of policies, the opportunity to reconsider them on a general level was missed.

The Steering Committee also helped to change officers' attitudes towards LARA. LARA's interest in the improvement of its area was so lively, positive and constructive that town hall officials were given a further incentive to use the resources they managed in the same manner. When dissatified, LARA was vocally critical: the slow rate of acquisition and modernisation of houses, the long delays in issuing home loss payments, the lack of maintenance of council properties - these and other issues were questioned at Steering Committee meetings. Replies, however, evasive, had to be given to the committee, and the officers responsible, aware of the close monitoring by LARA, at least took notice of requests coming from the area office.

The special interest shown by the St. John Ward councillors for the LARA area was resented in the town hall by officers who thought that it had been declared an HAA only because important councillors had wanted it, and that it continued to have priority treatment for the same reason. That there is a certain amount of truth in these suspicions shows only that without this 'special push' and left to the council's officers, the project would have probably never taken off.

Certain LARA personalities were also very significant to the association's success with the council, both on the front line and in less obvious ways. But if these people were crucial to the creation of LARA, they necessarily inhibited the active involvement of less vociferous members of the community. It took a long time and the development of a whole range of other activities (e.g. nursery, community hall, social events organisation) to encourage new activists to emerge. For the first three years in the life of the HAA, the same LARA representatives sat on the Steering Committee and influenced the LARA membership in matters of housing policy and allocation in the area. Only when it appeared that the main problems in the HAA had been resolved were a few committee members replaced by new ones. By this time LARA's general attitude was slightly changed; apart from having grown in membership and self confidence, the association had replaced its intransigence towards the council with a more conciliatory stance. This may have been the result of achieving some of the original aims, but the willingness to compromise could equally be a sign of accepting the shortcomings of the established system. Whatever the reasons,

there is no justification for complacency: even now
the LARA area is a long way from resolving its problems.

ACHIEVEMENTS

One of the main problems in the LARA area in 1974 was
the poor quality of housing.   The dual aim of the
HAA was to relieve residents from overcrowding and
lack of amenities, and to improve the existing housing
stock.   The Labour Council believed that this aim
should be achieved mainly by acquiring privately rented
houses and by grant aiding owner occupiers with the
improvement of their homes.

A substantial part of the project therefore involved
offering council accommodation to those families who
needed rehousing.   By November 1978, 210 households
resident in the area had been rehoused in modernised
council and housing association flats and houses:
144 of them remained in the area whereas 66 moved to
council accommodation outside the HAA.

Residents who qualified for rehousing assistance
were given a choice of staying in the area or going
elsewhere within the boundaries of Wandsworth Borough.
Many of the people who initially expressed the wish
to move out of the area later changed their minds,
some because of the type of housing offered elsewhere,
and others because they saw a chance of being rehoused
sooner if they chose to stay until an HAA improved
unit was available.   The majority of the people who
stayed in the area, however, chose to stay because
of their involvement with the neighbourhood.

The Labour Council believed that it could resolve
housing problems in the LARA area by reducing the number
of dwellings managed by absentee landlords and by replacing
them with modernised council-owned units.   To achieve
this aim, the council acquired 70 houses during the
first three years of the HAA, adding them to the 65
it already owned.   It modernised 66 of the total 135,
to provide 143 dwelling units.   Most of these are
now let to residents; a few that were not needed locally
were offered to families living elsewhere in Wandsworth.
In the private sector during the same period, 58 house
owners improved or carried out major repairs on their
houses.   The majority of people benefitting from improvement grants have been owner occupiers.   Similarly,
the environmental grant which was at LARA's request
used to redecorate the facades of private houses, benefitted owner occupiers most directly.

Whereas the quality of housing has improved in both
public and private sectors, no housing gain has yet
been achieved: 53 houses were totally empty and a

further 20 partly occupied in 1974; in November 1978
58 houses were totally empty and a further 20 partly
occupied. The main difference seems to be that whereas
in 1974, only 41 empty and 4 partly occupied houses
were in the public sector, in 1978, 50 empty houses
and 10 partly occupied were owned by the council and
housing associations. This is partly due to the fact
that the rate of acquisition, including three compulsory
purchase orders totalling 21 houses, has been more
rapid than the rate of modernisation, but more dramatically
to the standstill that followed the May 1978 elections.
In total effect, the number of housing units in 1978
is largely the same but the proportions in private/public
ownership are very different (Table 4.1).

Table 4.1
Tenure of Housing Units in the LARA Area, 1974 and 1978

	1974 %	1978 %
Council Tenants	8	31
Private Tenants	53	27
Housing Association Tenants	7	10
Owner Occupiers	33	32

CHANGE OF POLICY

Since the Conservatives became the majority party in
the Wandsworth Council a major policy change brought
all rehabilitation programmes to a halt. The Tories
propose to resolve the housing problem by offering
council houses for sale, in principle to existing tenants,
in order to enable more people to become owner occupiers.
In the LARA area the council would like to sell unmodernised houses for homsteading or owner occupation, and
to sell converted flats and modernised houses instead
of letting them.

These plans have not met LARA's approval: if they
are carried out, families who cannot afford a mortgage
and who require the council's aid with rehousing will
remain in old and decrepit accommodation. Furthermore,
the majority of houses available for sale are not suitable
for single family occupation: large four storey Victorian
properties with long back additions lend themselves
to conversion into two or three flats, but not into
single family houses. This may well mean the return
of the private landlord and with him a step backwards
into the problems existing in 1974.

Housing associations which were brought in to smooth

the problem and help the worst off, are no longer as welcome as they were; their conversion standards are lower than the council's, and management problems affecting their tenants' welfare have given them an unfavourable reputation in the area.

The Tory housing plan is not the only council policy unpopular with LARA. LARA remains determined that the council should continue hearing and considering the opinions of the local residents through the Steering Committee but in 1978 the newly elected council, both because of its weak majority and its fear of confrontation with the public, made it known that it wanted to have as few public meetings as possible. On 31 May 1978, soon after the election, a letter from the Department of Administration to resident members of Steering Committees in HAAs, announced that the council had decided to suspend meetings of all HAA Steering Committees because it is a 'difficult problem for the council to man all the many committees, sub-committees and panels which were set up under the previous administration'. LARA immediately invited councillors Chope and McKenzie-Hill (Housing Committee and Sub-Committee chairpersons) to attend a meeting with the view to convincing them of the usefulness of the Steering Committee.

To the great disappointment of the residents neither councillor accepted the invitation. On 2 August, encouraged by the unpopularity of this decision, the Labour opposition called a special meeting of the Housing Committee to discuss the effect of new policies on the HAAs and criticised the council for suspending the Steering Committee meetings. Residents' representatives expressed their wish for the continuation of these meetings. Councillor Chope compromised with a proposal to hold meetings of all HAAs together. His proposal was totally rejected by LARA who insisted on continuing the programme established by the previous council. Pressure from the public, and, perhaps, the advice given by council officers, finally convinced the Tory Council to give in. On 1 October LARA was officially informed that formal Steering Committee meetings were to start again 'as soon as possible'. The first such meetings took place on 17 November in the form the residents had wanted.

This victory, together with the discussions about forming a cooperative to manage council owned houses and so to avoid selling them gave LARA new hope. Again it proved its ability to influence the council and to participate in decision making. Although all is not lost because of the outcome of the May 1978 election, the disruption that occurred in the area improvement programme should not be underestimated. By the end of 1978 although no council houses had actually been sold, no definite plans have been prepared for them either.

CONCLUSIONS

It would not be fair to make here a final assessment of the success of thte LARA area improvement programme. Certainly a number of families now live in better conditions, but there are others who still live in bad housing. Certainly a substantial number of houses have been improved, but the actual increase in the number of empty unmodernised houses can hardly be considered an improvement. The programme has not been completed, however, and some of its shortfall must be attributed to the disruption brought by the change of council.

Whether new solutions will be considered in the next few years or whether housing associations will take over the improvement programme started by the council, it is certain that LARA's opinion will count. This is an achievement which is itself worthy of account. The combination of factors which contributed to LARA's successful involvement in affecting the fate of the Louvaine neighbourhood can be summarised as follows:

a) The idea of public participation was generally acceptable in the mid-seventies; the Town and Country Planning Act (1968) and the Skeffington Report (1969) had already recognised the need to involve the public in decisions affecting their livelihood and had established the procedure for their participation.

b) The demolition and redevelopment approach, which had been the dominant feature of urban renewal throughout the sixties, went 'out of fashion' in the seventies for reasons we have discussed in the Introduction.

c) LARA had members who could speak for the association and who were well connected with the elected local council. Local residents with knowledge of community development legislation and local authority proceedings, as well as social connections with councillors were of vital importance to LARA.

d) Government legislation made special allowances for public participation and recommended residents' involvement in HAAs. Department of Environment circulars concerning HAAs insisted that the support of the local population was essential for the success of these programmes. (DoE Circulars 13/75 and 14/75).

e) In the particular case of the Louvaine HAA, the councillors and the local team of officers involved were in agreement with the idea of public participation: Town Hall based officers were soon persuaded not to impede it.

f) Public resources were made available by both central and local governments to assist the improvement of the area. The council was therefore able to acquire and modernise a considerable number of houses for people in need of rehousing, a strategy which also improved the physical appearance of the area. A team of officers was employed exclusively to serve the residents of the HAA. Increased and special grants were available for house improvement in the HAA. Further environmental grants were provided for use within the HAA. An urban aid grant was obtained and used by LARA to provide a community centre and a nursery.

Finally, LARA was both able to demand to be part of every decision that could affect the area, and successful in this demand. LARA was generally assisted by the council in improving the neighbourhood, but was also able to fight, and in most cases to win against the council when its members or officers were hindering this improvement programme. On both counts the achievements of the Louvaine Housing Action Area stand substantially to LARA's credit.

Chapter Five continues the discussion of livelihood, picking up the question of participation as an indicator of involvement. It considers local amenities, local contacts and local networks as local resources which are taken up by various households in various ways; and it uses patterns of take up to compare the extent to which different categories of respondent in LARA are involved in the south London/Battersea/LARA areas.

The comparisons show that age, family stage, work commitments and social class affect residents' involvement in the local area, but that ethnic origin, on the contrary, does not. Nor does it seem to be significant to relationships at the neighbourhood level. It is a combination of length of residence and participation in local activities which makes a 'local'. Because ethnic origin is no bar to either, it has no direct effect on insider-outsider status.

The fact that 'outsiders' of any origin can become 'insiders' so readily is consistent with Battersea's traditional openness to foreign immigrants and minorities of every sort. The openness of the LARA networks described in this chapter challenges the stereotype for 'mixed' urban neighbourhoods just as Battersea's political and economic style goes against expectations for inner city areas. The smaller area is a microcosm of the larger in both respects. Certainly residents tend to have a lot of local contacts and to spend a lot of time in the area. In the Battersea context at least, there is good evidence that these practical involvements go along with strong local ties.

5 Livelihood II: Local involvement

YVONNE DHOOGE

LIVING IN THE CITY

How far does the everyday behaviour of people in a residential inner city area indicate what meaning the area has for them? Is it a place in which they invest a lot of time and energy, or is it just a place to sleep? This chapter interprets localised behaviour as evidence of residents' involvement in the LARA area and in Battersea as a whole. Three measures are considered: the use of local amenities, the number of social contacts in the area, and the extent of involvement in the neighbourhood itself.

Each of them depends on the availability and use of resources of some kind. The range of items counted as 'resources' here includes local amenities such as shops, the community centre and the statutory services, all of which are formally available to everyone, and the kinsmen, friends and neighbours of the separate households in the area. These last are resources in two senses: they may be combined with or used instead of public support systems to help the household solve its practical problems; and they inevitably affect the way its members feel about city life.

The neighbourhood survey centered round the question: How do households of different origins who now live in the same area manage their separate livelihoods in relation to that area? This chapter therefore takes explicit note of the origins of residents in the LARA area. Here as elsewhere, however, the categories employed are not ethnic categories in the strict sense of the term; all are based on the birthplace of the informants except for the New Commonwealth ethnic category which is based on the birthplace of parents, and a distinction is made between people born in south London, north London and outside London but in the UK. At the same time it should be emphasised that ethnic origin is only one factor which might influence local involvement and access to local resources. Factors such as length

103

of residence, age, family cycle, social class and work commitments are also important. Where these factors vary together there is a danger that a focus on ethnic origin obscures the possibility that it is other factors or combinations of factors that determine differences between residents.

Mr and Mrs X were not born in south London, but have been living in Battersea for over ten years. They are in their fifties. Mr X has a full time job and his wife does some part time work. Their children have left home. Their children and some other relatives live in other parts of south London and outside London but in the UK. Mr and Mrs X shop locally and use some of the local statutory services. They never, however, go to the local community centre, do not participate in neighbourhood activities and are more or less outside the neighbourhood network. But this limited degree of local involvement is better explained by their work commitments and the importance they attach to close contact with their children and other relatives than by their ethnic origin - whether as it affects their own behaviour or as it affects the way their neighbours respond to them.

METHODS OF DATA COLLECTION

Two kinds of data are used: data based on answers to the LARA neighbourhood survey questionnaire itself, and data which stem from the survey procedures.

The first kind is limited by the fact that, while this was a household survey and information was collected about all household members, only one adult member answered the questionnaire. A household is in some respects one social unit; in others its members operate as separate individuals whose use of local facilities and social networks differ, and who may attach separate meanings to the local area. Furthermore, the knowledge household members have about each other's lives is not always complete. Consequently, respondents were asked to answer the questions about use of local amenities and the presence of significant local ties on their own account as individuals, and the discussion of them refers to respondents only.

Except for answers to the question 'Do you have plans to move?' which was incorporated in the questionnaire, the data on involvement in the neighbourhood itself stem from our having employed local residents to do the survey interviews, and from encouraging them to choose the households they interviewed. Some interviewers preferred to have households assigned to them, but two thirds took the opportunity to make their own selection. Recording the households selected by each interviewer in this latter category and noting the sequence in which they were selected produced maps which show each interviewer's contacts in the neighbourhood. Put together week by week, these separate maps produced a kind of neighbourhood network map. On the grounds that those interviewed first can be considered 'closer' to at least one interviewer and so more involved in local networks, we have used it to distinguish which households were relatively in and which relatively outside the local system. These data are impressionistic. Nevertheless, systematic differences between households interviewed first and households interviewed last do give some indication of the principles governing social relationships at neighbourhood level, and of the indices used by the local residents to define insiders and outsiders.

A PROFILE OF THE RESPONDENTS

There were 446 households in the survey; one adult member of each household answered the questionnaire for his or her whole household. Predictably the proportion belonging to each local or ethnic category matches the proportions for each category in the neighbourhood as a whole (Table 5.1). One third of the respondents were born in south London and another third in the New Commonwealth; 10 per cent came to Battersea from north London, 15 per cent moved in from other parts of Britain, and the remaining 11 per cent are either Irish or 'other foreign born'. Nearly two thirds of the respondents are women. This is not demographically significant, but confirms that more women than men are at home during the day when interviewers made their first calls. The bulk of male respondents by contrast were interviewed in the evening or on weekends.

In 1978 the majority of respondents had been living in Battersea for over five years but some of the ethnic categories have a higher proportion of well established household members than others. Of respondents born in south London, 61 per cent were born in Battersea and another 16 per cent had been living there for more than 20 years. Nearly half the respondents who were born in north London and a full third of those born in other parts of Britain and Ireland have also been in the area for over 20 years. In the aggregated New Commonwealth category, only a very small proportion (8 per cent) are residents of such long standing, but there are great differences between the sub-categories within it: a good number of the Caribbean born respondents have, like their households, been resident for twenty years, while most of the African born are very recent arrivals (Chapter 3).

There are significant age differences between the

ethnic categories.   41 per cent of south London born
respondents are over sixty, and only 29 per cent are
under forty.   The much smaller north London born category,
contains a similar percentage of elderly people, but
the proportion under forty is higher (40 per cent).
Respondents born in the UK outside London have a somewhat
younger profile: 21 per cent are over sixty, and 59
per cent are under forty.   But the age contrast is
sharpest in the case of the New Commonwealth born:
only 3 per cent are over sixty and 61 per cent are
under forty, the Irish and 'other foreign' born categories
hold a middle position on the respondent age ranges
(Table 5.1).

These age differences are reflected in the employment
patterns of the respondents.   The south London and
north London born show the same pattern;   around one
third have retired - i.e. are of retirement age - slightly
more have a full time job and 16 per cent do part time
work.   The number of retired people is of course smaller
among the younger ethnic categories: 15 per cent of
the UK, Irish and 'other foreign' born and 3 per cent
of the people of New Commonwealth origin are listed
as retired.   While more than half of all respondents
are economically active, the proportions who engage
in full time and part time work differ: among the
Irish born 41 per cent have a full time job and 29
per cent work part time;   among the New Commonwealth
born, 57 per cent work full time, and only 9 per cent
have part time work.   For respondents born outside
London but in the UK and the 'other foreign' born,
the figures are 50 per cent in full time and respectively
12 per cent and 10 per cent in part time work.

USE OF LOCAL AMENITIES

The LARA area is predominantly residential, but it
contains some small industrial premises, shops and
pubs.   Most of these are situated on the main road
which forms the area's eastern boundary.

a) The Community Centre

As a Housing Action Area LARA succeeded in getting
a grant from the government to convert part of an underused
church into a community centre and day nursery.   In
it a full time community worker assisted by a group
of part time workers and volunteers now runs a variety
of activities - a pensioners' club, a youth club, information and handicraft sessions for housewives, a darts
club, social evenings and discos.

The community centre was not and is not the centre
of social life and leisure for local residents.   In
1978 there was in the immediate vicinity a cinema (now

closed), a bingo hall and the Battersea Arts Centre, and the 'west end' of London is always in easy reach. In any case the availability of consumer goods encourages people increasingly to spend their leisure time at home (Gershuny and Pahl 1980). But the large number of respondents who had never used the community centre at the time of the survey gave more personal reasons for not doing so: some said they were new to the area and did not yet know what it offered and others said they had never liked community centres of any kind; the majority however reported having no time for it because of work or other social commitments.

The popularity of the centre apparently varies with ethnic origin: a bigger proportion of native Londoners use it than of respondents born in the New Commonwealth or outside London but in the UK. But this apparent ethnic difference is readily explained by other factors: most residents participating in activities organised at the centre were either housewives or retired people and, among the London born there is a relatively high proportion of elderly people, and of women of child rearing stage who tend to stay at home or to work only part time. On the other hand the respondents of New Commonwealth and UK (outside London) origin are younger and many, including those with children, have a full time job. It is important that while they do not themselves go to the centre, they do send their children to it: the centre's nursery is a great asset to working mothers and is particularly well used by those born in the New Commonwealth. There is also a core of women born in the UK (outside London) who are very active in the organisation of the residents' association and the community centre.

b) Statutory services

Living in a welfare state implies that housing, medicine, food and clothing will when necessary be provided by the state through a whole range of statutory services. The use of these provisions however, is not solely a matter of need and availability. It also depends on the discretion of officials (Flett 1979); on the potential user knowing his or her rights and the rules of eligibility and access to the services required; and on his or her assessment of their appropriateness. Some people, although eligible, do not claim supplementary benefits because they do not know the provisions or because they perceive the benefits as a humiliation instead of a right. Similarly, some unemployed people do not register as unemployed because relatives are taking care of their basic needs, because they object to the bureaucratic entanglement involved, because registering reduces their options to work in the informal economy or because, they find their relatives or friends more effective resources than job centres in the search for work (Chapter 6).

Few people in the neighbourhood have ever used advice
centres or counselling services; those who report
having contact with the social services are largely
elderly or people dealing with a specific crisis.
More residents have contact with the Department of
Health and Social Security: and still more use the
hospital services, but even in this case it is only
either a few times a year for chronic complaints, or
once off following an accident or sudden illness.
Use of the DHSS and the hospital run parallel with
the stages of the family cycle; among the respondents
it is mainly child rearing or elderly women - of whatever
origin - who are in regular contact with these government
services.

c) Shopping facilities

Besides small cornershops situated along the main
road, the survey area has three other shopping facilities
close by: Clapham Junction with its selection of chain-
stores, supermarkets and small specialised shops is
only five minutes and the Northcote Market ten minutes
walk away: the Arndale Centre can be reached by a
short bus ride. The majority of respondents shop
locally, using cornershops for daily groceries and
supermarkets for their once-a-week supplies. Northcote
Market and Clapham Junction are more poular than the
more modern and uniform shopping facilities offered
by the Arndale Centre.

The size of the household and the time and transport
available to the household influence the respondent's
choice of shops. Large supermarkets, for example,
do not normally cater well for one person households,
and buying food and other household articles once a
week is much easier when you have a car than when you
have to go on foot or by bus. A car is even more
necessary if you want to use shops outside the local
area. The same factors influence 'ethnic' shopping
patterns. Many of the south London born are elderly
and live alone or with a partner or an adult child
so that purchasing large quantities of groceries once
a week is neither necessary nor feasible. On top
of this, age tends to tie them physically to the neighbourhood. Thus most of the south London born shop in
Battersea and they often use cornershops. The majority
of north London and New Commonwealth born respondents
also shop in Battersea, but a small proportion of them
also use shopping facilities in other parts of south
London. Being younger and more mobile they are more
likely to use supermarkets and street markets than
cornershops. While over half of the people born outside
London but in the UK shop in Battersea, compared with
the other categories a much higher proportion of them

shop in other parts of south London and London and use the whole range of shopping facilities.

SOCIAL CONTACTS IN BATTERSEA

Each household manages its livelihood with reference to its traditions, its aims and expectations, and to the resources available to it. Kin and friends are an integral part of these. But the part played by kin and friends in the organisation of day-to-day life depends on what kind of resource they are. What are they good at? What can they be used for? Most obviously status counts to some extent since it allows one party to influence the actions of others, whether by greater wealth, more education or an occupational position with some degree of control over the allocation of scarce resources (Blau 1964: 12-33; 115-43). But no status counts always in the same way and the value of kinship or friendship, varies with context. Distant contact with a foreman or a manager may, in the context of job hunting, be more valuable than close contact with ten working friends; and a woman may find her mother a source of help when the childrern are ill, but a liability during an emotional crisis. In any case, it would be wrong to imply that family and friends are used only in a calculating or instrumental way. They can also be sources of identity and emotional support. Being part of an extended family group or having a large circle of friends may make you feel good even if in practical or economic terms these kinsmen or friends are quite 'useless'.

We do not know exactly the resource value of the people listed as kin or friends in the neighbourhood survey. Only one person reported the contacts for the whole household and, except in the questions about job hunting, we did not ask what kind of resource each contact was. More important, it should be noted that the presence or declared presence of kinsmen and friends does not of itself say anything about the quality or the content of the relationship (Wallman 1974). Our limited 'aim' here is to consider whether and to what extent kin and friends are among the resources available to the households in the survey area; we do not pretend to know how or how often the option to 'use' them is taken up.

The focus is on contacts in the locality for two reasons. One is that locally based relatives and friends are within easier reach than those living further away so might more readily be called in to help with practical daily problems. Their localness implies also that they have information about the area which may improve their chances of access to other resources and expand options available to the neighbourhood as a whole. The successful declaration of the neighbourhood as a Housing Action Area was in part due to the presence of local residents who had the right information as well as access to people with valuable information (Chapter 4).

Information is also essential to the more individual aspects of livelihood. People have no access to formal or informal employment unless they know where it is available and how to get it. Similarly, they cannot make proper use of 'welfare' or statutory services unless they know what their rights are, what benefits are offered, how to apply for them and how to deal with the officials. And as the most valuable information is, by definition, exchanged through personal and non official networks, an outsider excluded from such networks has no access to a whole chain of essential information.

Local social contacts are significant resources in another sense too. As some neighbourhood studies have shown, the meaning an area has for its residents correlates with the extent to which social relationships are localised. Thus while the physical characteristics and political traditions of an area may serve as identifying features (Chapter 2), people tend to feel emotionally attached to a neighbourhood when they have kin and friends in the locality. (Elias and Scotson 1965; Gans 1962; Young & Willmott 1957).

KIN IN BATTERSEA

'Blood is thicker than water'. Although this saying is generations old it continues to summarise English ideals. And if the English family system is no longer what it was kin still retain an important place in the normal universe of personal relationships.

In this section we look at the close relatives of each ethnic category in turn, describing patterns of interaction with parents, parents-in-law, absent children and relatives who are perceived as of special importance to the household. For the purpose of comparison we will start with the residents who have longest connections in Battersea, the south London born. Age influences the number and age of intimate kin in a social network, and the south London born category includes a high proportion of elderly people. Two thirds no longer have parents and three quarters have no parents-in-law; close relatives outside the household are for many of them restricted to adult children and special relatives of the same or younger generations.

The family ties of all south Londoners who have kin at all are local ties. This is not only because they are locally born. The south Londoners in the LARA area are predominantly of working class background; manual workers are generally less mobile than people involved in middle class occupations and so tend to stay in the area in which they grew up. All the respondents were, by selection, adult and few still live with their parents. Those who do are in situations where combining two households makes practical housing sense, or makes it easier to give an elderly person necessary care. Typical combinations consist of a widowed mother and an unmarried son, or of a nuclear family and an elderly parent. Of the south London born with parents still living, 85 per cent of those parents live within the boundaries of south London - one third of them in Battersea. The reverse picture is similar: of the 42 per cent of south Londoner respondents who have children living independently, one third has at least one child living in Battersea, and another third has a child somewhere else in south London. Although nearly all reported having relatives outside their immediate family, not all regard them as important or 'special'. But of the 70 per cent who claim to have relatives at all, over half have a 'special' relative in Battersea and the rest have one in some other part of south London. These patterns of local concentration and continuity are the defining features of 'south London ethnics' group (SLEO, Chapter 3). They do not always pertain to both sides of a family. The fact that of south Londoners who still have parents-in-law one third report them living in Battersea and another third in other south London areas shows a striking degree of marriage within the local area.

The north London born are somewhat younger and the proportion of them without parents and parents-in-law is slightly lower than among the south Londoners: approximately half have no parents and around two thirds have no parents-in-law alive. Considering that this population has moved into the area, its kinship networks are surprisingly localised. Of those with parents, over a third have their parents living nearby - 8 per cent in Battersea, 30 per cent in other parts of London. Geographically speaking, the parents of the north London born seem to have been unusually mobile: less than one third of them still live in north London. Besides the one third who had moved south of the Thames, a similar proportion had left London altogether. It is the parents-in-law and children of the north London born who give them their present ties with the local area: no less than 60 per cent have parents-in-law in south London, equally distributed over Battersea and the rest of south London. It appears that many north Londoners migrated to work in south London and married locally, or that they moved southwards because of their marriage with a south Londoner. Forty seven per cent have children living away from home. In this case too, there is a marked tendency for these children to settle near their parents. Of north London born respondents with adult children, 30 per cent have at least one child in Battersea, and another 38 per cent a child living somewhere else in south London.

The behaviour of the north London born towards more distant kin is consistent with that reported in other studies of English kinship: they attach great importance to ties with these relatives as such, but do not feel obliged to keep in touch with them: contact is a matter of preference and personal choice (Young & Willmott 1957, 1960; Firth 1956). A large proportion of their more distant relatives live outside south London, but of the three quarters who specified their relatives at all, 44 per cent have at least one living close by - 20 per cent in Battersea, 24 per cent in other parts of London.

The residents born outside London but in the UK show a rather different picture. They tend to be younger than other residents and more of them are professional people. By virtue of their age, the number among them without parents and parents-in-law is comparatively low: less than half no longer have parents, while slightly more than half have no parents-in-law. On the other hand only one quarter of these families have adult children; those children that they do have tend still to be living at home. London's large administrative and service industry provides a whole range of economic opportunities for young professionals. This is clearly the main factor which has pulled this group of people to Battersea. That it has meant leaving relatives behind is not an overt source of conflict or distress. Middle class people are used to geographical and social mobility and tend to emphasise independence from parents and other relatives. Their relationships with kin are generally less strong than in working class families (Bott 1970; Young & Willmott 1960).

From these factors combined it follows that few kin contacts of the people born outside London but in the UK are local: their parents, special relatives and adult children tend to live outside London. But even this population is not without local kin. Of those with children who have set up independent households, 42 per cent have a child nearby, although other areas of south London have attracted them more often than Battersea itself. In this case also the number of parents-in-law in the immediate vicinity is surprisingly high: one third of the parents-in-law live in south London, largely concentrated in Battersea.

The fourth category of respondents to be considered here are of New Commonwealth origin. In the LARA area, most of this population arrived in England in the late 1950s. Virtually all of them will have left parents, parents-in-law and children behind when they came to England. But their arrival as it occurred in the 1950s and 1960s followed the pattern of chain migration: the migrants often joined or were joined by kinsmen. Some of these were intimate kin such as wives, children and elderly parents. Others were more distant relatives. And as the already established migrants usually assisted relatives in finding employment and housing, the new arrivals tended to settle in the same area (see Watson 1977).

In the LARA area, the chain migration process seems to have involved partners, children and young economically active kinsmen, not parents or parents-in-law. Around half of our New Commonwealth respondents have parents still living and slightly less than 40 per cent have parents-in-law. But while the majority of these have left their parents and parents-in-law in their country of origin, a quarter have parents and a similar proportion have parents-in-law in England. This last group are predominantly parents and parents-in-law of people who were born in England or came to England as children - i.e. they are the parents of the black English. Their residential patterns are therefore indicators of the future position of people of New Commonwealth descent with respect to local resources.

The survey data suggest that they are beginning to resemble the south and north London born. Two thirds of the NCW respondents' parents residing in England are living in south London with Battersea as the major place of residence. For the parents-in-law the proportion living in south London is less, but they still concentrate in Battersea. The same tendency to remain in the local area and close to relatives is evident in the residential patterns of adult children: of the 30 per cent of NCW respondents who had children living away from home, nearly half had children in Battersea or other parts of south London.

Finally, the 'special' relatives. In accordance with Caribbean, South East Asian and African kinship ideologies, the extended family group is perceived as relatively more significant than amongst the English, and ties with more distant relatives are less a matter of personal selectivity than of blanket acceptance. While English respondents tend to specify which of their kin count, the NCW respondents are more likely to insist that all their kin are equally important to them. But even here there is a strong localist bias. Over half of the New Commonwealth people specified their more distant kin; one half of these have a 'special' relative nearby - 31 per cent in Battersea, 21 per cent in other parts of south London. The fact that for many these 'special' relatives are the only local kin ties they have suggests that it is their very localness

which makes them special.   Only in the case of the
younger generation are 'special' relatives defined
out of a larger local kinship network.

WOMEN AS KIN KEEPERS

In all four ethnic categories, some people have relatives
in the LARA area itself.   For example:

> Mrs V lives next door to her parents and sees a
> great deal of her mother.   She drops in regularly
> for a chat and a cup of tea, or to ask her mother
> to keep an eye on the baby.   And Mrs P has a sister
> in one of the adjacent streets.   Whenever she goes
> out to do her shopping she calls in at her sister's
> to see whether she needs anything.

But locally based relatives more often live outside
the neighbourhood, scattered over Battersea and other
parts of south London to an extent to which makes daily
interaction impossible.

While everybody with kin has 'regular' contact with
them, there are variations in the frequency of contact.
These can often be attributed to residential proximity
alone: people of English origin are more often in
contact with their parents and parents-in-law than
are New Commonwealth respondents whose parents and
parents-in-law more often live outside the UK.   But
sometimes frequency of contact varies with the closeness
of the kin tie: contact with parents is regularly
more frequent than with parents-in-law for all except
the north London born.   In their case residence is
apparently a more determining factor than genealogical
proximity.

Among those with adult children, the south and north
London born have more contact with them than do the
New Commonwealth parents and the parents born in other
parts of the UK.   The age of the parents and the children
seems to have as much influence as geographical distance.
Parents are likely to play a less important role in
the lives of young single people or young couples without
children.   On the other hand parents with children
in their twenties are themselves still relatively young
and so less likely to need their children's care and
support.   Once parents have grown older and children
have established their own families, contact tends
to become more frequent.

Every household has a number of resources to manage,
and household members may each take responsibility
for a particular task.   In the survey neighbourhood
women are the principal housekeepers (Chapters 6 and
7).   They do most of the household tasks and the shopping,
and they contact the health and social services when

other household members need medical care or specialist help. They also play the central role in managing relatives or kinship resources. In this respect LARA women match the evidence of kinship and network studies which describe women as kin keepers, pivotal in maintaining contact with family members (Firth 1956). If we consider women and men respondents separately, it is evident that the former have far more contact with relatives than the latter. This affects the relationship married couples have with various kin. The difference in rates of contact suggests that the relatives of the woman form the nucleus of the household's kin contacts and that her mother is the key kin person - a pattern reminiscent of Bethnal Green in the 1950s (Young & Willmott 1957). But as the women have more contact with their parents-in-law than men have with either parents or parents-in-law, it indicates that they are also crucial to keeping in touch with their partners' families. It is not particular kin but kin in general that they keep.

KIN AS A RESOURCE: A COMPARISON

Table 5.2 presents an overall picture of local kin claimed by the respondents in each ethnic category. The numbers of Irish born and 'other foreign' born are rather small and they are only included in the table to give complete information. The social significance of the figures depends on family stage, the needs of the household in each case.

It is clear that most of the south London born are well placed in terms of access to kin as a local resource. The elderly have children and special relatives nearby for company and support. Sons and daughters are able to rely on parents and other relatives for advice and practical help. Their local kin networks include various generations and consequently their knowledge of and information about the area are likely to be extensive and effective. The latter point shows very clearly in relation to acquiring employment (Chapter 6).

Of those who have moved into the area, the north London born are also relatively well off in this respect. A large proportion live close to their adult children, and although their parents are on the whole not living nearby, this absence is compensated by parents-in-law; many of the north London born seem to be embedded in their partner's family network and to have close contact with their parents-in-law. But the locally based kinship networks are not as extensive as those of the south London born and are largely restricted to parents, parents-in-law or adult children. This implies that they probably do not have access to local information as diverse as the south Londoners', many of whom have also aunts, uncles, cousins and even grandparents in the local area.

The position of people of New Commonwealth origin is, in respect of local kinship resources, better than that of people born outside London but in the UK. But in real terms the comparison is misleading since the two categories have different needs for practical help and local information. The majority of NCW residents belong to the manual working classes and many have young families. By contrast, those born outside London but in the UK, are predominantly professional class people and many are young without children. Thus for instance in the business of finding a job or looking after children the NCW households might find their local relatives useful resources, while in the lives of the UK born such help is not so much needed; kin, however important in other respects, can have no value as job finding or child minding resources if jobs and child minders are not required.

Compared to the north and south London born the NCW households have fewer locally based kin. Nevertheless there is evidence of mutual support between the young and the elderly and their parents/children, and many, in addition, have special relatives living nearby. At present it is the newcomers in their thirties and forties who have only very limited access to kinship resources. Without parents or adult children in England they have only special relatives. And although in crisis situations these relatives are likely to give support, the fact that they tend to be of the same generation, still economically active and with their own children growing up, reduces their ability to assist in day to day problems.

This is of course a static picture. The local kin ties of NCW residents in Battersea are likely to increase: the tendency among adult children to settle in Battersea and other parts of south London indicates that the NCW residents have started to follow the residential pattern of the local population. If this trend continues the NCW households will eventually match the south and north London born residents in the matter of access to local kinship resources.

CLOSE FRIENDS IN BATTERSEA

Local friendship ties are another reflection of involvement or investment in an area. The relationships people have with those whom they call 'friends' are not all of the same quality. Recognising this and focussing the enquiry on people as potential resources, we asked respondents only about their 'close' friends. Definitions of a 'close' friend no doubt vary, but the term does imply some degree of intimacy and emotional investment, and people tend to turn more readily to 'close' friends than acquaintances when in serious need.

In the survey area friends form an important part of people's social contacts: between 80 and 90 per cent have or claimed to have at least one close friend, and people are more often in contact with friends than with relatives. Many got to know their close friends because they lived nearby. But while frequent physical contact does facilitate the development of friendship, people do not become 'close' friends merely because they live next door or in the same street. Friendship between neighbours is likely to develop because they meet each other also in other settings. People who have grown up in the same neighbourhood will have had the opportunity to develop ties of friendship at various stages of their lives. Newcomers on the contrary need a kind of integrating force. An old friend already living in the area or a next door neighbour might serve as such a force. More often it is neighbourhood clubs which give new inhabitants the opportunity to make local friends. In the LARA neighbourhood the social activities organised by the local residents' association have this function and many of our informants mentioned this as one of the positive aspects of the Housing Action Area.

Mrs B moved into the neighbourhood because it offered better housing conditions. But having most of her kin and friends in other parts of south London and being tied to the house by her small children she felt initially very isolated. When the area became a Housing Action Area this changed; the neighbourhood acquired its own community centre and the residents' association started to organise a variety of programmes for young mothers and their toddlers. This gave Mrs B the chance to go out, meet local people and establish relationships with some that are now her friends.

Work, family ties, children and school or college also provide opportunities to get to know people and make friends. Among the respondents as a whole, work and family ties rank highest as ways of making friends but many of the NCW people and of those born outside London but in the UK also have close friends whom they met at school. Because of the various ways in which people got to know their friends, not all those called 'close' live locally, and not everyone has close friends within the boundaries of south London. Overall however, the proportion without local friends is small. The people born outside London but in the UK are an exception; the fact that around one quarter of them have no close friends in the south London area underlines the relatively loose ties of this population with its area of residence.

The immediate neighbourhood is a particularly important source of friends for the south and north London born; nearly half of them have close friends in the survey area itself compared with slightly more than one third of the people in the other categories. Although length of residence is of some influence here, the difference also reflects the fact that the south and north London born tend for quite other reasons to be physically tied to the neighbourhood. Many of them are retired or are housewives, consequently depending more on neighbours for companionship than younger residents who go out to work would do.

Both these characteristics apply to people born in the New Commonwealth and to those born outside London in the UK. While the friendship ties of the latter are the least localised, it should be pointed out that where they do have local close friends, they are more likely to live in the immediate vicinity than in other parts of Battersea or south London. In this respect they differ from the NCW residents who more often have close friends in other parts of Battersea than either in the rest of south London or in the survey neighbourhood. As in the case of kin, the local friendship ties of NCW respondents are ties with Battersea.

INVOLVEMENT IN THE NEIGHBOURHOOD

Besides keeping contact with kin and close friends, people are also engaged in a whole range of other neighbourhood relations. Some people visit each other at home, others meet in the street, in common garden areas, local shops and pubs or at the community centre; some only know each other by sight, others acknowledge recognition by saying hello or stopping to talk. The cumulation of these exchanges gives the LARA area its own internal network and defines the boundaries between core and peripheral members.

Whether people are more or less 'in' or 'out' of that local system is partly a matter of personal choice. People absorbed in non local activities or in relationship with their kin and friends will have neither the time nor the reason to become part of a neighbourhood network. But patterns of local involvement and detachment are also governed by the kind of indices local people use to define insiders and outsiders.

In neighbourhoods with a significant proportion of many generation residents, it is generally these residents who set and mark any boundaries against the outside. In the past Battersea people have been tolerant of minority groups and foreign immigrants and have come in the course of time to accept them as insiders, ordinary neighbours. It is even more significant that they have always looked for local commitment and involvement in their choice of political leaders: the ethnic origin of aspiring candidates has been irrelevant (Chapter 2). The employment of local interviewers in the LARA area and the recording of their progress through the area week by week allowed us to draw up maps of the local contacts of each interviewer and a kind of network diagram of the neighbourhood itself. The maps and the diagram show that similar principles to those operating in old Battersea still govern relationships at neighbourhood level: throughout the survey neighbourhood insiders are defined in terms of their local involvement, not by their ethnic or national origin.

Not all interviewers wanted to choose the households they interviewed. Those who did started by calling on those they knew well. These households tended to be dispersed over the area. Interviewers who stopped after having completed these addresses were largely those for whom the neighbourhood was a relatively unimportant focus of social interaction. A striking feature of the interview pattern of those who continued was that having visited the households they knew well, they returned to and stayed in their own street. Within the boundaries of the neighbourhood their networks seemed to be largely concentrated in the streets in which they lived. Most of the residents in other streets are seen by contrast as 'the others'.

Maps 5.1 and 5.2 illustrate these points. They represent the neighbourhood contacts of two interviewers at the time of the survey.

> Mrs N is 26, married with two small children. While born in south London she had been living in Battersea for less than ten years. Both her own and her partner's kin are living in other parts of south London and they keep in close contact with her. She has only one 'close' friend. Since she invests a lot of time and energy in her relatives and the one friend, she knows relatively few people in the neighbourhood well enough to feel that she could call upon them for an interview. Her local social contacts consist only of people she has met through activities at the community centre.

> Mrs C is 65 and a widow. She is of south London origin and has lived in Battersea since birth. She has two sons, both living outside London, a sister-in-law in Battersea and a twin brother in Clapham with whom she is very close. Her 'close' friends all live in Battersea and other parts of south London. Although these relatives and friends form the inner core of her social network, she also knows a relatively large number of people in the neighbourhood. In her case the street is an important arena for knowing and interacting with

local people. Except for five out of the 31 she
visited, all the households with whom she has the
kind of relationship which she felt made an interview
possible are clustered in her part of the road.

The local contacts of both interviewers include a
full range of people in terms of age, occupation and
ethnic origin. They are similar only in respect of
a relatively long residence in Battersea or involvement
in the community centre's activities.

The analysis of the local network diagram underlines
this. The majority of core members - defined as those
households interviewed during the first period of the
survey - had been living in Battersea for at least
five years. Those with a shorter length of residence
qualify as core members because of some extra involvement
in local activities or because of strong links with
established residents. By contrast, the periphery
of the area's local network mainly comprises people
who have either moved into the Battersea area quite
recently, or who, while of longer standing, still have
few local commitments. The LARA area constitutes
a relatively open local system, so that 'newcomers'
of whatever origin can acquire local status on the
basis of long residence and local involvement.

Tradition is only one of a series of interrelated
factors which help to explain the style of the neighbourhood and its residents' attitudes to newcomers. The
type of social networks of the local indigenous population
might also have some explanatory value. Although
'good' neighbourhoods are often assumed to be those
with close knit networks, close integration can also
imply the total exclusion of newcomers (Elias and Scotson
1965). The survey area does not have closely integrated
networks. The local relatives of the indigenous south
London 'ethnic' category, are spread over Battersea
and south London, and contact with kin is not so intense
that there is no room for non kinship ties. Furthermore,
'close' friends are defined in a variety of ways and
they live in different parts of Battersea and south
London as well as outside the locality. These features
of kin and friendship ties suggest that the various
spheres of interaction do not overlap to the extent
that kin or close friends are also neighbours, workmates
and playmates. The social networks of the south Londoners
are dispersed in a way which makes the integration
of newcomers feasible.

PLANS TO MOVE

From the previous sections we can infer that many residents
invest much of their time, energy and affect in the
LARA area and Battersea. It might therefore not be

a coincidence that the majority of respondents have no plans to move out of the neighbourhood. This of course does not mean that the neighbourhood has no unfavourable aspects. Like most inner city areas it has too much traffic noise and too little open space and it has been affected by deteriorating housing conditions. While Housing Action has started to reverse the latter trend, house purchase and improvement is a slow process and a substantial number of people are still waiting to be rehoused (Chapter 4).

The condition of housing is therefore one of the major reasons why people want to move. In 1978 21 per cent of the respondents wanted to move in order to get better accommodation. For some however the advantages of the neighbourhood outweighed its disadvantages and they only wanted to be rehoused within the survey area. Others were hoping to move to other parts of Battersea and south London, or want to leave London altogether - some because they want to live closer to relatives or to work, not for want of decent housing.

Only 9 per cent of respondents want to move because they do not like the neighbourhood. Their dislike of the area is couched in two ways. Some people (5 per cent of all respondents) give reasons for moving which have more to do with city life than with the neighbourhood itself. They want to get away from city noise and pollution and/or they feel that a suburban or country area is a more suitable environment in which to bring up children. They perceive such areas as safer and healthier than the inner city and expect them to provide better educational facilities.

A total of 3 per cent of respondents give reasons for wanting to move which are specifically related to features of the neighbourhood. Some few (1 per cent) want to leave because they are fed up with the physical disorder of particular streets or because they have problems with their neighbours. Only 2 per cent of all respondents made explicit reference to ethnic or racial difference: the whites among them object to the presence of too many blacks, and the blacks to racially prejudiced whites in the area. This is a very low percentage. It is possible that residents have inhibitions about expressing racial hostility during interviews. Considering the social character of Battersea and the survey area it is however more likely that within the local context - which would include talking to local interviewers - ethnic origin and colour are not significant, and that they become relevant only when talking to outsiders. This possibility is enhanced by the fact that three of the seven respondents who refer to ethnic or racial difference were interviewed by one of the two non local interviewers.

Local ties in and commitment to an area are likely to influence plans to stay or leave. In the survey neighbourhood the degree of local involvement varies for the different ethnic categories and this difference is evident in people's plans to move. The south London and north London born - two categories with a high degree of local involvement - have a lower proportion of respondents who are thinking of leaving the neighbourhood than the NCW category or the category born in the UK outside London. And while the percentage of NCW respondents with no plans to leave the area is only slightly lower than the percentage of UK (outside London) born, the NCW respondents' stronger ties with Battersea and south London are reflected in the fact that most of them do not want to leave the Battersea or the south London area. On the other hand the UK born, a category with weak local ties, have a relatively high proportion of people who want to move away from London altogether. Here the difference in local ties is only one explanation; there is also the socio economic factor. The NCW respondents belong predominantly to the manual working classes and many are council tenants. Moving to a suburban or country setting is therefore less feasible for them than for the UK (outside London) born, many of whom are professional class people who are or aspire to be owner occupiers. There is also a cultural difference. Traditional English culture idealises living in 'the countryside' and the middle class or upwardly mobile Englishman living in a city often aspires to a more rural life (Thorns 1973; Williams 1973). People born in the New Commonwealth, like other non English minorities are more likely to take the opposite view. In their perspective it is town life which offers them the best options (Deakin & Ungerson 1977; Flett 1979; Kosmin & De Lange 1980).

Even when people are locally involved family considerations may make them decide to leave a particular neighbourhood. Children are often a decisive factor (Young & Willmott 1957; 128-30). There are also residents, perhaps young people who have not yet settled down, for whom the area is no more than a transitory place. In the survey area the household stage of respondents seems to be as significant to the desire to move as are ethnic origin and local ties; compared with other household categories higher proportions of couples and respondents with young children have more or less specific plans to move.

It appears that more among the younger and socio economically mobile households than among the elderly households have plans to leave the neighbourhood. But even if those with plans to move were to follow them through, LARA will not lose its heterogeneous population, or come to resemble those inner city areas in which only the elderly and the 'socially disadvantaged' have remained. Even those few who talk of leaving are a reasonable cross section of the whole.

CONCLUSION

This chapter has considered a number of dimensions of local involvement. At the level of individual respondents we have looked at the use of local amenities, social contacts in the local area, and any plans they have to move. Because one objective of this study has been to examine the extent to which people of different origins now living in the same area differ in the way they organise livelihood and relate to the local area, we have analysed the material in terms of ethnic origin. Our data suggest that it has markedly less effect on local involvement than age, family cycle, work commitments and social class. Similarly, in the matter of indices used by well established residents to define insiders and outsiders at neighbourhood level, ethnic origin is relatively insignificant. This small area follows the traditions of Battersea as a whole: incomers of any origin can 'become insiders' on the basis of long residence or active participation in local activities.

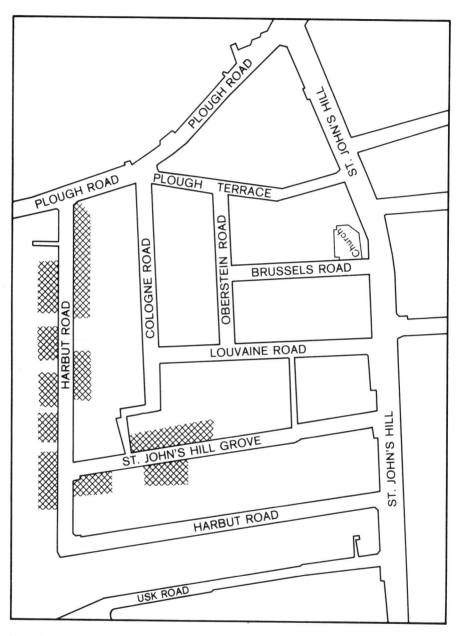

Map 5.1

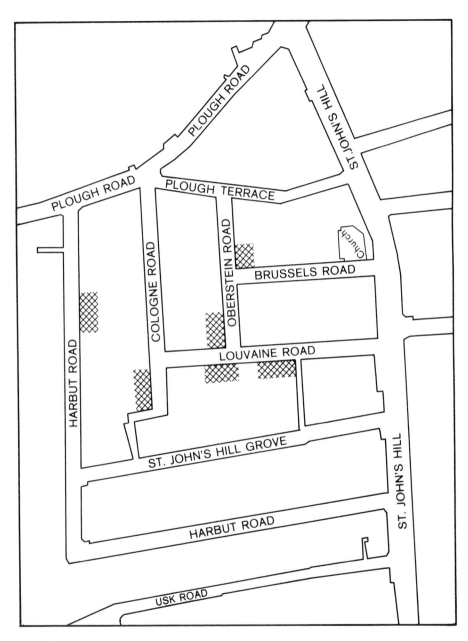

Map 5.2

TABLE 5.1

LENGTH OF RESIDENCE OF THE RESPONDENTS

(expressed as percentages of each ethnic category)

	All Resp.	South London	North London	Other UK	NCW	Irish	Other Foreign
Total Number	446	140	43	66	146	31	20
Time in Battersea	%	%	%	%	%	%	%
N.I.	3	–	2	5	3	3	–
Under 1 year	9	4	12	14	11	6	15
1-5 yrs	22	9	23	21	32	23	40
5-10 yrs	13	7	14	12	19	16	10
10-20 yrs	15	3	2	18	26	23	25
Over 20 yrs	18	16	47	30	8	29	10
Since Birth	20	61	–	–	–	–	–

TABLE 5.2

KIN IN BATTERSEA AND SOUTH LONDON (RESPONDENTS ONLY)

expressed as percentages of existing kin in each category (N)

Resp's Bth Plce	Mother				Father				Mother-in-law				Father-in-law				Adult Chldn outside Hh		
	(N)	Hh	Bat	SL	(N)	Hh	Bat	SL	(N)	Hh	Bat	SL	(N)	Hh	Bat	SL	(N)	Bat	SL
All Resp	(227)	2	16	18	(178)	1	15	18	(152)	3	21	15	(120)	1	19	15	(138)	26	35
S London	(49)	3	34	49	(43)	0	32	45	(39)	4	32	25	(29)	3	34	28	(60)	33	37
N London	(20)	0	10	30	(18)	5	5	29	(14)	0	36	29	(8)	0	38	25	(20)	30	34
Other UK	(39)	0	5	5	(29)	0	9	7	(33)	4	22	6	(26)	0	21	10	(19)	5	37
NCW	(98)	4	12	4	(72)	0	10	6	(54)	3	8	3	(41)	0	11	4	(42)	21	24
Eire	(14)	0	7	7	(11)	0	9	9	(8)	0	0	25	(5)	0	0	20	(7)	0	28
Foreign	(10)	0	0	0	(7)	0	0	0	(4)	0	0	25	(4)	0	0	25	(5)	40	20

Notes: Hh: Same household
        Bat: Battersea (including LARA)
        SL: other South London

Chapter Six returns to the economic aspects of livelihood. It analyses the work patterns of the neighbourhood population, including both paid employment and 'informal economic activity' in the discussion.

The evidence for informal economic activity is patchy and difficult to evaluate, except where household tasks are concerned: in the domestic sphere women do most of the work. The evidence for 'formal employment' patterns is more complete. LARA men pursue a wide variety of occupations and the majority have jobs outside the Battersea area; LARA women, presumably because they are under pressure to accommodate to family and household needs, have a narrower occupational range and show a preference for part time or flexible time jobs near home.

But wherever they are employed and no matter how far outside Battersea, men and women alike consider local sources of information more effective than any other in the search for work. Most currently employed residents found out about the job they now have on informal networks centering in or around the LARA area.

Since 'insiders' have by definition more and better access to information resources of any kind, residents of 'south London ethnic origin' (i.e. those born in south London of south London parents) are least likely to be unemployed when jobs get scarce. But ethnic origin does not of itself keep anyone out of the local information system - evidence the fact that the work patterns and expectations of 'ethnic south Londoners' and Caribbean born south Londoners of long standing are very alike.

6 Livelihood III: Employment and work

IAN BUCHANAN

THE SCOPE OF WORK

The LARA area survey set out to discover the ways in which people organise livelihood in the inner city, and work in its widest sense covers the management of all the resources necessary to livelihood. This chapter deals only with work in the narrower 'economic' sense: it covers remunerated activities like regular paid employment and unremunerated tasks like housework. Labour is the primary resource involved, but since information about work determines access to it and how it is done, information resources are also taken into account.

The focus is the individual and the relationship of the individual's sex, age, social class, ethnic origin and position in the household to a wide range of work activities. The underlying theme is change and continuity in the LARA area because even though many individuals travel widely in the course of their jobs, the neighbourhood remains the main arena of everyday life. At the same time employment inside or outside a residential area is vital to its general livelihood. Studies of other parts of London, notably those done in Bethnal Green in the East End in the 1950s, leave employment out of account when its pursuit carries the population beyond the physical boundaries of the residential neighbourhood (Young and Willmott 1957). Our evidence for LARA in south London however, shows that patterns of seeking, finding and getting a job vary with the extent of integration and involvement in the neighbourhood and in turn affect community process.

THE BACKGROUND TO EMPLOYMENT IN LARA AND BATTERSEA

The neighbourhood survey was residentially based and covered the entire population living in the LARA area. But not all residents work in that area or even in Battersea. The appropriate context for the study of their work is therefore the whole area over which they range to work rather than work in the LARA area or Battersea. Local authorities tend to look at the employment prospects of their residents in terms of the availability of work locally - probably because any influence they might have on labour markets is mainly limited to their administrative constituencies - but there is rarely a close correspondence between residents in and workers in the administrative areas of great cities.

The distinction between the employment of residents of a particular area and employment in that area is an important one because it is not only suburban commuters who travel to work. Our inner cities are not closed communities, and the inner city worker normally sells his labour in the same labour markets as the suburban commuter, and may travel to them in the same way. Battersea itself illustrates this point. At its genesis, long before it qualified for the inner city label, modern Battersea was a suburb. Although its population was initially varied, the working classes and poorer clerks in the north and the middle classes in the south shared the need to travel to work. This need has persisted. Since 1921 the proportions of the Battersea population travelling outside Battersea Borough to work have remained constant at around 60 per cent for both men and women; so have their destinations. Westminster has always been the primary source of employment particularly in the case of women, whilst Wandsworth (which was separate from Battersea before the reorganisation of London government), Lambeth, the City (for men) and Chelsea (for women) have remained prominent. (Census 1921, 1951, 1961, 1971).

The LARA area is apparently even more reliant on dispersed labour markets; in 1978 77 per cent of employed men and 71 per cent of employed women travelled outside the old Battersea Borough to work. But LARA lies in the extreme west of Battersea and within walking distance of Wandsworth, which means that a larger proportion of comparatively local jobs will involve travel outside Battersea. The similarities between LARA in 1978 and Battersea in 1971 and earlier are therefore more significant than the differences.

These travel to work patterns reflect the variety of occupations which the Battersea population has pursued. Although changes in census classification and job descriptions make it impossible to trace changes in employment in this or any other area with accuracy, the general picture is clear. Despite changes in national employment patterns involving an increase in white collar work and a decline in manual work, Battersea men have continued to spread themselves across a wide range of jobs. Throughout this century transport occupations have been the most important but clerks, engineering workers, building workers and those employed in commerce and finance have all been prominent to varying degrees; even at their height in 1921, transport occupations accounted for less than one in five of the male Battersea workforce. Nor is transport synonymous with the railways. In the misnamed Clapham Junction, Battersea houses the world's most famous railway junction, yet it has never had an overwhelming direct impact on local employment. Both road transport and the great Metropolitan labour market have employed more Battersea men than the railways at every census this century.

Despite increasing participation by women in the labour force, the occupations of Battersea women have remained strikingly constant during this century and show markedly less variation than the jobs taken by Battersea men. Since 1901 over half the economically active women in Battersea have been engaged in personal service and clerking/typing; even the movement of women into transport jobs since the war has not altered the dominance of these traditionally female occupations. Within these broad heads however, there have been some changes. In the personal service rubric domestic servants and laundresses have been superseded by charwomen and office cleaners and supplemented by a host of minor services like hairdressing, and the clerical/typing group tends now to centre less around clerical duties and more around typing or the more general office functions of the secretary. Nevertheless most women still fill subordinate positions which lack a career structure.

Over the last twenty years parts of Britain's inner cities have lost some of their traditional population and have received large numbers of immigrants - many of them non white people from the New Commonwealth. These immigrants rarely live entirely apart from the native population and may in time, by marriage and association, assume the role of natives themselves. Analysis by ethnic origin reveals similarity as well as difference in an area like LARA, or indeed Battersea where migrants have been settled for a generation. The present approach balances ethnic difference against the identity of community interests.

The ethnic classification used here is not simply a division into coloured and white populations. Asian, African, Caribbean and south London ethnic origins are distinguished, and the remainder of the population is divided into those born elsewhere in London, those born out of London but in the UK, the Irish born and foreign born residents. The category south London ethnic origin (SLEO) includes people born in south London of parents both of whom were also born in south London. It was created to counter the general inference that ethnic origin only differentiates populations by colour, but has special bearing in the LARA area;

the survey data indicate that jobs are not found locally,
but information about jobs is transmitted locally.
It is at this level that employment and community come
together. And because the SLEO category can be said
to incorporate the sense of identity and continuity
of an indigenous population, it is in this section
of the population, if in no other, that one would expect
to find extensive and efficient local information networks.
In 1978 people of SLEO accounted for 14 per cent of
the population of the LARA area and were distributed
across almost a quarter of its households. They were
a substantial presence in the survey neighbourhood
and, despite containing more than their share of LARA's
elderly, include a complement of children and the economically active. The SLEO population is not therefore
an historical appendix to urban decay.

SOCIAL CLASS AND THE COMMUNITY

The most generally used classification of people in
employment is social class. Social classes have been
identified in the census since 1911; the classifications
used in the 1971 census have been used also in the
analysis of the LARA survey. The social class distinction
is more appropriate to our present purposes than socio
economic group (SEG) because it has the virtue of simplicity. Socio economic grouping was introduced in
the 1951 census and by 1971 consisted of 20 categories
and sub-categories, each containing 'people whose social,
cultural and recreational standards and behaviour are
similar' (Census 1971). Since these were matters
for enquiry rather than assumption in this study, the
extra sophistication of the SEG would have been counter
productive.

  LARA in 1978 is predominantly working class - a feature
which reflects its Battersea context. Its overall
class structure is also similar to that found in Wandsworth
L.B. and greater London in 1971. Interesting differences
appear when the class structures of the various ethnic
categories in the area are compared. People of Asian
ethnic origin, African ethnic origin, Irish birth and
foreign birth are too few to contribute significantly
to the analysis, but are included in the tables to
provide complete information. People of Caribbean
and south London ethnic origin are numerically the
most important.

  Men of New Commonwealth ethnic origin are apparently
of a lower social class than the rest of the population.
When differentiated from the New Commonwealth population,
men of Caribbean ethnic origin are of even lower social
class. 78 per cent of Caribbean born men in the area
belonged to the traditionally defined manual working
classes (IIIM, IV and V), compared with 65 per cent

of all New Commonwealth men in the area. However, the tendency for more men of Caribbean ethnic origin to belong to the manual classes is paralleled in the disaggregated white population: over two thirds of men living in the LARA area who are of south London ethnic origin belong to the manual classes. This is a higher proportion than in the New Commonwealth population as a whole and, with the exception of the small number of Irish men, only men in the Caribbean sub-category filled more manual occupations. At the other extreme only a little over a quarter of men in the area who were born in the UK but not in London worked in manual jobs and two thirds of them belonged to the professional and intermediate classes (Table 6.1).

A clear social class pattern emerges among men in the LARA area. The men of south London ethnic origin, the category designed to represent continuity and local roots, are predominantly of the manual working classes, continuing the traditions of Battersea described earlier in this book. At the other extreme are men born outside London but in thet UK. Two thirds of this category worked in middle class occupations. Typically they are transient middle class people who have not put down local roots. Many are either not married or newly married young people living in privately rented accommodation. There is also a stable middle class element in the LARA area, some in the pleasanter and more compact residences of St. John's Hill Grove, where they are able to buy and improve their own homes. Much of the impulse for community action has come from this middle class element, but it is numerically small and not typical of those born outside London but in the UK.

Other sub-populations fit between these groups - between those with a stake in the community and those passing through. The category of men of Caribbean ethnic origin may be of lower social class than any other but its overall structure closely resembles that of men of south London ethnic origin. Both groups are essentially working class and have almost identical proportions of men working in skilled manual occupations. Although the Caribbean men do not have the traditional family roots which are the distinguishing feature of the south London ethnic population, many have established their own families in the area or belong to families which have settled there. On the whole the local Caribbean population is well established. Of those born in the Caribbean over half had been in the UK for 15 years or more and one in ten for over a quarter of a century. The vast majority of this population has lived in south London, mainly Battersea, since arriving in the UK. They have conformed to the traditional pattern of occupations found in the area and,

if intrusion is measured in terms of incongruence rather
than potential rivalry, are less intrusive in the local
systems than the population born outside London but
in the UK.

In sharp contrast to the men there are few differences
in the social class of women in the various ethnic
groups.   This is a function of the narrow range of
jobs engaged in by women.   There is one significant
variation from the general pattern in that compared
with other women in the area, women of south London
ethnic origin are underrepresented in professional
and intermediate classes and overrepresented in the
class involved in partly skilled occupations.   The
opposite holds for women born outside London but in
the UK (Table 6.1).   Thus LARA women who are involved
in the labour market are almost universally engaged
in service occupations which have the advantages of
requiring low levels of skill and of providing a demand
for part time workers.   Part time work is particularly
attractive to married women.   Of ninety one persons
in the LARA area described as part time workers, eighty
two are female.   The only 'ethnic' feature is the
preponderance of Caribbean women in 'professional and
related occupations in education, welfare and health'.
This reflects the take up by these women of jobs as
nurses and ancillary staff, mainly in the National
Health Service.

Much of the far greater variation in types of occupation
and industry pursued by men in the area is explained
quite adequately by social class.   Occupational classifications do, however, highlight some differences between
the Caribbean population and the south London ethnic
population.   The similarity in social class between
south London and Caribbean men is evident in the fact
that the largest number of men from both ethnic groups
(around a quarter) was found in 'metal and electrical
processing making and repairing occupations'.   But
the Caribbean men are distinguishable by the relatively
large number engaged in 'transport operating, material
moving and storing operations'.   Much of this employment
is provided by London Transport and British Rail and
probably reflects local opportunities in transport
as much as the legacy of earlier job patterns of Caribbean
immigrants (Patterson 1968: 96-7;   Smith 1977: 90).
It is striking that few south London ethnics had jobs
in transport; they were more frequently found in 'clerical
and related occupations'.   Although not engaged in
traditional blue collar work they were occupied in
another sphere long associated with Battersea - subordinate
office work (clerking).   They do not resemble the
migrant group from the rest of the UK for whom the
'professional and related occupations' designation
was typical.   By and large, SLEO white collar workers
remain within the occupational traditions of Battersea.

The vast majority of LARA residents 'in employment' are employees: 89 per cent of men and 96 per cent of women. Apart from two unpaid workers in family firms the rest of the working population is self employed. None of these however, employ over 25 persons; LARA is not the sort of area associated with large scale enterprises or entrepreneurs. Seven men run business enterprises which employ less than 25 persons and the rest of the self employed (25 men and 9 women) have no employees at all. Self employment is commonest in men of south London ethnic origin, 14 per cent of whom are engaged on their own account.

Not all of the LARA area population is in employment: only 55 per cent of men and 44 per cent of women have jobs. Those who have not cannot confidently be assigned a social class. Apart from children, the retired make up the largest number of those not active in the formal economy - i.e. those not 'in employment'. 8 per cent of men and 13 per cent of women are retired - a designation which means they receive a retirement pension, not necessarily that they were once employed. The retired population is important because it includes many of those who have an attachment to the area and are at home in the community. The typical retired person is an older member of the south London ethnic group.

INFORMATION AND EMPLOYMENT

This chapter cannot hope to uncover more than the broadest framework of employment in the LARA population. However, responses to the question how did each person find the job they have? throw up variations which reveal the operation of information networks. Except where random influences might have been important, the most common method of finding a job, irrespective of sex and, in the main, of ethnic origin, was by 'just applying at the place'. Other favourites were 'through a friend' and 'from an advertisement'. The large proportion finding work by 'just applying at the place' may be misleading because the question was answered by one person on behalf of the whole household and it is unlikely that they knew precisely how every household member found or finds each job. But it is also unlikely that aimless application at the workplace is common: work seekers normally act on some kind of information, even if it turns out not to be accurate. The number of people who report finding a job through friends gives still more grounds for this assumption (Table 6.2).

There is a marked contrast in the methods used to find jobs by members of different ethnic groups. Male migrants from the UK (outside London) report finding their jobs through friends, from advertisements, and from miscellaneous sources. Fewer of these men than of any other category 'just applied at the place', and still fewer took advice about jobs from family members. Apart from the possible effect of jobs and kin being in different parts of the country, the relatively high social status of these residents may account for the pattern since friends or colleagues are more likely to be useful in the search for higher status jobs and the jobs tend to be widely advertised, often nationally, or got by 'internal promotion' or transfers within the firm or organisation - contingencies covered by the 'miscellaneous' category in Table 6.2.

Similarly, men of Caribbean ethnic origin rarely use the help or advice of family members in the search for work. They are unique however, in being the only sizeable ethnic category to use Job Centres (Labour Exchanges) frequently. 14 per cent of Caribbean men found their present job in this way. Job Centres carry more than their share of less attractive vacancies and are used mainly by the unskilled and those for whom other sources fail (DoE 1979: 753-6). It is likely that a combination of a lack of skills and restricted access to local information networks accounts for the greater reliance placed on Job Centres by men of Caribbean ethnic origin. 'Friends' are for some of them an important medium of access to employment, but 41 per cent were reported as 'just having applied at the place'. Again, it seems unlikely that four out of ten Caribbean men walked aimlessly from employer to employer until they found work. It is more likely that the process only felt random because they made a large number of applications before finding work. In either case the experience of failure, whether caused by lack of skills, unwillingness on the part of employers to take them on, or faulty information, can lead to the distrust of any information offered (Table 6.2).

The best evidence of the effective functioning of information resources is the experience of the population of south London ethnic origin. Only among south London men is information about jobs obtained 'through a family member'. At the same time the proportion finding work 'through a friend' remains high and 'from a Job Centre' becomes even less popular. This evidence of the importance of information obtained through all kinds of local ties links directly with the criteria used to define the south London ethnic group: people living in the area where they and their parents were born are at home in that area and will be able to draw on a wide range of kin and friends for help in finding a job. The respondents' reports tend to confirm this assumption and certainly do not challenge it (Table 6.2).

It is important that these local information resources

are used to find jobs outside Battersea or south London. South London men are not significantly more likely than others to have a job in Battersea and more of their numbers (45 per cent) than of any other work outside south London. By this measure information networks produced by long association with Battersea/south London extend in a way which follows the traditional patterns of work of Battersea residents. Since the census first asked about workplace and residence in 1921, only about a third of the male working population has been employed in Battersea itself. Even in 1921 Battersea was an established community, a working class suburb whose residents were well used to operating in a dispersed labour market.

There is equally good evidence of efficient information networks in the job finding resources of women of south London ethnic origin. Jobs found 'through a friend' are as significant as for other categories of women, and jobs found 'through a family member' even more so. But the pattern for south London women differs from that of south London men in two respects: one third of the women found their jobs through advertisements, and a very large majority (85 per cent) work in the south London area. Local employment tends generally to appeal to unskilled women workers because transport costs in London are prohibitive to low wage earners and because many of them anyway have domestic commitments which make local work attractive, especially on a part time basis. Even those women who can command a reasonable wage may, in the face of domestic responsibilities, be put off by a high cost in time of travelling to work. Nevertheless, the proportion of south London women working locally is higher than of any other group of women residents.

The fact that such a high proportion of south London women found work 'through an advertisement' is further evidence of their local bias. The survey did not distinguish between types of advertisements, but the jobs they have would only have been advertised in local shops and local newspapers. Moreover, commercial employment agencies which tend to specialise in clerical and typing jobs were not used at all by women of south London ethnic origin. Agencies tend to carry information about vacancies well beyond their location; south London women can afford to ignore them because they are adept at using information resources leading them to work near at hand. Access to local information is not of course limited to the well established indigenous group, but the south London ethnic origin category is by definition one whose members will tend to use and identify with local resources more consistently and more successfully than newcomers to the area. ·By this token differences in access and use of local information resources among the various ethnic categories reflect levels of familiarity with those resources; neither cultural difference nor the active discrimination of employers need play any part.

Generally, both the Caribbean and the south London ethnic groups are settled parts of the community. The distinction between them in the labour market is that the Caribbean population is in the process of expanding its resource networks. It is still learning to be local. On the other hand the population born outside London but in the UK has relatively little incentive to identify itself with local resources related to employment.

UNEMPLOYMENT

Official unemployment statistics in the UK are a product of the welfare system insofar as they define the unemployed as those who have registered for unemployment benefit in the week of any count. The major drawbacks of the official figure are that it does not count everyone seeking employment, nor does it distinguish between those who are earning through informal or unenumerated work and those who are not. The Battersea Survey produced a fuller picture by allowing people three ways of describing themselves as unemployed: 'registered unemployed', 'unemployed, not registered, but looking for a job', and 'unemployed, not registered, not looking for a job'.

In 1978 the rate of unemployment in the area was 8 per cent for men and 7 per cent for women. (Percentages for December 1981 are given in the last chapter.) Even allowing for the more comprehensive definitions used in the survey this is slightly higher than in the UK and in London as a whole. The national rate was just under 6 per cent (6.7 per cent for men and 4.4 per cent for women) and declining slowly in the autumn of 1978; in the same period it was 3.6 per cent among men and 2.2 per cent among women in greater London (DoE 1978: 1407), reflecting the fact that during this century the rate of unemployment has been somewhat lower in London than in the rest of the country.

Although the rates of unemployment for men and women in the survey area were similar, there are striking differences in the nature of the unemployment. By asking the length of time each unemployed person had been out of work the survey revealed unemployment to be markedly longer term amongst women: half of all unemployed women had been without work for six months or more, while only 27 per cent of unemployed men had been so long out of a job; the same proportion of unemployed men (27 per cent) had been out of work for less than one month compared with 15 per cent of unemployed

women.   Respondents to the survey were then asked
to give an opinion on how soon each individual in the
household was likely to obtain work.   In the cases
where an opinion was expressed, respondents felt that
73 per cent of unemployed men would find work within
the month, and that 63 per cent of unemployed women
would take longer than six months to find a job.
The contrast is stark: the outlook was then optimistic
for men and pessimistic for women.   The number of
unemployed men expected to find work within the month
far exceeded the number who had been unemployed for
less than a month;   over half of the men who were expected
to find work within the month had been unemployed for
more than three months.   On the other hand respondents'
expectations of the future employment chances of women
were different.   The longer a woman was out of work
the longer the expected interval before the next job.

Several factors explain these different interpretations
of male and female unemployment.   Most significant
is the fact that position of women in the labour force
is equivocal.   Although women workers have become
more numerous and more permanent in recent years, they
continue to show a preference for part time employment
and remain the first to lose their jobs in recessions
(DoE. 1981: 167-73).   Also, women are still seen and
often still see themselves as having alternatives to
paid employment.   Single parents apart, most women
are not the household's only bread winner and a primary
or alternative earner makes their employment less critical.
This is also a factor for all single adults still living
in the natal household, but a combination of social
pressures and postmarital patterns sustain a division
of household labour which makes unemployed daughters
more acceptable than unemployed sons.

The marginality of female employment is based on
a very traditional interpretation of roles.   Any increased
participation of non professional women in the labour
force does not imply a feminist redefinition of their
world or the beginnings of a shift towards equality.
Employment represents for them an additional rather
than an alternative burden of work.   By and large
daily domestic work remains the preserve of women and
men's failure to take it up implies that they and perhaps
their women folk regard men as breadwinners first and
foremost - even when unemployed or retired.   Employment
is still considered more essential to a man's identity
than a woman's.   Hence perhaps the respondents' need
for greater optimism over the employment chances of
men as opposed to women.

The small absolute number of unemployed people in
the survey area restricts the usefulness of any analysis
of unemployment by ethnic group.   It would be misleading
to lump the sexes together, and division into single

sex ethnic categories produces perilously small cell
sizes.   Within this constraint it appears that the
unemployment rate was higher among men of New Commonwealth
ethnic origin (at 9 per cent) than among other men
(at 7 per cent).   Within the New Commonwealth origin
category Caribbean men were the majority of those unemployed and their rate was as high as 11 per cent.
Unemployed men of New Commonwealth origin counted together
had experienced longer terms of unemployment than other
men: a little over 40 per cent of them had been out
of work for six months or more, while a similar proportion
of unemployed white men had been without jobs for less
than a month.

Amongst women in the area the rate of unemployment
varied very little between ethnic groups.   It was
7 per cent amongst those of New Commonwealth ethnic
origin and for the Caribbean origin sub-category, and
6 per cent amongst the rest of the population.   Half
of unemployed women, irrespective of colour or origin,
had been without work for six months or more.

One surprising element in the unemployment statistics
for the survey area is that they number very few unemployed
among the young people of Caribbean ethnic origin.
Only two men and no women of Caribbean ethnic origin
aged under 25 were unemployed.   The two men represented
about 11 per cent of Caribbean origin men under 25
(excluding students) - the same rate as for Caribbean
men of all ages.   Other evidence suggests that there
ought to have been substantially more blacks unemployed
in youth than at subsequent ages (DoE 1975: 868-71),
but in the survey area the highest rates of unemployment
for Caribbean origin men occur between the ages of
25-39.   This is precisely the age range in which the
Department of Employment has found the fullest employment.

The unusual procedures of the neighbourhood survey
(which are described in detail at the end of this volume)
achieved a response rate of over 85 per cent.   This
level of response is very satisfactory - indeed it
is extraordinarily high for inner city survey research
- but it does not guarantee that there are no significant
omissions in the non responding residents.   It is
possible, for example, that young unemployed men of
Caribbean ethnic origin were overrepresented in the
small minority which refused to respond to the survey.
We can consider this unlikely on the grounds that non
response was not significantly more frequent in households
of Caribbean ethnic origin.   In any case it is household
structure rather than ethnic origin which correlates
most directly with response rate: single person households
constituted the most significant source of refusals.
We must therefore look for more general reasons for
the low unemployed rates reported for young black people
in the survey area.

Social surveys, even when they are based on a socially or ethnically stratified sample, cannot elicit information on people who refuse to answer them. Some sections of the community escape the surveyor even when he achieves his predetermined class or ethnic sample structure. The section of black youth living in squats or communal housing falls into this category. When they are approached and refuse to respond, there is a loss of quality in the survey even if they are subsequently replaced by individuals of the same social class, ethnic origin and age living in nuclear families or in other conventional households. In this instance the official employment statistics have the advantage that they are subordinate to the social security system: the only people without jobs who do not register as unemployed are those who are not entitled to benefits or do not wish to claim them. Black unemployed youths living away from home probably do claim basic benefits; they have little to lose.

Substantial numbers of young people living away from home would place a premium on cheap shared accommodation and squats. Given that the survey area provides little of this kind of accommodation it may be that some number of young unemployed blacks left home and the home area in one move. Whatever the case, it is clear that the meaning of youth unemployment figures may vary enormously. An unemployed youth, whether of south London or Caribbean ethnic origin, who still lives with his parents in his home neighbourhood is socially and economically less vulnerable than an unemployed black youth living in a squat in Brixton.

INFORMAL ECONOMIC ACTIVITY

Economic activity which escapes enumeration by the official system is a grey area between and around employment and unemployment which has lately attracted a great deal of attention. Popularly called 'the informal sector', it comprises the black economy, including moonlighting and the so called no receipt economy, and the household economy, which includes do-it-yourself production and maintenance as well as housework (See e.g. Gershuny 1979, Henry 1978). But while the neighbourhood survey is a rich source of information on the household economy, few people were at all specific about other informal sector activities. Nevertheless, the answers to some questions can be interpreted as qualitative evidence of informal economic activity in and around the survey area.

One south Londoner for example described himself as 'self employed' and at the same time 'unemployed'. An unemployed Caribbean man entered 'anything' as his occupation. A north London born man described his occupation as 'various - all over'. There were also examples of people with marketable skills who were registered unemployed: like an African car mechanic and a single parent who was a dressmaker. Some evidence of moonlighting also appeared as a by product of the survey method. Interviewers themselves resident in the area with a resident's knowledge of local patterns and habits. During debriefing, they were therefore able to report a rich variety of economic activities. One interviewer confided that a friend, an ethnic south Londoner, worked in a bar on Saturdays and that this was work 'on the side', adding that 'any chance of working on the side and "X" knows about it'. Needless to say the identity of 'X' is not relevant to the point.

In doing the survey the interviewers could themselves be said to be engaged in 'informal' work. They adapted and fitted the interviewing to their ordinary routines. Because earnings were small and few interviewers were anyway liable to tax or national insurance, there was no need to conceal it as a source of money. Even so it represented a piece of the black economy. The response, particularly from mothers, to the opportunity to earn small sums of money locally gives an indication of demand. (The extent to which close identification with the local area was also an important element in recruitment is spelt out in the Appendix.)

The income earning informal sector is incompletely reported in this survey of work because a questionnaire cannot be a suitable tool for researching the topic. It is likely however, that the indigenous south London population can use their experience of local life and their familiarity with local information resources to advantage in informal as well as formal employment. The same applies to self employment. In the survey area most self employment was in the service sector and was dominated by men of south London ethnic origin - 14 per cent of whom worked for themselves.

In the matters of the household economy it is the value of the activity not the activity itself which is concealed (Wadel 1979). Most people recognise the household tasks of cleaning, cooking and looking after children as work, but do not regard them in quite the same way as paid employment: those who are paid but do not travel work 'at home'; those who work in the home do 'housework'. The exclusion of housework from national income calculations is equally arbitrary. In principle there is nothing to prevent economists calculating the income deriving from the performance of household tasks and incorporating it in the national income computation (Clark 1958: 205-11). In a study of this sort, on the other hand, there is every reason to integrate domestic tasks into a complete picture of work. Individuals live in households which are, in their various forms, basic units of production and

142

consumption. A household requires an income and it must provide services for its members if it is to function successfully. But the household is more than an economic unit. It may be a family unit based on relationships which transcend simple economic needs, or it may be a single individual who has to look beyond the boundaries of the household for companionship as well as domestic services. But no family unit is self sufficient and all individuals also operate outside the household domain to some extent.

Since the industrial revolution, wage labour has been the preserve of men and domestic labour that of women in urbanised communities, but in recent years this division has become more flexible. More women have entered the 'formal' labour force and the increase can be attributed mostly to married women. In the survey area female participation in the labour force was normal for 1978: four out of every five women aged 16-60 were in employment; there were only 66 women solely occupied as housewives and the attraction of the labour market was such that there were rather more (81) in part time employment.

The numerical encroachment of women into the male world is clear. What is not obvious, however, is the extent to which men have or have not assumed trad- itionally female roles. The evidence varies. Young & Willmott (1973) take the view that the growth of women's paid employment is part of a larger process which originates with the increase in leisure, the decrease in physical labour of men, and the decline in family size. Consequently they argue that women's contribution to the household is declining with the reduction in the general work load because it allows men to contribute more at home; they draw the inference that sex roles are converging and the family becoming a symmetrical unit where paid and domestic work as well as leisure are shared. While they were at pains to point out that process of change is uneven, they did find that men made a significant contribution to household tasks: almost two thirds of married men whose wives did not work and 79 per cent of men whose wives worked full time had helped with cleaning, cooking or childcare in the fortnight prior to their survey.

The LARA survey asked about the performance of basic household tasks and the information sought was rather different from that obtained in the Young & Willmott enquiry. Households in the survey area were asked who usually performed a series of basic household tasks. The answers relating to couples and nuclear families indicate that the primary responsibility for housework still lies with the wife: only 5 per cent of men regularly prepare the main meal, and only 6 per cent regularly do the shopping. However, an additional 8 per cent of all couples share the preparation of meals, 13 per cent to 19 per cent did the routine shopping together, and 6-10 per cent shared in the 'weekly wash'. 5 per cent of men in nuclear families did the weekly laundry compared to 9 per cent of men in couples. This discrepancy is accounted for by the greater use of launderettes by married couples as opposed to nuclear families, more of whom owned their own washing machines. It would seem that carrying washing to and from the launderette is a more manly task than loading a machine at home. In all these 'necessary household tasks' the contribution of school age children in nuclear families was negligible. Wives therefore assumed the sole primary responsibility for preparing the main meal in 83-84 per cent of cases, for doing the routine shopping in 71-74 per cent of cases, and for the weekly wash in 80-84 per cent of cases (Table 6.3).

There was no significant variation in this pattern according to the ethnic origin or the social class of the men. Nor does occupation or the lack of it appear to make any difference: unemployed or retired men contribute no more to the household tasks than the employed although both of these groups can have time at their disposal, and no unemployed male youth living in the parental home has assumed primary respon- sibility for a basic household task.

These figures do not refute the Young & Willmott thesis. Indeed a back up question on who else sometimes performed necessary household tasks produced figures which are tolerably similar to theirs when allowance is made for men taking or sharing in primary respon- sibility for basic household tasks. What is clear from the LARA survey is that a woman's participation in the labour force does not necessarily change her role as domestic resource keeper. It seems certain that wives decide what is to be laundered and when, and that they draw up shopping lists and decide where to shop as a corollary to their continued primary respon- sibility for household tasks. The management and organisation of domestic resources is a major concern for most women, and it is one which, in the LARA area at least, does not yet seem to be shared by their men.

A central question for the symmetry thesis is the extent to which wives continue to assume responsibility for the management of domestic work. This issue poses questions about the allocation of time to various ends by members of the household, and about the effect of domestic technology on housework and other domestic tasks. These questions are taken up at length in the following chapter.

TABLE 6.1

THE SOCIAL CLASS STRUCTURE OF THE EMPLOYED LARA POPULATION, 1978
(Expressed as percentages of those employed)

SOCIAL CLASS

	I	II	IIIN	IIIM	IV	V	UN	N
A: MEN								
TOTAL POPULATION	5	22	13	30	24	5	1	(310)
NEW COMMONWEALTH E.O.*	4	13	17	29	28	8	1	(114)
ASIAN E.O.	8	28	24	12	24	4	–	(25)
AFRICAN E.O.	7	22	30	11	22	7	–	(27)
CARIBBEAN E.O.	3	7	11	39	30	9	1	(70)
WHITE POPULATION	6	27	10	31	21	3	2	(196)
SOUTH LONDON E.O.	2	14	17	40	25	2	–	(52)
OTHER LONDON BORN	4	22	9	34	22	3	4	(67)
REST OF THE UK	13	53	6	13	13	2	–	(47)
IRISH BORN	5	5	–	50	27	9	5	(22)
FOREIGN BORN	–	50	25	–	25			(8)
B: WOMEN								
TOTAL POPULATION	3	19	40	8	29	1	–	(266)
NEW COMMONWEALTH E.O.*	1	22	41	10	24	2	–	(98)
ASIAN E.O.	–	39	31	8	23	–	–	(13)
AFRICAN E.O.	4	20	40	4	32	–	–	(25)
CARIBBEAN E.O.	–	23	42	12	20	3	–	(66)
WHITE POPULATION	4	17	40	7	32	1	–	(168)
SOUTH LONDON E.O.	–	8	41	5	46	–	–	(39)
OTHER LONDON BORN	4	11	45	9	32	–	–	(56)
REST OF THE UK	5	30	42	10	15	–	–	(41)
IRISH BORN	5	21	32	–	42	–	–	(19)
FOREIGN BORN	8	31	23	8	23	8	–	(13)

* Subtotals amount to more than the total because some individuals
  fall into two categories.

SOCIAL CLASS:

```
 I.   PROFESSIONAL, ETC. OCCUPATIONS
 II.  INTERMEDIATE OCCUPATIONS
IIIN. SKILLED NON MANUAL OCCUPATIONS
IIIM. SKILLED MANUAL OCCUPATIONS
 IV.  PARTLY SKILLED OCCUPATIONS
 V.   UNSKILLED OCCUPATIONS
 UN.  UNCLASSIFIED
```

TABLE 6.2

SOURCE OF INFORMATION ABOUT LATEST EMPLOYMENT (LARA)

(Expressed as percentages of cases reported)

A: MEN

	JUST APPLIED	FRIEND	NEIGHBOUR	FAMILY	ADVERT	JOB CENTRE	AGENCY	OTHER	
TOTAL POPULATION	28	18	1	8	21	9	2	13	(294)
NEW COMMONWEALTH E.O. *	36	17	1	4	17	11	4	10	(109)
ASIAN E.O.	32	18	0	4	18	0	11	18	(28)
AFRICAN E.O.	30	26	0	0	19	11	7	7	(27)
CARIBBEAN E.O.	41	14	2	5	19	14	0	6	(64)
WHITE POPULATION	23	19	1	11	23	8	1	15	(185)
SOUTH LONDON E.O.	27	16	0	18	18	6	0	14	(49)
OTHER LONDON BORN	25	16	2	11	25	8	0	14	(64)
REST OF THE UK	18	25	0	5	21	9	0	23	(44)
IRISH BORN	24	19	0	5	24	10	10	10	(21)
FOREIGN BORN	14	29	0	14	43	0	0	0	(7)

B: WOMEN

	JUST APPLIED	FRIEND	NEIGHBOUR	FAMILY	ADVERT	JOB CENTRE	AGENCY	OTHER	
TOTAL POPULATION	31	22	-	5	18	5	9	9	(265)
NEW COMMONWEALTH E.O. *	34	24	0	2	16	8	10	5	96
ASIAN E.O.	25	42	0	0	25	0	8	0	(12)
AFRICAN E.O.	32	24	0	3	16	8	12	8	(25)
CARIBBEAN E.O.	38	20	0	3	16	9	9	5	(64)
WHITE POPULATION	29	21	1	7	20	4	8	11	(169)
SOUTH LONDON E.O.	23	18	3	15	33	3	0	5	(39)
OTHER LONDON BORN	34	21	0	7	7	2	12	17	(58)
REST OF THE UK	25	18	0	3	28	8	10	10	(40)
IRISH BORN	35	30	0	5	20	0	5	5	(20)
FOREIGN BORN	25	25	0	0	8	8	17	17	(12)

* Subtotals amount to more than the total because some individuals fall into two categories.

146

TABLE 6.3

BACK UP PERSONS SOMETIMES PERFORMING NECESSARY
HOUSEHOLD TASKS (LARA)

(Expressed as percentages of Couples and Nuclear Families)

PREPARATION OF THE MAIN MEAL	COUPLES	NUCLEAR FAMILIES
No One	53 (37)[2]	49 (32)[2]
Husband	41	25
Wife	5	5
Husband & child	N.A.	1
Child(ren)	N.A.	16
Others in/rest of family	N.A.	2
Others (i.e. outside the Household)	1	3

ROUTINE SHOPPING

	COUPLES	NUCLEAR FAMILIES
No One	67 (41)[2]	57 (28)[2]
Husband	30	24
Wife	2	1
Husband & child	N.A.	2
Wife & child	N.A.	2
Child(ren)	N.A.	12
Everyone	N.A.	1
Others (i.e. outside the Household)	1	2

MAIN LAUNDRY

	COUPLES	NUCLEAR FAMILIES
No One	79 (59)[2]	69 (43)[2]
Husband	18	11
Wife	2	3
Husband & child	N.A.	1
Wife & child(ren)	N.A.	2
Child(ren)	N.A.	13[1]
Others (i.e. outside the Household)	1	1
	N = 98	N = 115

NOTES

(1) Includes one case where daughters do their own.

(2) The figures in parentheses represent the proportion
of households where the wife performs the basic
household task without any other assistance.
Allowance has been made for the usual performance of
tasks by husbands and others, and for shared
domestic work.

Chapter Seven focusses on the distribution of work between men and women living together and so brings the discussion of livelihood home. Only households containing a couple are considered. The analysis charts the effect of age, family stage and wife's employment status on the extent to which particular household tasks are the special responsibility of men or of women, and on the total amounts of time each partner spends 'at work'.

Evidence for the sexual division of household labour is taken from LARA residents' answers to questions about the use of more than three dozen items of household equipment, each of which is associated with a particular household task. Each item has been 'scored' according to whether only women, men and women, or only men use it. By this measure LARA couples are quite 'traditional': cooking, cleaning and washing are female specialised tasks; 'odd jobs' and do-it-yourself repairs are male specialised tasks; only leisure time activities and entertainment are not specialised to either partner.

There is some variation within this frame. Tasks are much less specialised in younger couple households than in older ones; and a woman's full time paid employment increases the likelihood that her husband does some share of 'female tasks'. Even where both are employed full time however, domestic tasks tend to remain sex specific. Time budget data from several sources confirm that when paid and unpaid work are totalled together, employed women work considerably longer hours than their husbands.

But no division of labour is immutable. There are indications that the present cohort of young couples will not organise time and tasks the way their parents do even when, in the normal course of the domestic cycle, they come to match their parents' present age.

7 Livelihood IV: Household tasks and the use of time

J. I. Gershuny

INTRODUCTION

The purpose of this chapter is to throw some light on how domestic tasks are distributed in the LARA area of Battersea. It uses two different but connected research instruments. The first is embodied within the LARA survey: a new, extremely simple, but nevertheless very revealing indicator of the pattern of specialisation in domestic tasks within households. The second was started under the auspices of the LARA project, but has been developed for the more general purposes of a national, random-sampled, time budget survey (Gershuny and Thomas 1980). We shall consider in the following pages how much housework is done in LARA, and how the total of domestic tasks is distributed between the sexes, and will compare the picture that emerges with the findings of larger, national surveys of household tasks and the use of time.

There are two distinct reasons for carrying out local area studies of the kind reported in this book. The first is a specific interest in the unique characteristics of the local area itself - in the attributes which relate to particularly <u>local</u> circumstances. Where we are concerned, to choose a particularly pertinent example, with employment in LARA, with which sorts of people have which sorts of paid jobs, national statistics are not very much help to us, and accordingly our own survey of the area must be our primary, if not our only, source of information. The second reason is an interest in more general issues which can nevertheless only be investigated, or at least more conveniently be investigated, in the context of a particular locality. If there are grounds for believing that certain behaviour is roughly constant across a region or a nation, then we can use local studies as an alternative to regional or national research - as is done for example, in the local 'test marketing' of consumer products by market research organisations. And just as a special case can illuminate the general issue, so the general sometimes illuminates the special: under appropriate circumstances national data can be used to supplement the local picture.

The sexual division of domestic labour falls into the category of phenomena which are apparently constant across localities, and even across regions and nations. A multi-national time budget survey shows that domestic work is distributed in a very similar way between the two sexes in each of ten countries surveyed in the 1960s (Szalai 1972); comparison of UK data with information from the USA and from Canada shows very similar patterns for the 1970s (Robinson 1977, Meissner et al., 1977); and most important, the absolute amounts as well as the distributions of domestic activities shown in 1970 data for the London region (Young and Willmott 1973) compare very closely with our own data for the UK as a whole.

Before proceeding to it we should note that only the 225 'couple households' among the 446 households participating in the LARA survey appear in this chapter. It is concerned with what is usually called 'the sexual division of labour' and so focusses on the distribution of time and tasks only in households where men and women live together; single person, single parent, single sex and collective households are not included in the analysis. We have analysed patterns of the couples' household work in terms of job commitments outside the home (employment), age (life cycle), family stage (domestic cycle), and their access to household appliances or labour saving equipment. The sub-sample was too small to allow any test of the possible effects of ethnic origin or social class. The fact that these characteristics are not taken into account does not mean they have no significance to household organisation in Battersea or elsewhere. It means only that we have avoided drawing statistical inference where cell sizes do not justify it.

SEXUAL SPECIALISATION

In the study of time use, the most common measure used is the simple average time devoted to a particular activity either by the whole population or by some section of it. This statistic can give an indication of the behaviour of the community as a whole, but it is difficult to translate into individual terms. How useful is it to be told that the population as a whole spends an average of three minutes per week watching football matches? It would be more helpful to know that 2½ per cent of the population spend an average of two hours per week watching football, while 97½ per cent of the population does not participate in the activity.

So three different measures of time use need to be

distinguished: first, the average time spent in an activity over a period; second, the participation rate - i.e. the proportion of the population who engage in the activity over that period; and third, the average time spent by participants in the activity ('participants' time'). Obviously the three statistics are related. The participation rate, multiplied by the participants' time, equals the average time spent in the activity. We use two of these measures in this chapter - the participation rate and the average time - to illustrate two rather different but nevertheless easily confused, phenomena - the sexual specificity of participation in particular domestic tasks, and the sexual division of total household work. In this section we shall consider the participation statistics which emerge from the LARA survey.

In the literature participation data are found in conventional questionnaire results: the General Household Survey, for example, frequently asks its respondents directly whether they have participated in particular leisure activities during the past month (see Young and Willmott 1973). They are also found in the Time Budget Survey: any source that tells us how much time is devoted to a particular activity will also tell us whether or not any time is allocated to it - precisely the participation/non participation dichotomy.

We used two different versions of the first of these techniques in LARA (see questionnaire appended). First, we asked questions like: 'Who normally prepares the main meal?' and 'Who normally does the weekly wash?'. The answers we received were not very surprising. In most cases we found that the wife of the male head of the household 'normally' carried out these major domestic tasks. But what does 'normally' mean? Every day except Christmas, or four or five days a week? We therefore added the questions 'Who helps?' and 'How?'; 'Who else sometimes does it?' and 'In what circumstances?'. The range of answers indicated that it may be 'normal' for, say, a man to cook the main meal every Sunday, or every time his wife is working late even if she is defined as the cook; and that we cannot assume that the person who 'normally' does a particular task does everything required for its completion. Equally the person who 'normally' prepares the main meal or does the laundry may just take the responsibility for its organisation, leaving some of the less central activities associated with it - 'laying the table', 'putting out the washing' - to other household members.

These insights are valuable but only impressionistic. We need a more sensitive indicator, and one which will allow us to quantify its indications. The most promising solution would be the use of very detailed housework time budget surveys, but these surveys are extremely expensive, and their application would have swallowed up all our research resources. We therefore developed a new approach to measuring participation in housework to supplement the conventional direct questions.

On the assumption that particular pieces of household equipment are used for very specific tasks, we included in the LARA survey questions on the ownership and use of certain items of household equipment. Answers to these questions are the raw material out of which the argument in this section is constructed. They have given us a large body of extremely simple and unambiguous information concerning which households own particular household items, which members of these households use each item - and by implication, which members of the households participate in the domestic task or tasks associated with each item.

EQUIPMENT AND PARTICIPATION IN TASKS

Households differ in size and composition and these extra questions produced a mass of rather untidy information which we had to find some means of summarising. Since we are interested in sexual specialisation, we decided to identify 'husbands' and 'wives' within households, and to consider only the distribution of activities between pairs of spouses. We do lose information this way, since not all households contain such pairs, but the 'spouse pair' data does give us a neat first approximation to the sexual division of tasks.

For each spouse pair household we have three pieces of information for each of 40 pieces of domestic equipment: we know whether the household possesses the equipment, whether the 'husband' uses it, and whether the 'wife' uses it. These three pieces of information can be summarised, for each household, and each gadget, into one variable, coded as follows:

-1 = only the 'wife' uses the equipment
0 = both husband and wife use it
+1 = only the husband uses it
+9 = the household does not possess the equipment

Figure 7.1 shows the frequency distribution of this variable for thirty nine of the forty items on our list. (Data for the fortieth, - 'kitchen scales' had to be excluded because of a programming error.) We can see immediately that some of the gadgets are used mainly by the wives, while others are used mainly by the husbands. The distributions suggest a certain pattern of specialisation - wives being more likely to use cooking and cleaning equipment, husbands carpentry and repair equipment.

If we ignore cases where the household does not possess

the particular item and find the mean value for the remaining cases, we can calculate for each item - and hence, for each task - a single index of sexual specificity, whose potential values range from -1 (i.e. entirely female) through zero (not sex specific) to +1 (entirely male). Table 7.2 is a league table, showing the gadgets in order from the most female specific to the most male specific, together with indices for various subsets of the sample.

Three groups or 'clusters' of activities emerge naturally from the data. Figure 7.3 shows this quite clearly. 'Cluster 1' including just about all the cooking, house cleaning, clothes washing and sewing equipment covers the range from clothes wringers with a sexual specificity index of -1.00 to the automatic oven with an index of -0.44. The second cluster includes all the leisure equipment, and the indices range from -0.11 for the mono record player to +.10 for the stereo cassette player. Most of the indices in this cluster are close to 0, suggesting a neutral sexual specificity for leisure or recreational activities. 'Cluster 3' is very distinct indeed, consisting of the carpentry and similar equipment, with indices between +.61 (electric sander) to +.77 (electric drill). Remarkably few machines fall outside their expected clusters. The clearest exception is the motorbike: although it has a traditionally masculine aura, it emerges that 80 per cent of wives in households possessing the machines do ride them. But fridges, freezers and dishwashers whose use involves fairly minimal exertion, are considerably less sexually specialised than the rest of the cooking and cleaning equipment. Altogether a very clear, detailed and plausible hierarchy of sexual specialisation emerges: clothes washing being the most 'female' activities followed by cooking, and then by house cleaning; leisure activities show a low degree of sexual specialisation; transport activities and odd jobs are strongly 'male'.

There are different degrees of specialisation among various sorts of household. Figure 7.4 compares three different types: young couples (where the wife is less than 35) with no children, couples with children in the same household, and older couples (wife aged 35 or more) with no children in the household. Again there is a rather regular pattern, the older couples tending towards more specialisation within each activity than the younger. For the 'Cluster 3' male specialised activities, the patterns of specialisation are less marked among younger couples and the couples with children - the main contrast is between the older couples and the other two categories. For the 'Cluster 1' female specialised activities, the couples with children seem to be more similar to the older than the younger childless group. In this case the larger contrast seems to be between the younger childless group and the older two; the national sample (Figure 7.9) underlines this with direct evidence of a growth in the weight of the woman's responsibility for housework with the entry of children to the family. Yet some of the 'Cluster 2' leisure activities become less sexually specialised in older couples. Younger husbands are more likely than their wives to ride motorbikes, for example, whereas older wives are apparently not less likely than their husbands to do so.

There is a difficulty inherent in using this sort of 'cross sectional' data: we do not know whether the difference between younger and older couples is a genuine effect of getting older and more experienced (an 'age effect'), or an effect of difference between the culture and the historical experience of the different generations (a 'cohort effect'). When we find that older couples' activity patterns are more sexually specialised than younger couples, do we conclude that the experience of married life leads to specialisation (because of 'age')? Or do we conclude that the older couples formed their sex role expectations in an era of greater sexual specialisation than the present (a 'cohort' effect)? Statistical analyses (of variance and covariance) might help to disentangle some of these questions, but the (discontinuous) nature of our special- isation index makes their interpretation rather difficult.

We can go some way towards answering these questions, however, through the techniques of display used in Figures 7.3 and 7.4. Figure 7.5 shows the different sorts of households grouped according to the employment status of the wife (we only include couples with husbands in employment). Consider the older couples with no children in the household: there is a marked difference in the extent of specialisation between the couples in which the wife has a full time job, and those in which the wife is not employed. The 25 year age range within this group is wide enough to explain some of the variation in the specialisation indices (older women being less likely to have paid jobs than younger women – see Figure 7.9), but it does not account for all of it. We may still suspect that households where the wife is employed full time are less task specialised than those where the wife is not employed at all.

Households with children however, show no clear trend towards sharing tasks when the wife has a job. But there is a problem of aggregation here; the category of non-employed wives includes a significant number of women with very young children who are only temporarily non-employed. When this group is <u>averaged together with</u> the group of wives who will remain non-employed, even when their children have left home, the effect of employment is statistically less clear than in the case of the older households with no children.

These questions could be resolved if age and family circumstances were more severely controlled and a larger sample (of around a thousand couples) used. We would then have age controls adequate to testing the possibility that wives' employment leads to a decrease in task specialisation; given that each successive cohort of wives shows an increasing propensity to have paid employment, we would have strong grounds for arguing that the lower levels of sexual specialisation shown by younger couples is a 'cohort' rather than an 'age effect'. But even the evidence presented here concerning older couples without children leads us to suspect that the 'cohort' hypothesis is in fact correct - i.e. that there is a gradual change in the division of household tasks between men and women.

FROM PARTICIPATION RATES TO TIME USE

From time use statistics, the other source of information on participation rates, we can develop indices from our national time budget sample to parallel the data from direct questions in the LARA survey. Figure 7.6 gives time budget derived frequency distributions equivalent to those in Figure 7.2. The activity categories are much less detailed, of course, and for this reason show a rather higher male participation rate in cooking and cleaning, and a much higher female participation rate in 'odd jobs' - i.e. almost everyone does some of these rather general categories, even if the probability of doing each of the detailed categories is rather low. Figure 7.7 compares the time budget derived indices directly with the LARA data. It seems plausible to suggest that they are reflections of the same reality.

Turning to the more comprehensive, though less detailed, data available from the national time use survey, we see a rather similar pattern to that in the 'participation' data. Table 7.8 gives the amounts of time devoted to particular activities by husbands and wives in different sorts of activities. We see that husbands spend a large proportion of their housework time in the 'non routine' household activities, with wives concentrating on the routine. But an additional fact becomes plain: though there may be a certain symmetry in the specialisation patterns there is no equality - the time devoted to the female specialised tasks in general outweighs that devoted to the male by a factor of three or four.

This book as a whole is intended to give a picture of how life is lived in LARA. But interesting as the LARA area is in itself, we study it in such detail with the aim of coming to some broader understanding of the larger picture, of British cities, and of Britain in general. It seems quite likely that the pattern of sexual specialisation in domestic tasks that emerges from our small scale study is the pattern that holds for the country as a whole. So the detailed and clear patterns that emerge from our survey may be viewed as a contribution to the general literature on sex role specialisation in Britain. And conversely, perhaps to a greater extent than in the other chapters in this volume, we can use national statistics on time use to augment the information obtained specifically from the LARA survey. So our view of the domestic division of labour in LARA is a composite, made up of some information originating from LARA itself, and some coming from the more general time budget surveys.

WHAT DO WE KNOW?

The most reliable information we have on the sexual division of domestic labour comes, paradoxically, not from data on unpaid work but from data on paid work. We find that women's economic activity rate (the proportion of women with paid jobs) varies according to their domestic circumstances. Men's economic activity rate by contrast, shows no significant variation in relation to their domestic conditions. It would seem sensible to infer from this contrast that women bear a much heavier responsibility for domestic work than men do.

Why should it be that in 1971 very nearly twice as many non married as married women between the ages of 25 and 35 had jobs? (Figure 7.9). There cannot be any very substantial direct causal connection from employment to marriage: we can hardly explain away the difference by a tendency of employed women not to marry although in the past this sort of connection did exist in certain professions). It is more likely that the causation proceeds from marriage - or some attribute of marriage - to employment. And on this evidence it would seem quite sensible to argue that it is the unpaid domestic work responsibilities of married women which take priority over paid work. We can identify these unpaid work responsibilities more precisely by considering the paid employment pattern of women with children (Figure 7.10). The participation rate varies inversely with the age (and hence the independence) of the youngest child. Around 80 per cent of women between the ages of 25 and 45, with youngest children able to take care of themselves, have paid jobs - a total not far short of the male participation rate. Women with much younger children, by contrast, have very much lower participation rates, while the male participation rate remains at around 90 per cent irrespective of their family circumstances. The difference between men and women in the official statistics on paid employment must reflect the division of unpaid work within the household.

But this conclusion is merely a matter of inference; something must explain the difference between male and female paid work patterns, and it is plausible to suggest that it may be the differential in unpaid work. There are no official national statistics which show unpaid work patterns, but we can use our time budget evidence to make the point more directly. Figure 7.11, taking a sample of husband and wife pairs in the UK in the mid 1970s, expresses the husband's unpaid work as a proportion of the total of unpaid work done by the couple. It emerges that husbands do, on average, rather less than one quarter of the total domestic work. This proportion includes 'odd jobs' as well as the more routine cooking and cleaning activities; when we look at the routine chores, the husband's average percentage declines to below 10 per cent - though they do on average approximately half of the non routine work (Figure 7.12).

Another familiar finding is that wives' unpaid work does not decline proportionately as they increase the amount of paid work they do, while their husband's unpaid work totals are hardly affected. Canadian data suggests that full time employed housewives do about half as much housework as non employed wives - in effect exchanging about fifteen hours of routine housework per week for about thirty hours of paid work, giving them a total work week (paid plus unpaid work) about ten hours or (20 per cent) longer than that of their employed husbands. Our own UK data support this conclusion - we shall return to consider this data later in this chapter.

But before continuing, we must express a caution. Some writers have sought to demonstrate sexual inequality in total work time by comparing the average amounts of work done by employed men and employed women (Meissner 1977). This is an analytical fallacy because it is logically possible that the average employed woman works longer hours than the average employed man while each employed husband works exactly the same hours as his employed wife. This is quite simply explained. Assume for a moment that in all married couples with an employed wife the husband and wife work the same length of time, and that such couples work longer hours on average than married couples with no employed wife. If under this assumption we compare the average work time of employed women with that of employed men, we would still find that the average employed woman works longer hours than her male counterpart - simply because it is more likely that an employed man has a non employed wife than that an employed woman has a non employed husband.

In fact the empirical evidence does not really fit the assumption. Our UK data do reveal a limited tendency for couples with employed wives to work slightly longer hours than couples with non working wives, but this goes only a small way towards explaining the discrepancy, most of which does genuinely come from employed wives working much harder than their husbands. Nevertheless the point is clear: argument about the sexual division of labour must rely on data on households, not on the comparison of data on individuals. And this is one great strength of the LARA survey and of our time budget data, and also of the Canadian survey cited. By giving us information on whole households rather than just on individuals, they allow us to look at the activities of individuals in their microsocial context.

Table 7.10 gives evidence of the process whereby wives employed full time gain new 'formal economy' work responsibilities without losing an equivalent proportion of their unpaid domestic work, so that the total amount of work they do rises in relation to that done by their husbands. Table 7.13 illustrates this tendency: it shows the average proportion of all the couple's work (paid and unpaid) done by the husband. We should note that there is a systematic bias in these estimates. Housewives completing our time budget diaries tended to be more conscientious about noting breaks in the working day than working men and women were about noting their meal times and rest breaks. Housewives work time therefore may be greater relative to other categories than is shown in the records. This suggests that Table 7.13 should probably look more symmetrical, with full time housewives with no children doing perhaps 45 per cent of their household's total work, and full time employed wives doing 55 per cent.

So the 'no exit for wives' conclusion - that their disproportionate responsibility for domestic work must hamper their access to paid jobs, and particularly to success in paid jobs - does emerge quite clearly from the time budget data. But an element of hope for the future can be derived from 'average time' results that parallel some of the LARA 'participation rate' findings. Table 7.14 shows the husbands' proportion of unpaid work in the different sorts of households. Just as in Figures 7.5 and 7.8, it shows an increase in the proportion of the domestic responsibilities shouldered by the husband both in the younger households and in households where the wife goes out to work. In younger couples with employed wives, husbands carry out more than four tenths of the household work. Again there is the danger of mistaking 'age' effects for 'cohort' effects. But the large scale entry of women into thet paid workforce is a recent phenomenon and we might expect the process of cultural adaptation to its effects to take a generation or so; Table 7.14 may be evidence that this adaptation is beginning to take place.

Within the overall category of unpaid work, however, sexual specialisation still remains marked. Table 7.15 shows the husbands' proportion of 'routine' (cooking and cleaning) and 'non routine' (odd jobs) tasks. The husbands' proportion of routine work does increase very considerably with the wives' paid employment, but still in the most liberated, young, two job household, the husband does on average only 15 per cent of the routine work. And indeed in such households the male proportion of non routine housework actually increases. So even those couples with more equal shares in the total housework burden may show more sexual specialisation within the various categories of housework.

We can make this point more explicitly by classifying households according to the proportion of the total unpaid work done by the husband. In Figure 7.16, the horizontal axis groups couples according to the total proportion of paid work done by the husbands; the vertical axis shows the husbands proportion of routine and non routine work for each of the groups. Even in the group of households where the husband does half the couple's total housework, on average he does rather less than a quarter of the routine work - and it is only in households where the husband does around four fifths of the total housework that he can be expected to do half the routine housework. Conversely, when the non routine housework is shared, husbands tend to do less than a quarter of the total housework.

On this basis we can advance a rather important proposition: sexual specialisation in domestic tasks is not the same as unequal sexual distribution of total domestic work. A move towards sexual equality in total domestic work time could, and on the evidence of both the LARA and the time budget data does, lead to a substantial degree of sexual specialisation in particular tasks.

So far we have discussed housework as distributed between husbands and wives. Before leaving the question of household time use, let us look briefly at the contribution of other people in the household. Table 7.17 includes the whole of our national time budget sample and covers children and other adults who are not members of 'couples' in addition to husbands and wives. We find that 'couples' are responsible for about 57 per cent of household work. Of the remaining 43 per cent, about 13 per cent is contributed by children and 30 per cent by 'other adults'. Among the children, boys contribute about half as much as girls do, and among the 'other adults', women do nearly three times as much as men. The sexual inequalities are not confined to husbands and wives.

Returning now to our specific case, Table 7.18 breaks down the LARA sample of 'couples' into the different family and employment types. This is a cross-sectional view which tells us nothing about the sequence of employment patterns experienced by a couple, but let us pretend for a moment that these data cover the same cohort for successive life stages. What picture would emerge?

Table 7.19 which is calculated as the column percentages of Table 7.18 (excluding cases where the husband has no job) gives us some such conjectural view. We see that for most young couples with no children, husbands and wives both have jobs, there is no part time employment. By contrast, most wives (62 per cent) leave the paid workforce altogether while the children are of preschool age and most of those in employment are in part time jobs. As the children grow up and go to school, so more of the wives return to the paid work force, and an increasing proportion of these return to full time work. And for older couples below retirement age, most (61 per cent) have two full time jobs, and only 15 per cent of older wives with employed husbands do not themselves have any paid employment.

There are errors built into using information about different sets of people of different ages as though it applied to one set of people at different ages. Women's employment rates have been rising over time, and the large proportion of women with children who currently work part time may well seek full time jobs as they get older, following a life pattern different from their mothers'. It is therefore likely that our synthetic sequence underestimates the future employment levels of the present generation of young women.

Similar sorts of arguments can be applied to the working time data. Consider the cross-sectional evidence: the distribution of households in LARA between the various family and employment categories (Table 7.20) can be added to the time budget data to give us a composite picture of the distribution of work between couples in LARA (Figure 7.21). The width of the columns in Figure 7.21 is proportional to the numbers of households in the various categories; the height above the central line is proportional to the average wives' work time in each category; and the depth below it is proportional to the husbands' work time. If we were to try the same experiment and transpose this from a cross-sectional into a longitudinal view, we would arrive at a rather gloomy conclusion. We would see couples, as they get older, dividing work less equally, with full time working wives spending a much larger proportion of their lives in work activities than their husbands do.

But this is not necessarily an appropriate conclusion. Working wives are less rare than they were, and our evidence shows that today's younger couples share work more equally than do older couples. The increasing inequality of total work time caused by the entry of more women into full time employment may be compensated on other levels by the more egalitarian lifestyle of the present cohort of young couples.

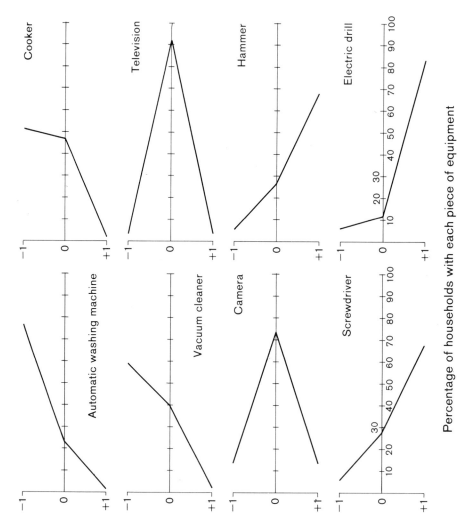

Percentage of households with each piece of equipment

Figure 7.1

162

TABLE 7.2 a

USE OF HOUSEHOLD ITEMS IN COUPLE HOUSEHOLDS IN LARA
WHERE HUSBAND IS EMPLOYED FULLTIME: BY FAMILY STAGE

Household Item	% with Item	Whole Sample	Younger Hh w/o Chldrn	All Hh with Chldrn	Older Hh w/o Chldrn
1. Wringer	0.4	-1.000	-	-	-1.000
2. Ordinary Washer	12.4	-.929	-1.000	-.875	-.933
3. Tumble Dryer	8.9	-.850	0.000	-.857	-1.000
4. Elec.Sew Machine	39.6	-.787	-.500	-.878	-.758
5. Automatic Washer	34.2	-.753	-.375	-.792	-.810
6. Spin Dryer	20.7	-.739	-.667	-.750	-.744
7. TwinTub Washer	11.6	-.731	-1.000	-.429	-.824
8. Hand Sew Machine	19.1	-.721	-.500	-.688	-.783
9. Electric Mixer	44.0	-.717	-.375	-.800	-.758
10. Electric Iron	94.7	-.685	-.417	-.657	-.793
11. Pressure Cooker	32.9	-.608	-.462	-.551	-.550
12. Vacuum Cleaner	84.0	-.566	-.150	-.631	-.600
13. Carpet Sweeper	54.2	-.541	-.462	-.551	-.550
14. Cooking Stove	97.8	-.495	-.333	-.429	-.625
15. Automatic Oven	27.8	-.444	-.286	-.423	-.500
16. Freezer	22.0	-.278	0.000	-.273	-.367
17. Fridge	92.3	-.133	-.037	-.112	-.188
18. Mono Player	21.1	-.114	0.000	-.088	-.156
19. Radio	92.9	-.038	-.037	-.042	-.034
20. Colour TV	56.0	-.008	0.000	-.016	0.000
21. Black & White TV	47.6	0.000	0.000	+.019	-.022
22. Dishwasher	0.4	0.000	-	0.000	-
23. Camera	76.9	0.000	+.083	-.047	+.031
24. Movie Camera	7.1	0.000	0.000	0.000	0.000
25. 'Workmate' Bench	5.8	0.000	0.000	0.000	0.000
26. Stereo Player	67.1	+.007	+.042	0.000	0.000
27. Push Bike	23.1	+.058	-.167	+.103	0.000
28. Cassette Player	54.2	+.098	+.200	+.103	-.051
29. Motor Bike	6.2	+.214	+.500	+.167	0.000
30. Electric Sander	20.4	+.609	+.571	+.500	+.765
31. Hammer	94.2	+.623	+.538	+.550	+.733
32. Screwdriver	96.0	+.625	+.577	+.559	+.716
33. Electric Saw	15.1	+.676	+.600	+.471	+1.000
34. Car	44.4	+.680	+.375	+.689	+.795
35. Van	4.4	+.700	0.000	+.750	+1.000
36. Carpenters Bench	10.2	+.739	+.400	+.714	+.909
37. Hand Saw	69.8	+.745	+.688	+.735	+.767
38. Hand Drill	55.1	+.758	+.706	+.698	+.833
39. Electric Drill	39.1	+.773	+.727	+.657	+.881

Groupings (vertical labels): Cooking, Cleaning Equipment (items 1–17); Leisure and Recreation Equipment (items 18–26); Transport, 'DIY' Equipment (items 27–39)

- = item not present

163

TABLE 7.2b
USE OF HOUSEHOLD ITEMS IN COUPLE HOUSEHOLDS WHERE HUSBAND
IS EMPLOYED FULLTIME: BY FAMILY STAGE AND WIFE'S EMPLOYMENT

Household Item	Younger Hh w/o Children*		All Hh with Children			Older Hh w/o Children		
	F.T.	None	F.T.	P.T.	None	F.T.	P.T.	None
1.	-	-	-	-	-	-	-	-
2.	-1.000	-	-	-1.000	-.500	-1.000	-.500	-1.000
3.	-	-	-1.000	-.833	-.800	-1.000	-1.000	-
4.	-.571	-	-.800	-.875	-.875	-.900	-.500	-.833
5.	-.333	-	-.778	-.733	-.882	-.900	-.800	-.600
6.	-.750	-	-.750	-.818	-.500	-.727	-.625	-1.000
7.	-1.000	-	0.000	-.500	-1.000	-.667	-1.000	-1.000
8.	-1.000	-	-1.000	-.833	-.571	-1.000	-.500	-1.000
9.	-.583	-	-.906	-.750	-.733	-.417	-.889	-1.000
10.	-.500	-1.000	-.550	-.750	-.677	-.786	-.750	-.750
11.	-.375	-	-.500	-.500	-.714	-.625	-1.000	-1.000
12.	-.267	-1.000	-.529	-.571	-.692	-.571	-.500	-.857
13.	-.500	-	-.333	-.625	-.765	-.500	-.455	-.833
14.	-.300	-1.000	-.286	-.548	-.344	-.567	-.600	-.750
15.	-.167	-	-.125	-1.000	-.444	-.400	-.500	-.667
16.	0.000	-	-.286	-.333	-.222	-.071	-.625	-.667
17.	-.050	0.000	-.053	-.133	-.069	-.100	-.313	-.500
18.	0.000	0.000	0.000	-.071	-.145	-.222	+.167	0.000
19.	0.000	0.000	-.190	-.033	+.037	0.000	0.000	0.000
20.	0.000	-	0.000	-.042	0.000	0.000	0.000	0.000
21.	0.000	0.000	-.091	+.091	+.118	0.000	0.000	0.000
22.	-	-	-	-	0.000	-	-	-
23.	0.000	0.000	0.000	0.000	-.040	+.083	0.000	+.143
24.	0.000	-	0.000	0.000	0.000	0.000	0.000	0.000
25.	0.000	0.000	0.000	-	0.000	0.000	-	0.000
26.	0.000	-	+.067	0.000	-.083	+.045	0.000	0.000
27.	-.200	-	-.111	+.067	+.400	-.250	+.500	-
28.	+.100	-	+.154	0.000	+.250	+.059	+.222	-.200
29.	+.500	-	0.000	0.000	0.000	0.000	0.000	-
30.	+.750	-	+1.000	+.200	+.571	+.714	+1.000	+1.000
31.	+.684	+1.000	+.650	+.387	+.567	+.643	+.800	+.714
32.	+.632	+1.000	+.545	+.452	+.567	+.621	+.813	+.714
33.	+1.000		+1.000	+.143	+.833	+1.000	+1.000	-
34.	+.385	+1.000	+.800	+.500	+.813	+.842	+.778	+1.000
35.	-	-	-	+1.000	+.750	+1.000	-	-
36.	+.500	-	+1.000	+1.000	+.500	+1.000	+1.000	+1.000
37.	+.818	-	+.833	+.680	+.773	+.667	+.923	+.667
38.	+.750	-	+.727	+.563	+.813	+.737	+1.000	+1.000
39.	+.857	-	+.800	+.429	+.800	+.857	+1.000	+1.000

Side labels: Items 1–17 — Cooking, Cleaning Equipment; Items 18–26 — Leisure and Recreation Equipment; Items 27–39 — Transport, 'DIY' Equipment

* No part time work recorded
- = item not present
FT = wife employed full time
PT = wife employed part time
None = wife not employed

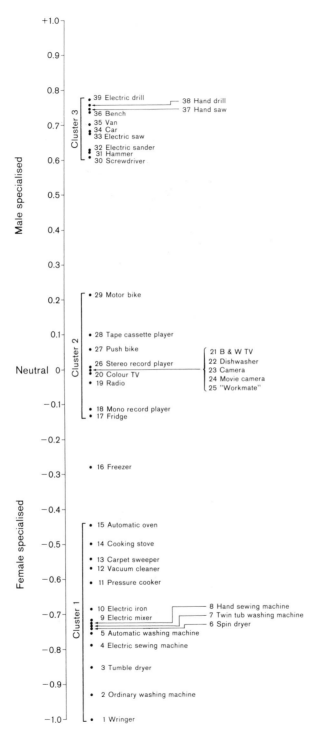

Figure 7.3

165

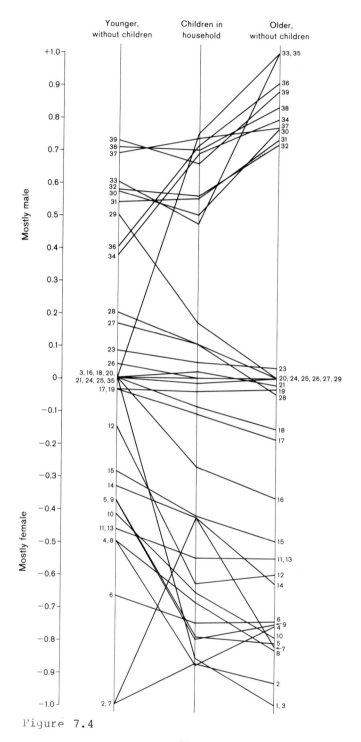

Figure 7.4

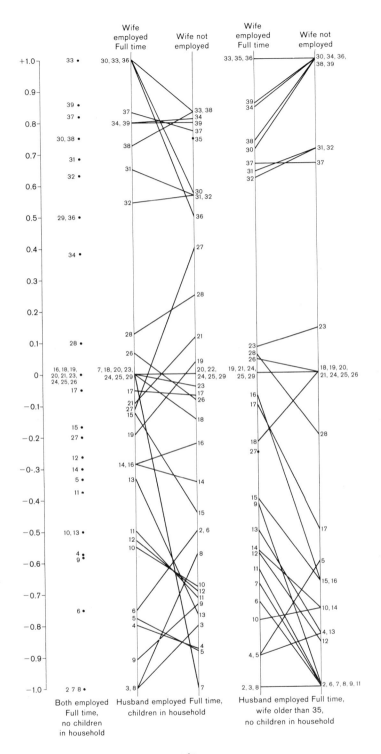

Figure 7.5   167

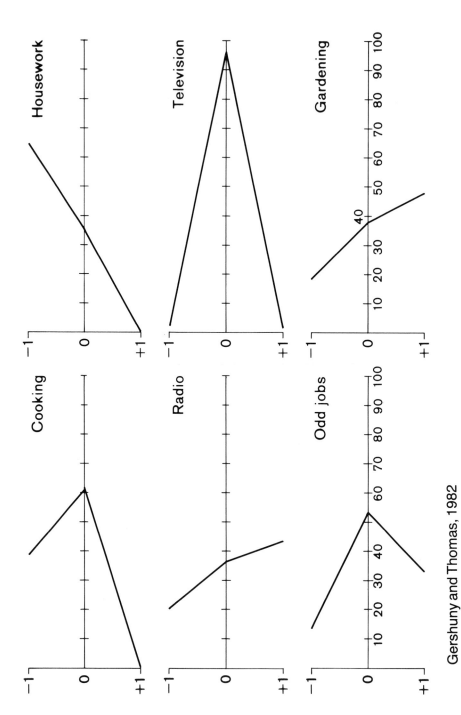

Gershuny and Thomas, 1982

Figure 7.6

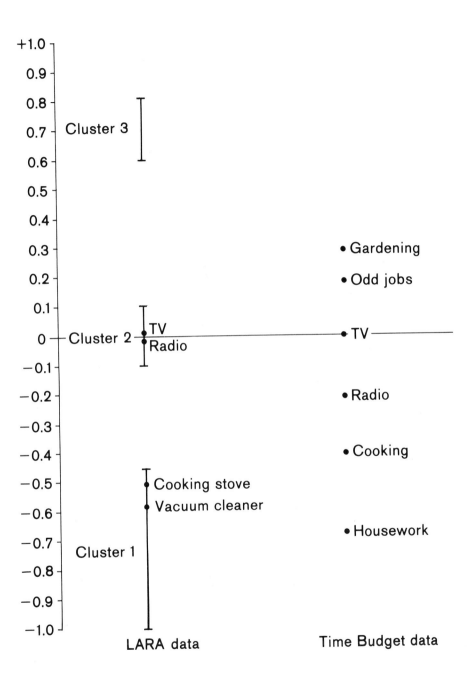

Figure 7.7

TABLE 7.8
WORK TIME IN VARIOUS SORTS OF HOUSEHOLDS: MINUTES WORKED PER AVERAGE DAY

Minutes per Average Day	Husband and Wife Employed Full Time			Husband Employed Full Time, Wife Employed Part Time			Husband Employed Full Time, Wife Non Employed		
	Ynger, No Chldrn in Household	Chldrn in Household	Older, No Chldrn	Ynger, No Chldrn in Household	Chldrn in Household	Older, No Chldrn	Ynger, No Chldrn in Household	Chldrn in Household	Older, No Chldrn
Husband: Paid Work	382	390	383	463	404	401	417	370	373
Unpaid Work	106	101	76	75	84	68	75	99	81
Total Work	488	491	459	538	488	469	492	469	454
Wife: Paid Work	339	304	354	286	172	179	26	6	–
Unpaid Work	147	216	194	171	296	267	290	404	339
Total Work	486	520	548	457	468	446	316	410	339
Couple: Paid Work	721	694	737	749	576	580	443	376	373
Unpaid Work	253	317	270	246	380	335	365	503	420
Total Work	974	1,011	1,007	995	956	915	808	879	793
Number in each Sample	42	95	22	6	164	28	17	234	41

Source: Gershuny and Thomas 1982.

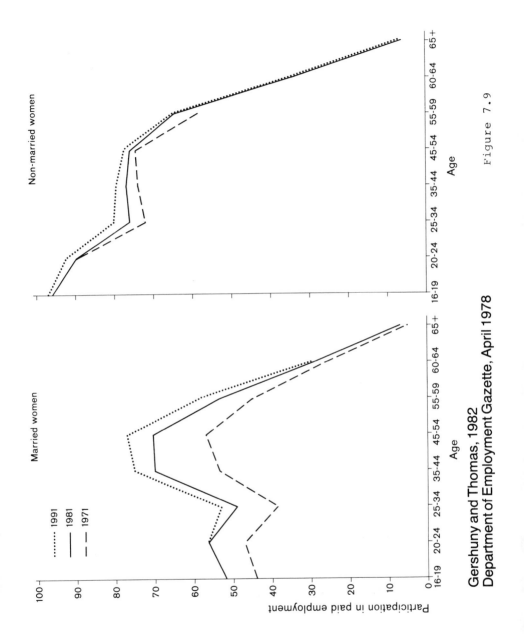

Married women

Non-married women

Participation in paid employment

Age

Age

1991
1981
1971

16-19 20-24 25-34 35-44 45-54 55-59 60-64 65+

Gershuny and Thomas, 1982
Department of Employment Gazette, April 1978

Figure 7.9

171

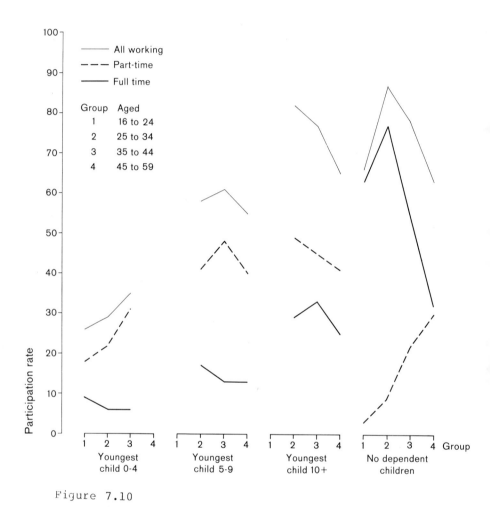

Figure 7.10

General Household Survey, 1978

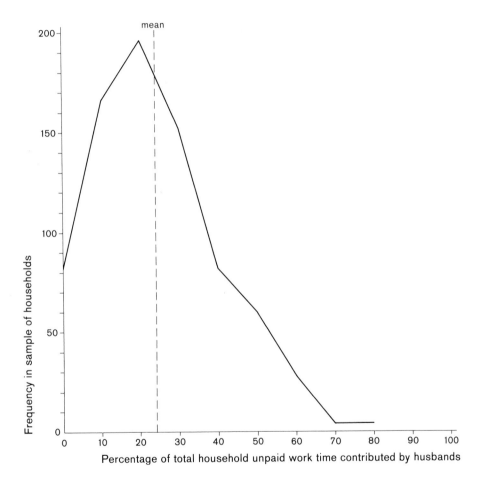

mean

Frequency in sample of households

Percentage of total household unpaid work time contributed by husbands

Gershuny and Thomas, 1982

Figure 7.11

173

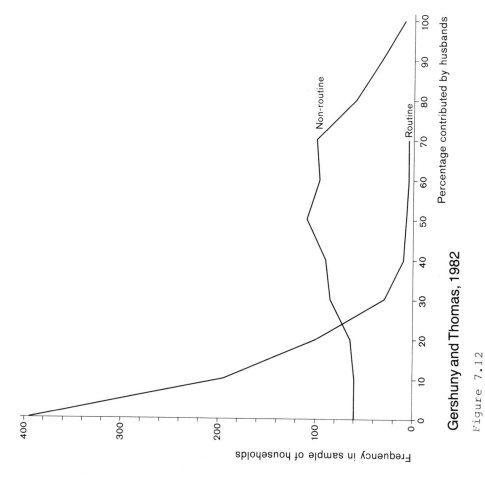

Gershuny and Thomas, 1982

Figure 7.12

TABLE 7.13

HUSBANDS' PROPORTION OF ALL WORK

% of All Household Work	2 Jobs	1½ Jobs	1 Job
Younger, No Children	50.1	54.1	60.9
Couple with Children	48.6	51.0	53.4
Older, No Children	45.6	51.3	57.3

2 Jobs - Husband and Wife both employed Full Time
1½ Jobs - Husband Full Time, Wife Part Time
1 Job   - Husband Full Time, Wife Non Employed

Source: Gershuny and Thomas 1982.

TABLE 7.14

HUSBANDS' PROPORTION OF UNPAID WORK

% of Household Domestic Work	2 Jobs	1½ Jobs	1 Job
Younger, No Children	41.9	43.9	20.6
Couple with Children	31.9	28.4	19.7
Older, No Children	28.2	20.3	19.3

Source: Gershuny and Thomas 1982.

TABLE 7.15

HUSBANDS' PROPORTION OF ROUTINE AND NON ROUTINE UNPAID WORK

	% of Routine			% of Non Routine		
	2 Jobs	1½ Jobs	1 Job	2 Jobs	1½ Jobs	1 Job
Younger, No Children	15	7	4	64	53	59
Couple with Children	12	7	5	66	55	53
Older, No Children	14	4	5	56	58	50

Source: Gershuny and Thomas 1982.

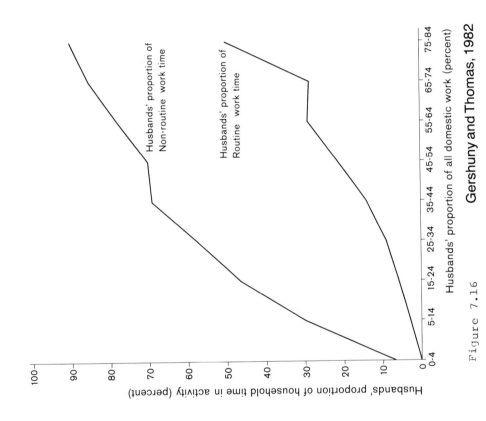

Figure 7.16　　Gershuny and Thomas, 1982

177

TABLE 7.17
DISTRIBUTION OF HOUSEWORK BETWEEN HOUSEHOLD MEMBERS

Minutes per Average Day

	All	Husband	Wife	Boy	Girl	Other Man	Other Women
Child Care	40	6	25	0	2	2	5
Routine Chores	383	23	210	9	28	14	79
Non Routine Chores (Odd jobs, gardening)	116	48	13	7	14	27	7
Shopping etc.	142	19	44	13	19	15	32
Total	681	96	292	29	63	58	143

Percentage of All Housework

	All	Husband	Wife	Boy	Girl	Other Man	Other Women
Child Care	6	1	4	0	0	0	1
Routine Chores	56	3	31	1	4	2	14
Non Routine Chores	17	7	2	1	2	4	1
Shopping etc.	21	3	6	2	3	2	5
Total	100	14	43	4	9	8	21

Percentage of Household Members' Time

	All	Husband	Wife	Boy	Girl	Other Man	Other Women
Child Care	6	6	9	0	3	3	3
Routine Chores	56	24	72	31	44	24	69
Non Routine Chores	17	50	4	24	22	46	5
Shopping etc.	21	20	15	45	30	26	22
Total	100	100	100	100	100	100	100

Source: Gershuny and Thomas 1982.

TABLE 7.18

NUMBERS OF COUPLES IN THE HOUSEHOLD CATEGORIES IN LARA

	Younger without Chldrn	Pre School Chldrn	School Aged Chldrn	Wife Aged 35-60 No Chldrn	Wife Aged 60+ No Chldrn	Total
2 Jobs	20	4	18	28	2	72
1½ Jobs	0	10	22	11	5	48
1 Job	1	23	9	7	1	41
Other[1]	6	14	8	6	30	64
Total	27	51	57	52	38	225

[1] Mostly Husband Unemployed or Retired

TABLE 7.19

EMPLOYMENT TYPE BY FAMILY STATUS IN LARA

% of Couples with Husb.in Employment	Younger without Chldrn	Pre School Chldrn	School Aged Chldrn	Wife Aged 35-60 No Chldrn	Wife Aged 60+ No Chldrn	Total
2 Jobs	95	11	37	61	25	45
1½ Jobs	0	27	45	24	63	30
1 Job	5	62	18	15	12	25
All Couples with Husb. Employed	100	100	100	100	100	100

TABLE 7.20

DISTRIBUTION OF HOUSEHOLD TYPES IN LARA

	Younger No Chldrn	Chldrn in Household	Older, No Chldrn	Total
2 Jobs	9	10	13	32
1½ Jobs	0	14	7	21
1 Job	0	14	4	18
Other	3	10	16	29
Total	12	48	40	100

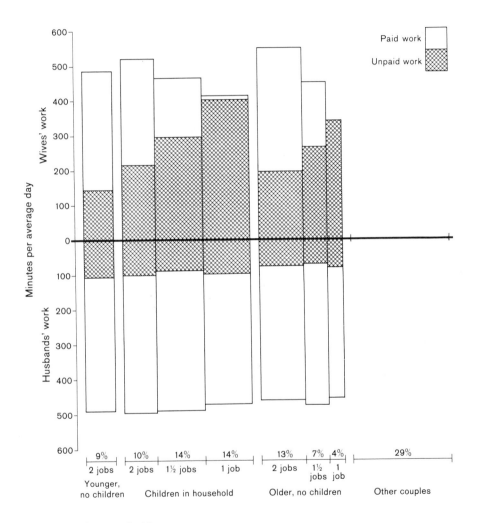

Figure 7.21

8 Epilogue and conclusion
SANDRA WALLMAN

Three years after the 1978 Neighbourhood Survey, things have changed in the LARA area. Given that the housing action programme is that much older, it would be extraordinary if they had not. On top of this, the Conservative local government council which came to office in 1978 has had time to alter the housing policy of its Labour predecessor, tailoring it to fit cuts in public spending as much as political conviction; and the percentage of the UK male labour force officially counted as unemployed has risen from 6.7 to 14.8 per cent. It is striking however that the area's response to change, even to the traumatic effects of recession, is consistent with the style identified as characteristic of Battersea throughout this book.

In the matter of unemployment both the extent of joblessness and the characteristics of the unemployed go against popular expectation for inner city areas. In the first respect the area is surprisingly resilient. There is an appalling increase in the number of men without jobs: a follow up neighbourhood survey completed in December 1981 shows that the percentage of men unemployed has risen from 8 to 14.2 per cent in three years. But relative to the nation as a whole, the LARA microcosm of Battersea has not done so badly. Both our neighbourhood surveys have included those who are 'registered unemployed' and those who are 'unemployed, not registered, but looking for a job' in the total number of unemployed (Chapter 6). Because national figures include only people registered as unemployed - i.e. only those who stand to benefit from 'signing on' - they represent a smaller category. Even so, LARA's rate of increase in unemployment is lower than the national. If the difference in definition of 'the unemployed' were taken into account it would be lower still.

In the second respect, a profile of the unemployed confirms the strategic importance of local ties and local involvement. Amongst LARA residents, men born outside south London are almost twice as likely to be unemployed as those born in it; and men who have lived in south London for one to five years are three times

182

as likely to be unemployed as those resident for more than five and less than ten. These probabilities are largely independent of colour.

In the matter of housing, change is no less marked. According to official figures, only slightly over 15 per cent of LARA properties are now 'in bad repair' compared with the 83 per cent listed when the housing action programme began; and the proportion of households lacking 'exclusive use of basic amenities' has dropped from 70 per cent to less than 12 per cent. The pattern of tenure in the area is also very different: the proportion of owner occupied remains around one quarter, but there has been a massive transfer of ownership from private landlords to housing associations and the local council.

These changes have together brought the neighbourhood to a point at which the number of improved housing units available for letting exceeds the number of residents who need rehousing; they are unequivocal evidence of the successful management of LARA's housing resources. But the same success has diminished its control over those resources, altering patterns of access to information and the boundaries on which local identity had come to be based.

Recent developments are indicative. The overall improvement in housing has combined with cuts in public spending to encourage the council to cancel the area's HAA (Housing Action Area) status. Being now expert in effective protest (Chapter 4), LARA managed to win for itself the alternative G.I.A. (General Improvement Area) status from March 1982, although strictly speaking the housing conditions are too 'good' and the number of owner occupiers too low to warrant it. The new status anyway reduces the area's entitlement to manpower and financial input from the council, and has lost it the convenience and focus of its own housing office. The new office is some distance away and deals also with two other housing action areas. On both counts it is less accessible and less 'ours' than before, and it is said that complaints and requests for repairs are now handled much more slowly because they have to go through extra bureaucratic channels. True to form however, the LARA committee has carried out a survey of local households which will allow it to itemise the need for repairs and to prepare the strongest possible case for efficient local authority backing.

The challenge to local identity assumptions is not so explicit. Who belongs in the LARA area anyway? In 1981 most of the residents on the original housing list have been accommodated, and the council has begun to implement Conservative Party policy by selling its properties to the private sector - to present tenants if they are both willing and able to purchase, and to buyers on the open market if they are not. At the same time the letting of council and housing association property is now controlled by the borough, not the neighbourhood office, and all new claimants must join the borough queue. Even residents with long standing connections or kin in the area have no guarantee of accommodation in it and inevitably wait longer to be rehoused than their neighbours did.

Both procedures have brought new people into the area and have focussed attention on the LARA boundary. There is no real evidence that newcomers are being housed at the expense of established residents, but some say that 'outsiders' are moving into housing units which should have been allocated to 'locals'. There is a persistent rumour that a local family did not get the house promised to it because the housing association 'gave' it to a family from outside. The local family is of Irish origin, with kin in the area, and although it moved a short distance away from LARA to get better accommodation, it still participates in local activities. The incoming family is of Indian origin and has no ties with the area. Discussion of the conflict within LARA pays scant attention to the origins of the competing families but emphasises the priority of insider over outsider status. It is characteristic of Battersea that the significant boundary between 'us' and 'them' should be drawn in terms of local involvement and without reference to ethnic difference; and that local opinion is in favour of both families being encouraged to settle.

*   *   *   *

Each of the chapters in this book has brought a perspective on Battersea itself, or on livelihood in a small south Battersea neighbourhood. Together they spell out a kind of dialogue between continuity and change.

The continuity inheres in what we have called Battersea style. All the expressions of it put some kind of emphasis on local over ethnic identity, and on hetero-geneous over homogeneous forms. On the first account there is minimal interest shown in status ascribed by ethnic origin, and there is maximum scope for newcomers to achieve local status. On the second there is both an unusually wide variety of resource stock and relatively open access to it: housing and jobs and people are 'mixed' and there are so many separate 'gates' into local resources that no one group or institution or ideology can claim a controlling share.

Change here as anywhere is not all of one kind.

184

Although the events that make it up are related, they belong to different time scales. The three most readily distinguished are historical, personal and situational.

In the historical frame we have described social and economic changes happening to Battersea over the last century. Some of these changes were explicitly imposed on it from outside - although it is likely that no one intended all their consequences. Certainly Battersea did not choose to dissolve its own metropolitan status, lose 'grass roots' access to its elected politicians or decrease the number of jobs available in local industry. Other changes came as implicit reactions to national or international events: wars of one kind or another, population movements in and out, industrial growth and recession, fluctuations of interest in the Commonwealth, the spread of state services and welfare bureaucracies, renegotiations of the social division of labour between men and women, rich and poor, white and black... No subset of people can have been immune to trends like these. And if it is true that densely populated inner city areas react first and strongest to social and economic developments of every sort, then this specific study of Battersea may also serve to illuminate their general effect.

Other changes have happened and continue to happen on quite another level. They are the effects of ordinary social process - changes within the local system which do not alter it overall, and which in a bird's eye view, would happen even if the world outside went away.

The most obvious of them follow on the passing of life time - as opposed to historical time - and are repeated in every generation: families progress through their separate domestic cycles; daughters grow into mothers and babies into grandfathers; households get bigger and again smaller; houses and flats and corner shops change hands... An outline of these processes emerges from our descriptions of livelihood in the LARA area.

Changes in the position and content of the boundaries which divide 'insiders' from 'outsiders' are less obvious but no less normal. Social boundaries reflect the ordinary permutations of social context. Because they are processes in situational time, they move in rhythms apart from historical trends or individual cycles. Yet they are not independent of them. There is no one measure which defines 'us' - the people entitled to share the resources we call 'ours' - but the continual shifting of the boundary of 'us' is not random. Social process at any level is not 'free'; it is constrained by other things happening in and around the local environment,and on the scope of the resources it offers.

People who live in or move into an area can only take

up the options that are there. Similarly public policy and generalised 'social change' have different effects even in different parts of the same inner city because each local area has a characteristic style of response.

Battersea's particular style is cumulated in the body of this book. Two summary items will serve to spell it out here; at the same time they underline the context of the continuities and changes reported in the epilogue. The first refers to Battersea's consistent boundary style; the second to the creation of the identity defining the south Battersea neighbourhood we have described.

One: the population of Battersea is mixed in a way that leaves plenty of scope for ethnic solidarity or discrimination, but ethnic origin has little bearing on the business of livelihood. Nor did it mark significant boundaries in historic Battersea. On the one hand no incoming population category has been exclusively associated with one industry or one industrial role, and there is no evidence of ethnic niches or ethnic specific patterns of employment. Despite demographic and economic change, Battersea residents have 'always' been prepared to spread themselves across a wide range of industries and industrial locations: national labour statistics over several decades show the majority of men in the Battersea workforce travelling outside the borough to work. On the other hand, while it has 'always' been polyglot by London standards, it has 'always' considered outsider status to be more a matter of newness or non involvement in the area than of colour or foreign origin.

Two: at the start of housing action the LARA area existed only as half a dozen streets within a rectangle clearly demarcated on the map, distinct only because it was bounded on two sides by main traffic arteries, on two more by fenced, now derelict ground designated for a new council housing estate. Although the Housing Act (1974) provides that grants for rehabilitation can be made available only to established communities (in technically appropriate areas) residents tend to date the beginning of 'community' from the beginning of 'housing action'. On this basis it is less than ten years old.

Of the 500 households in the area, more than one third are put into the official category 'New Commonwealth origin' - which is to say that their members, or most of their members, are non white. But neither colour and language, nor the presence of 'blacks' or 'Greeks' are central or persistent issues. Those most often cited are: faceless bureaucrats, ambitious politicians, people who ignore the council's skips and leave their large rubbish by the dustbins, council employees who will not take this large rubbish away, people who have noisy and frequent parties, and worse, are thought to charge a gate fee and so to admit strangers to those parties. Also, a looser category, those newly arrived, perhaps eccentric, certainly without connections 'in this part of London'. Thus: a Newcastle man, three years' resident, with a wife from the other side of London - he is called a 'foreigner' by a Jamaican woman resident of ten years standing who clearly is not.

As the regulations for housing action entail, the houses and flats are being refurbished for established residents of the area. Households may move or be moved within the area, either temporarily while their own quarters are rehabilitated, or permanently, into accommodation better matched to household size. They may on no account be ousted from the area, although some few do profit from their special bureaucratic status to acquire council accommodation elsewhere in the borough. But even without mass exodus, better use of the housing stock has created a surplus over the residents' requirements. This must, again according to the rules, go into the council's hopper to be allocated to 'anybody' on the housing lists.

This possibility is a focus of anxiety:... 'Anybody' will not be known to us...will only use the place to get a house...will not really want to live here...will not have people here...will not care about the place... will run it down...will move on... Residents therefore encourage each other to find amongst their acquaintance 'somebody' who wants to live in the area; who would move in and would stay; who would become 'us'.

Even in this context, ethnic ratios and affiliations are beside the point. 'We' are, in the most general sense, those who belong here. Specifically, 'we' are defined as those who were in the area when it was earmarked for housing action and so designated a 'community'. (That this occurred very shortly ago does not prevent its having the force of tradition.) At that time the area was distinguished only by being marked off on an official map. But the cartographer's boundary marked a categorical difference between those entitled to particular political and economic resources, and those not eligible for them. It became a <u>social</u> boundary only when residents identified themselves by it. This happened when it began to be used to define 'us' - the people entitled to share the resources we call 'ours'.

*   *   *   *

Economic change in this small part of south London created new local boundaries and identities. This process in turn altered the meaning and management of

'local' resources.   Similar change can be expected
similarly to affect boundaries and resource management
wherever it occurs.   But it need not affect them in
the same way: its outcome depends in each case on the
kinds of people included and excluded in the new local
system, and on the style and scope of local livelihood.

   Our findings for Battersea cannot therefore be generalised
to all 'inner city' areas.   The point to be taken is
that even where comparable areas have equal access to
the same resources, they may not have the same organisational options.

Appendix on the survey

Living in the City

BATTERSEA SURVEY 1978

In September/October of this year an interviewer will invite you to answer a set of questions about living in London.

We are interested in the ways in which people use the resources of Battersea and how they travel to them; whether they have family and friends in the area or further away; what kind of work they do — both in and out of the house — and how much they use household appliances.

You will be able to tell us how much people know about local services and facilities, how far community needs are met, and what other facilities you would like to have.

Everyone's view is equally important. Without *your* co-operation we cannot get a complete picture. But nobody's name will be used in anything written or said about the area. Everyone's privacy will be protected.

The survey will be carried out by a Social Science Research Council team. It is not associated with any political party or commercial interest. It will cover all households in the housing action area of L.A.R.A. and has the moral support of the Residents' Association and the Community Centre.

We look forward to your co-operation.

Battersea Survey Team
Telephone: 223 7703

A Field work strategy

ETHNOGRAPHY IN THE CITY

Until quite recently the settings of ethnographic enquiry were always rural. This is not only because social anthropology was from its beginning defined by a specialist interest in small scale and 'whole societies' whose members expected no change in their relationships with each other or with the natural environment. It is also because the discipline built its reputation on an appreciation of the context in which events occur and are evaluated, and it knows these contexts to be dauntingly hard to perceive, let alone to control, in town. We have therefore a number of durable professional excuses for not venturing into cities at all - particularly our own cities - and all kinds of professional anxieties to face when we get there. Significant on both counts is the fact that other social scientists seem to have pre-empted the study of 'us' in general and of the urban setting in particular. Even now we are curiously willing to connive in the rumour that we are working in our own (urban) countries because we cannot get the money or the 'research permission to go back to (rural) Africa, and to accept the small exotic corners of the urban scene, the residuum of the other disciplines, as our only and proper due. Indeed, what conceptual room is there left? What is there in our professional repertoire that is worth transposing and can be transposed out of the setting in and for which it was developed - out of the periphery and into the centre of the social research map?

The popular answer tends not to go beyond participant observation. In the popular image, social anthropology is a technique of enquiry, nothing more. By this logic, its means are equated with its ends, its method with its methodology; if it is not possible to 'do' participant observation - which, in the traditional paradigm, requires year round isolation from one's own ordinary life and clock round immersion in the ordinary lives of others - then it is not possible to 'do' social anthropology. In these terms it is difficult to work as a social anthropologist in any town and impossible in your own.

But these are not the right terms. The proper criterion of the craft is in the perspectives we bring to the analyses we attempt, not in the deceptively simple act of 'hanging in'. Participant observation is a means to understanding social life in the round, to the appreciation of context and meaning, and to the relational perspective, all of which are distinguishing marks of social anthropology. Leach has put it more elegantly: '...the typically anthropological assumption (is) that a social field does not consist of units of population but of persons in relation to one another' (1967: 80).

This assumption is fundamental to the present enquiry into the ways in which people of different ethnic origin define and manage the resources of the urban environment which they share. Whether a study done in the domestic urban setting and without participant observation can be legitimate anthropology is certainly not an issue for the non anthropologists involved, nor is it even interesting to general readers of this book. It is important, however, that the crucial problem has been to devise research strategies that are feasible in a dense urban setting - as participant observation is not - and yet do not distort the realities of ordinary life by dealing with people as 'units of population', classified only by characteristics which can readily be seen and counted by outsiders, in the way that conventional social survey tends to do.

This is then a summary account of the survey stage of fieldwork in a programme of research into aspects of livelihood in 'inner' London. The work, which is continuing, is not and has not been a purely anthropological venture. Researchers from several different disciplines have been so closely associated in its design and execution that there is a sense in which this is the report of a collective effort in interdisciplinary ethnography.[2] Nor does the neighbourhood ethnographic survey stand by itself: it is backed by local historical sources of various kinds (as Chapters 2, 3 and 4 above), and enriched by the detail of a series of household case studies which will appear in a separate and subsequent volume.

The results of the survey are reported in Chapters 5, 6 and 7; here we are concerned only with the way it was done. We have been explicitly aware of the methodological charters of sociography (Jahoda et al. 1972) and mass observation (Harrisson 1976) and have borrowed heavily from the perspectives of traditional ethnography throughout.

THE PRACTICAL CONTEXT

The constraints on mapping relationships in a densely populated setting are probably standard elements of the practical context of ethnography in the city. Others are peculiar to particular urban areas and to the political and economic conditions affecting them. It is significant to this programme of study that our designated field area is not just 'city', but 'inner city', and that the label implies and entails a number of special assumptions. Summarised here with reference to the British scene they provide the first level context for an ethnography of London.3

The 'inner city' districts of the great metropolitan centres have been considered problem areas by politicians, administrators and researchers in Britain for a number of years. They are the new <u>terra incognita</u> of the establishment: no one knows what really goes on in them, and they are thought to be too remote and too hostile for anyone to find out. This 'no go' reputation is only half founded in fact, but the facts are persuasive. The inner city has traditionally been described by urban geographers as an area of transition and population turnover. Both the turnover and the loss of population have lately been accelerated by housing stress and blight, 4 and all of these have assaulted the fabric of the physical environment. Anyone who can leave is assumed to have left. The population 'remaining' must, by this logic be 'socially disadvantaged' and, whether as cause or effect, deprived of ordinary resources and amenities. The same districts are characterised as containing concentrations of minority ethnic groups and/or by unusually high proportions of people classifed as deviant. In short, the inner city is by current definition a problem area, more often identified by economic, social or political pathology than by the spatial criterion implied in its name.

These conditions and prejudices entail that it is more difficult to gather information about the people living in inner city areas than about those living in suburbs, new towns or rural villages. They are underenumerated in the National Census and on the electoral rolls and they show exceptionally high non response rates in market research surveys. Their relative lack of participation in the national political process is indicated by a below average turnout to vote in elections, and a lower than average rate of membership in formal organisations.

It is of course in terms of 'formal' and official structures and processes that the inner city is remote or hostile. This is the environment in which 'the informal economy' flourishes - which means only that many inner city transactions and activities cannot be enumerated because they do not fit into the categories and specifications which the official system imposes. It is also true that the population of the inner cities is largely low status, socially distant from the political and managerial elite and from the majority of social researchers.

But if people living in these areas are alienated from the mainstream, they should not be assumed to be passive about it. Certainly they are more articulate and openly suspicious of enquiry than they were in Victorian times. Charles Booth's interviewers, who were mainly clerics and school board officials, could apparently enter a person's home on demand and badger the residents with their questions (Booth 1891). The period of such obedient cooperation with high status investigators has long passed.

The clearest and most recent evidence of the contrast between the uncooperative inner city and the rest of Britain appears in the field results of the 1977 National Dwelling and Housing Survey (NDHS). The London results alone indicate that survey success varies with social and spatial indices - i.e. inversely to inner-city-ness. The overall success rate at the sample addresses in Greater London was 75.9 per cent, but the range within London is enormous: the (suburban) borough of Bexley shows a response rate of 85.4 per cent against the (inner) borough of Kensington and Chelsea's 60.7 per cent (DoE 1979). Moreover, in sixteen London boroughs the NDHS fieldwork had to be extended as so many addresses needed to be revisited even after four calls. 5

The NDHS report itself suggests that non response was most likely in pre1919 properties, and that problems arose with 'properties sub-divided internally'. Doubts about the validity of the results for inner London led local authority officials to publish a paper itemising their reservations. The 'most frequently mentioned criticisms' were that the number of pensioners, of one person households in shared dwellings, and of house-holds sharing facilities were all underestimated in inner areas. The statistical corollary multiplies the effect of the fault: it entails that other types of household are overrepresented as proportions of the total, and that the total number of households is itself underestimated. Non identification of addresses and non contact at sample addresses were described as inner city phenomena, and the paper concludes: '...It seems likely that non response is the prime cause of doubts concerning the reliability of the 1977 NDHS as a basis for policy and decision making in inner city areas' (London Housing Research Group 1979).

The central aim of the survey was to study the ways
in which people of different ethnic origin now living
in the same inner city area use the resources available
to them, and to examine the significance of ethnicity
as one of those resources.   The underlying assumption
was that inner city residents are, like all social
creatures, involved in systems of relationships: they
do not function without a context, or as units of population.   The survey was therefore carried out in a
relatively small area, covering the total population.
This made the process of communicating with the potential
respondents easier than when the sample of people to
be surveyed is dispersed but the problem of gaining
credibility and acceptance and of getting the cooperation
of the residents of the area remained.   The decision
to employ local people as interviewers as well as informants, was made on that basis: one member of the research
team had pioneered the approach in an earlier study
of a dispersed ethnic community (De Lange & Kosmin
1979).   At the time of the survey the area improvement
programme had reached its fifth year (Chapter 4).
There was a need for updated demographic data, particularly
since a change in local government had made the continuation of the housing improvement programme uncertain
and the local organisers were aware they might have
to defend the area's rights to 'renewal'.   The survey
could collect new population figures and could at the
same time enquire into the residents' perception and
use of local facilities, and their expectations of
the area's future.   For the second purpose the questionnaire section on 'Neighbourhood' was devised.   The
inclusion of locally oriented questions in turn enhanced
the general acceptability of the survey: the fact
that residents/respondents could identify with some
of its aims increased their willingness to cooperate
with the study.

   The involvement of local people in the survey as
interviewers as well as respondents had a similar effect.
Although it could be justified simply as a means of
injecting extra cash into the local economy, it was
taken in the light of several more strategic considerations.   The first is that some of the difficulties
experienced in trying to get people to cooperate with
social investigations in inner city areas are a product
of their concern that personal information might fall
into the wrong hands.   This concern is more likely
to be directed against the authorities and outsiders
than against friends and neighbours who probably already
have it by informal or indirect means, and who constitute
quite a different kind of intrusion into ordinary life.
On all these counts amateur local interviewers are
more likely to get willing cooperation than professional
non local interviewers.   Second, the success of a

survey in terms of response rate and completeness of information is also related to the level of motivation of the interviewers. Employing interviewers who are interested in the survey because it is of some direct relevance to their own livelihood ensures a highly motivated fieldforce. Of course the promise of payment for interviews achieved was significant, but not to an overriding extent: at best the fees constituted only a small additional income. Third, local interviewers are more knowledgeable about gaining physical access to households: they know the layout of buildings and the number of occupants. Fourth, local interviewers are less worried about calling on homes after dark, not having the inhibitions about walking in their own neighbourhood which outsiders have. And fifth, the use of local interviewers has a time and money saving effect: it minimises the time spent travelling to and from respondents, and as local interviewers often know when people are at home, it reduces the number of unsuccessful calls.

Figure A.2 represents a flow chart of the survey sequence and shows that the participation of residents as interviewers constitutes the mainstream of the survey activity. The left hand side 'technical and support activities' and the right hand side 'methodological functions' are common to most social survey procedures - except perhaps for the fact that the latter have in this case combined the approaches of a number of different disciplines.

The remainder of this section will be concerned with the organisation of the survey, and of the way in which it reflected and benefitted from the personal networks of the interviewers and the researchers.

PREPARING THE FIELD

While the survey itself took only a few weeks to complete, it took place in the second half of a five year research programme. As a research strategy it was dependent on the fact that some members of the research team had made informal contacts in the area many months before the survey began. The most influential of these was a longstanding resident who had been active in the setting up of the local residents' association and in applying for the government grant to convert a part of an underused local church into a community centre. Through him other local organisers were approached and the general intention of the survey explained. It is striking that at that stage the content of the questionnaire was less interesting than the local connections of the research team. We were encouraged nevertheless to write a formal letter to the residents' association (LARA) in which we set out the purpose, method and sponsorship of the study and asked for their cooperation with it. This letter was printed in the association's monthly newsletter the LARA Echo to inform the residents at large. The survey was then discussed at a public meeting of LARA which allowed the residents to ask questions about it. It was during these initial contacts with local organisers that the questions relating to local interests were suggested and added to the questionnaire.

The more detailed fieldwork preparations began in August 1978. A small survey office was set up in the main road bounding the survey area and an able and experienced field researcher was appointed to coordinate the preliminary work, recruit and train interviewers and supervise their fieldwork - all tasks whose crucial importance to the success of a survey tend to be under-estimated. The next step was to build up a descriptive profile of the houses and the households in the area. The presence of a housing officer (who is the author of Chapter 4) facilitated this task enormously. She had been involved in the housing programme since the declaration of the Housing Action Area and although in her official capacity she dealt only with properties owned by the borough council and by housing associations, she had extensive knowledge of the total area. With her help a detailed map of the survey area indicating the number of households in each building, the size and ethnic composition of each household, and the empty housing units in the area was drawn. Over the same period the fieldwork supervisor (who is the author of Chapter 5) extended our contact with local organisers and spent time in the community centre, but since it was necessary to build up a social network among residents other than these leaders and to gain more general credibility and acceptance, participation in local activities was no less crucial. August was the month in which the community centre organised a holiday programme for local children; as extra help was needed, she volunteered to assist as a playgroup leader. In this role she met a range of local people and so prepared the ground for the recruitment of interviewers. Conversation with residents on and about these children's outings was also an invaluable source of data on inter-action processes and attitudes towards living in the area.

The publicity campaign was another important aspect of preparing the field. Besides personal communication about the survey, more formal methods were used. Advertisements were placed in the monthly newsletter issued by the residents' association. In the middle of August children participating in the holiday programme were asked to design posters around the theme 'Living in the City'. Every child who did so was given a small prize and was eager to show the results (which were displayed in and outside the community centre

and the housing office) to his or her kinsmen and neighbours.   Closer to the fieldwork data, professionally
printed posters were distributed to the local pubs
and shops.   Finally, in the second week of September,
one week before the fieldwork started, a card was sent
to each household, explaining the aims of the survey
and asking for cooperation.   (The card is reproduced
as Figure A.1 above).

RECRUITMENT OF INTERVIEWERS

On the basis of the information obtained from the housing
office the number of households living in the area
was estimated at 526.   To survey these households
we anticipated a fieldwork period of six to seven weeks.
The closing date was announced in the beginning to
make it clear that the survey period was limited and
our intrusion temporary.

We recognised that working with a fieldforce which
had no experience in interviewing would require intensive
training before the fieldwork started, and continuous
guidance while it was happening.   We knew also that
a good relationship between the interviewers and the
survey staff was vital for successful field performance
and that therefore the number of 'supervisors' involved
should be kept to a minimum.   Accordingly, only 3
researchers appeared in the field area throughout.
Although we had aimed for a fieldforce of 30, we achieved
the survey with 22 local interviewers.

The interviewers were recruited through four channels:
1) personal contacts with local organisers and residents;
2) announcements in the community centre and the housing
office;   3) advertisements in the residents' association
newsletter and 4) the social networks of interviewers.

The success rate of these channels differed.   Advertisements in the newsletter and the announcements in
communal buildings produced only a small number of
replies (3 of 22).   On the other hand · recruitment
through personal networks was very effective (the remaining
19).   This points to the importance of a preparatory
stage in which members of a research team are seen
to be actively interested in local life, and supports
the observation that the willingness of people to cooperate
with social investigations depends to a large extent
on their knowledge and opinion of those in charge of
the project (see e.g. Whyte 1955:   300).   And there
is no doubt that the mere existence of a community
centre and a residents' association helped the recruitment
procedure.   It made it easier to contact people and
to participate in local activities.   Once the first
contacts with prospective interviewers were made, they
tended to talk about and to recommend our proposals

to their relatives and friends and so opened up their social network to recruitment.

A PROFILE OF THE FIELDFORCE

All but two interviewers were residents of the survey area. The two outsiders were taken on when it became clear that there were some households that local interviewers preferred not to visit, and a few which refused to cooperate at the first call. Except for the two boundary roads (which are busy urban throughways), all streets were represented in the fieldforce; but nearly one third of the interviewers lived in one street - the one whose residents had taken the initiative to oppose government plans for the area and who had played a crucial role in the formation of the residents' association. The fact that their interest in the area was still very much alive and many were involved in local activities explains their overrepresentation in the fieldforce; the survey had achieved the status of a local activity.

The interviewers came from different backgrounds: they included 5 housewives, 3 clerical assistants, 2 old age pensioners, 2 teachers, 2 employment advisers, 2 students, 2 unemployed persons, a nurse, a domestic help, a market researcher and a computer operator. The level of education of the fieldforce also varied: 8 interviewers had no formal qualifications, 2 had CSE certificates, 3 had 'O' levels, another 3 had 'A' levels and 6 had postsecondary school qualifications. Classified by ethnic origin, 2 interviewers were Irish, 2 West Indian, 1 European, and the great majority English. In terms of our enquiry it is significant that 9 of the 17 English were born and bred in south London, having lifetime knowledge of and identifying with the survey area - a category that we have constituted as 'south London ethnics' in the survey analysis (Chapter 3).

Of the 22 interviewers, only 2 were men. This could be attributed to the difference in work commitments between the sexes, the necessity to declare the earnings from the interview sessions to the Inland Revenue, and the fact that interviewing is generally regarded as a female job. 12 of the total were under 30 years of age and 2 were pensioners over 60. A handful of the young women had pram stage babies and regularly took them interviewing or brought them into the survey office. The most diligent and successful of all was a woman under 20, with a small baby, and without formal education or job experience.

It would not have been useful, even had our situation allowed it, to have recruited interviewers on the basis of particular characteristics or experience. Interviewing is a self selecting process; people who feel ill at ease conducting an interview or trying to get cooperation give up of their own accord soon after their first interview sessions. The questionnaire designed for the survey was highly structured; the range of answers to the closed questions were set out in columns and only had to be circled; open questions were kept to a minimum and any necessary instructions for the interviewers were printed on the form, and the questionnaire took thirty five minutes to complete. In combination, these design features made it relatively simple to administer but the skills involved in carrying out any interview should not be underestimated. Even with a highly structured questionnaire, people unfamiliar with interview techniques cannot be expected to achieve a good performance unless attention is paid to training and debriefing them, and continuous support is given during the fieldwork period.

TRAINING THE INTERVIEWERS

The preparation of the prospective interviewers was organised in three stages spread over one week. One week before the fieldwork started, they were invited to an introductory session, most of which was devoted to explaining the questionnaire and telling them how to record answers to the various questions. The aims and administration of the survey were also discussed, and we gave them guidelines on how to introduce themselves and the survey to potential respondents. All these points served equally to explain the survey to the interviewers themselves. At the end of this session they were given printed notes referring to specific questions and ways of recording answers and a copy of the questionnaire. They were asked to look at them at home and to write down anything they did not understand or wanted more information about.

At the end of the week an individual training session was arranged with each interviewer. Because the interviewers were also residents of the survey area, they were included in the survey as respondents. The individual training sessions were used to interview them, but served also as a practical demonstration of how to handle the questionnaire and to record the answers given. When the interviewer's own interview had been completed, any difficulties he or she had experienced with it or while reading through the questionnaire and the notes at home were discussed.

Throughout the training the interviewers were told that the success of the survey depended importantly on the precision with which they handled the questionnaire. But since they tended more often to underestimate than to overestimate their ability to conduct interviews, the need to make them aware of the problems of interviewing had to be carefully offset against their need for reassurance. We sought the necessary balance by training them in stages, by encouraging them to select the addresses they were to visit, and by debriefing them regularly and at length about every interview they attempted or completed.

FIELDWORK MANAGEMENT

The seasons appropriate to a survey of this kind are limited by the annual cycles of livelihood and climate. In the inner London setting one such period comes in early autumn - after the schools have reopened and anyone taking a summer holiday away has returned, and yet before the days become so short and the weather so unpleasant that sensible people stay indoors to avoid the dangers and discomforts of the street. We therefore started the fieldwork during the third week of September. The interviewers were given an identity card, questionnaire and a list with ten addresses. Where they had no preference for particular addresses, the lists were compiled by the survey staff. In most cases, however, the interviewers selected the addresses. While going through address lists we compared our data on the number of households in each dwelling and on vacant housing units with the interviewers' knowledge of the neighbourhood. We asked them to check the number of households in each building and to tell us of any inaccuracies in the status of vacant properties. In the first week of fieldwork the interviewers were instructed to return to the survey office as soon as possible after they had completed a single interview so that one of us could go through each person's first questionnaire with them in detail. This round of checks showed such a high standard of accuracy that we told them instead to report back once a week, or after every five completed questionnaires, whichever was the sooner. Some consistently called in more often, whether because they preferred to be paid as each questionnaire was completed, because the survey office or the survey staff had for them some extra social or personal function, or for some combination of these reasons (see Debriefing, below).

An address list was made out in duplicate - one copy given to the interviewer and one kept in the office. The form of these lists was such that interviewers could readily record completed interviews, appointments, refusals and reasons for refusals. At the debriefing sessions the information on the interviewer's copy was transferred to the office copy and any information on empty housing units or households not recorded in our files added to our list of households. We also kept a list for each street on which we entered the interviews obtained, the names of the interviewers who had made the calls, refusals and reasons for refusals. The same information was therefore recorded by street and by interviewer. Because the interviewers were so familiar with the area's residents we were able even to record accurate basic information on non respondent households. When asked about his or her neighbour, everyone knew or could find out the size of the household, age of the household members, ethnic origin and in many cases also the type of employment. Weekly maps of the survey's progress were drawn. Through these different methods of record keeping we kept a full and up to date account of each interviewer's performance and of the level of local cooperation throughout the survey period.

Our response to refusals varied. When a household refused cooperation because of a serious illness or a long term crisis, we did not revisit it. Where the refusal seemed to be due to a temporary problem, we postponed the second call till the end of the survey. In cases where the respondents seemed to refuse cooperation because the interviewer was either too closely acquainted with the household or totally unknown to it, a second interviewer would be sent, sometimes on the specific recommendation of the first, to conduct the interview. Finally, the households who objected to the questionnaire itself were approached by a personal letter from the fieldwork supervisor before any other visit was attempted.

We had planned a fieldwork period of six to seven weeks, but we had not taken into account factors which could slow down the progress of the survey. For example, we lost three interviewers at a very early stage of the survey: one interviewer withdrew because she felt ill at ease during interview sessions, while two others were unable to continue for medical reasons. But the most influential factor was the necessity to declare earnings to the Inland Revenue: many interviewers, particularly the pensioners, the unemployed and those with part time jobs, literally could not afford to be taxed on their interview earnings. 6 They therefore adjusted their weekly performance to the amount of money they were allowed to earn tax free. After six weeks of field work 25 per cent of the households had still to be interviewed. As this shortfall was connected not with an unwillingness to cooperate but with a lack of manpower, we felt it justifiable to extend the fieldwork period. The number of available addresses was by then so small that it was difficult to supply all interviewers with enough addresses to keep them going; only four were kept on to visit the remaining households. The fieldwork operation was finally terminated at the end of November.

The debriefing was a one-to-one procedure and enormously time consuming both for the researchers and the interviewers, but it was crucial to training and data gathering, and was an invaluable source of informal ethnographic detail about the neighbourhood.   For the interviewers it provided a routine source of support and assistance and the chance to discuss experiences and anxieties which they might not otherwise have had the confidence to initiate.   On each occasion the returning interviewer was asked how the respondents had reacted to the questionnaire, and whether he/she had had any special problems getting or recording answers.   Most interviewers found the residents very cooperative and their involvement in the survey enjoyable and interesting: those who consistently did not would have dropped out of the fieldforce.   But even the more successful of them sometimes expressed frustration, particularly after having failed to get an interview.   In such cases a debriefing session helped them to rationalise a bad experience or refusal.   At the same time it involved a detailed examination of each questionnaire and ensured that every entry was checked for accuracy, completeness and legibility.   Whenever information was missing, the interviewer would be asked to drop in to the respondent's home a second time to get it.   This follow up was only possible because we were working with interviewers who lived locally and knew the respondents as neighbours;   it was nearly always successful. The debriefing procedure as a whole also made us aware of weaknesses in the questionnaire which we could take into account when we came to analyse the data.

Finally, as we have said, the debriefing sessions were a major source of qualitative data about the area. Some of it came through as interviewers filled out what was written on the questionnaire with their insider knowledge of the informant or the neighbourhood. More was added as the researchers themselves became significant nodes in the interviewers' local networks. The fact that the survey office was always manned by one of only three researchers, that it was situated so near to where the interviewers lived, and that it could be contacted twelve hours a day contributed to the development of this kind of relationship.   Initially, the interviewers visited the office only to ask for assistance with their interviewing or to be debriefed. As the survey progressed and relationships between researchers and interviewers became more friendly, many began to regard the office as a place where they could drop in for refreshment and chat.   When they stayed on after a debriefing session the conversation automatically became more informal, sometimes centering around personal, family, employment or educational problems.   Although some interviewers occasionally asked for advice, on the whole they just wanted somebody who was prepared to listen and to talk. Because we were known to the interviewers but at the same time outsiders, we were structurally appropriate to this intermediary function.

In relation to the respondents we played a similar role, but less directly. Some respondents came to regard the survey staff as people who had access to all kinds of information. They used the interview sessions to indicate what they wanted to know about, and the interviewers brought back to us their requests for information on creche facilities, English language classes, training courses, provisions provided by the community centre and even on accommodation. Some enquiries we could handle ourselves, others we referred to the organisers of the community centre. Either way we came to know the ordinary problems and preoccupations of the residents and of the area.

THE FIELDWORK RESULTS

By employing a local fieldforce we had hoped for a higher than usual response rate, but we had not anticipated the quality and extent of its effect. The results were impressive. Of the 526 households - an estimate based on the data from the local housing office - 446 households were successfully interviewed. This is an interview success rate of 84.6 per cent. As housing tenure in inner city areas is extremely fluid, the estimate of the housing office might have been inaccurate. An alternative way of calculating the survey response rate is to add all non respondents, including households not contacted or located, to the number of completed interviews and to exclude only the vacant dwellings. On this basis there were 76 non respondents out of a total of 521 households and the overall response rate was a 'suburban' 85.4 per cent.

The 76 fieldwork failures comprised 41 refusals, 10 households where cooperation was not possible because of serious illness or a crisis, 24 addresses where the residents could not be contacted or located, and 1 household which gave inaccurate information. The non response profiles were very similar to those of the respondents. Except for single person households, who constituted 41 per cent of the non responding compared with 27 per cent of the responding households, the proportion of all other types of household amongst the non responders corresponded with their proportion amongst the responding households. As for 'ethnic origin', by which we mean here only place of birth, the main discrepancy occurred in the figures for residents born in the Caribbean: 24 per cent of the non respondents were of Caribbean 'ethnic origin' compared with 17

per cent of the respondents.   The other groups showed
no great difference and none is overrepresented among
outright refusals.

Non respondents were not distributed equally over
the various streets.   63 per- cent of the total were
concentrated in three streets.   But since these three
are the largest in the survey area, the figure tells
us nothing about reasons for refusal or non contact.
If however, we calculate non response per street, as
a proportion of the total number of households in that
street, the size of the street becomes insignificant,
bottom place is taken by a different set of three,
and a number of possible explanations of low rates
of survey response can be offered.   One clue is given
by the type of household living in these roads.   They
contain a large proportion of young single and two
person households.   Because of work commitments they
could not be contacted during the day, and they tended
to spend the evenings and weekends away from home.
Another possible reason is the type of buildings.
Two of the same three were the only streets in the
survey area which had buildings with three or more
housing units.   As other surveys have demonstrated,
areas containing such buildings tend to produce a relatively high non response rate.   The fact that we worked
with local interviewers did not solve this problem
completely.   Indeed, the interviewers' networks coincided
with it.   Many preferred to interview households they
knew or at least recognised; none of the interviewers
lived in either of the two roads with multi-occupied
housing; and a large proportion of the households
who refused to cooperate or could not be contacted
or located were marginal households, not involved in
local activities and not personally known to any of
the interviewers.

THE PERFORMANCE OF THE INTERVIEWERS

It took the interviewers about ten weeks to try to
contact the 526 households and to complete 446 interviews.
During the first and second week of the fieldwork period
the interviewers obtained 122 interviews (27.4 per
cent of the total interviews), during the third and
fourth weeks 164 interviews (36.9 per cent), during
the fifth and sixth weeks 110 interviews (24.7 per
cent).   At this point we decided to continue the fieldwork
with a reduced fieldforce of four interviewers.   In
the extended period 49 households (another 11 per cent)
were contacted and successfully interviewed.

The performance of the interviewers differed.   Three
completed less than 5 questionnaires;   two managed
each more than 50.   The rest were distributed across
the range between, the mode being 10 to 15 questionnaires

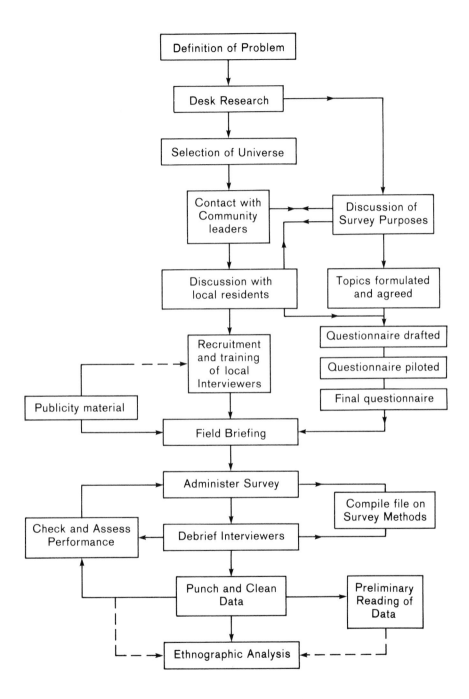

Figure A.2   SEQUENCE OF THE NEIGHBOURHOOD SURVEY

per interviewer. There was no relationship between interview performance and educational qualifications. The interviewers without any formal education completed 40 per cent of all interviews, those with CSE, 'O' or 'A' levels 24 per cent, and those with postsecondary qualification 19 per cent. The remaining 17 per cent were done by the fieldwork officer and a social science student from outside the area.

Job and family commitments and outside interests were more significant to the difference in performance, and we have already noted that the amount of money interviewers could earn before being taxed affected their output. Our data on the interviewers' performance suggest that differences can also be explained in terms of the extent to which each interviewer was involved in the neighbourhood (see Chapter 5). The progression of the survey through the neighbourhood demonstrated the various levels of the interviewers' individual local networks quite graphically. They first interviewed households whose members were relatives, friends or acquaintances of some kind. These households were dispersed over the area. They then started to operate in their own streets. The roads not represented in the fieldforce and marginal households were left to a much later stage of the fieldwork period.

Figure A.2 indicates that the tasks and procedures of the neighbourhood survey were in many ways the same as those used in conventional social survey. Our innovation is represented by the extent to which the area's residents participated in the survey not simply as respondents, but also as contributors to the question-naire and as interviewers. We involved the neighbourhood in these ways in an attempt to compensate for the low response rate which characterises survey work in inner city areas. On the evidence of the response achieved, the strategy was by this measure successful. Further, on the basis of the checks carried out during and after the fieldwork period (a 10 per cent sample of households was interviewed a second time), we can be confident that the employment of local residents as interviewers did not reduce the validity of the survey results. On the contrary: the survey's ethnographic scope - i.e. its validity as an indicator of patterns of social relationships as well as a count of units of population - is a direct product of their involvement.

NOTES

(1) This item is abridged and adapted from Wallman
    et al 1980.
(2) The disciplines involved in the programme include
    social anthropology, political and applied sociology,
    economic history, systems analysis, urban planning
    and psychotherapy.
(3) It will be obvious that this context has not been
    extended to include the wider issues of colonial
    immigration and industrial or urban decline.
(4) 'Blight' refers to the deterioration of an environ-
    ment said to be caused by uncertainty and spec-
    ulation about its future.   See e.g. Wallman
    1975.
(5) Evidence for the City of Bradford underlines
    these patterns.   In 1979, in the same national
    survey, the overall response rate was 80 per cent.
    But in the inner city wards of University and
    Manningham it was 55 per cent, and in the suburban
    wards of Baildon and Tong it was 83 per cent
    and 86 per cent respectively.
(6) The recipients of particular kinds of state benefit
    in Britain were (in 1978) only taxed if they earned
    above £15 per week; they run the more significant
    risk of having the benefit stopped altogether.

B Survey questionnaire

This questionnaire was administered by local interviewers in the neighbourhood survey in the way described under the heading Fieldwork Strategy (A: above). Two changes were made in its early days to cope with difficulties which had not arisen in the pilot stages.

The first was that Section 1: ACTIVITIES was moved to the end of the questionnaire on the grounds that it made too frivolous a beginning. The survey had been advertised (as in the postcard reproduced here) in a friendly but serious tone. It seems that questions on sports, hobbies and outings contradicted people's expectations; indeed, some were openly irritated by them. The section was no more enthusiastically received at the end of the questionnaire (a point which may be significant to leisure studies in inner city areas if not to 'leisure studies' in general) but at least in that position there was no risk of it spoiling the whole encounter from the start.

A second change was made by the elision of the question 'Is it used often?' which was asked of each of the appliances listed in Section 5: HOUSEHOLD MACHINERY. Some respondents found the whole section bizarre, many were amused by it; neither of these reactions were counter productive but everyone had trouble with the fact that the question 'Is it used often?' could not sensibly and equally be applied to all the items listed. Since the questionnaire was designed to avoid ambiguities or questions requiring either the interviewer or the respondent to ponder on meaning, the question should not have been posed in this context at all.

One final comment: those interested in the Data Processing (C: below) may wish to note that the questionnaire generates more variables than are indicated by the numbers in the lefthand column.

1. ACTIVITIES *(mark "yes" answers only)*

A

		ARNDALE CENTRE	NORTHCOTE MARKET	CLAPHAM JUNCTION	WEST END	OUT OF LONDON	OUT OF ENGLAND
1–6	**When did you last go to**						
	1 last week	1	1	1	1	1	1
	2 last month	2	2	2	2	2	2
	3 two to six months ago	3	3	3	3	3	3
	4 more than six months ago	4	4	4	4	4	4
	5 never been	5	5	5	5	5	5
7–12	**How did you get there?**						
	1 on foot or bicycle	1	1	1	1	1	1
	2 by private car or motorbike	2	2	2	2	2	2
	3 by public transport	3	3	3	3	3	3
	4 by taxi	4	4	4	4	4	4
	5 by some combination	5	5	5	5	5	5
13–18	**What was your main reason for going?**						
	1 connected with work	1	1	1	1	1	1
	2 personal business	2	2	2	2	2	2
	3 social outing/holiday	3	3	3	3	3	3
	4 shopping	4	4	4	4	4	4
	5 family reasons	5	5	5	5	5	5

B

		PLAYING SPORT (which?)	WATCHING SPORT (which?)	BINGO	CINEMA	DANCING	DARTS	DOMINOES	JUST RELAXING	PLAYING CARDS	IS THERE SOME OTHER HOBBY OR ACTIVITY THAT IS IMPORTANT TO YOU?
19–29	**When did you last do each of these things?**										
	1 this week	1	1	1	1	1	1	1	1	1	1
	2 within this month	2	2	2	2	2	2	2	2	2	2
	3 one to six months ago	3	3	3	3	3	3	3	3	3	3
	4 within this year	4	4	4	4	4	4	4	4	4	4
	5 more than a year ago	5	5	5	5	5	5	5	5	5	5
30–40	**Where do you prefer to do each of them?**										
	1 at home	1	1	1	1	1	1	1	1	1	1
	2 at the pub	2	2	2	2	2	2	2	2	2	2
	3 hall or stadium *(entrance fee)*	3	3	3	3	3	3	3	3	3	3
	4 in breaks at work	4	4	4	4	4	4	4	4	4	4
	5 friend's house	5	5	5	5	5	5	5	5	5	5
	6 park/open space	6	6	6	6	6	6	6	6	6	6
	7 community centre	7	7	7	7	7	7	7	7	7	7
	8 private club	8	8	8	8	8	8	8	8	8	8
41–47	**Who are you most likely to do them with?**										
	1 spouse	1	1	1	1	1	1	1	1	1	1
	2 other family	2	2	2	2	2	2	2	2	2	2
	3 work mates	3	3	3	3	3	3	3	3	3	3
	4 friends	4	4	4	4	4	4	4	4	4	4
	5 neighbours	5	5	5	5	5	5	5	5	5	5
	6 other	6	6	6	6	6	6	6	6	6	6

48   **Do you belong to any clubs or societies?** *(mark yes or no)*
     1 Yes   1
     2 No   2

49   If yes, which?..

50   **Do you ever take holidays away from home?** *(mark yes or no)*
     1 Yes   1
     2 No   2

     If yes –
51   Where do you usually go?..

52   Where did you go this year?...

2. NEIGHBOURHOOD

53 How did you happen to move into this house/flat?
    1 lived here since childhood   1
    2 spouse lived here before marriage   2
    3 Council housing list allocation   3
    4 Housing Action allocation   4
    5 purchase on the open market   5
    6 purchase as a sitting tenant   6
    7 private rental arrangement   7
    8 got it through friends   8
    9 got it through relatives   9
    10 inherited it   10
    11 other   11

54 Where did you live immediately before coming to this house/flat?
    1 in LARA area   1
    2 Battersea   2
    3 other south London   3
    4 other London...   4
    5 elsewhere in UK   5
    6 outside UK..   6

55 Have you any plans to move in the next five years or so?
    1 Yes, possibly   1
    2 Yes, definitely   2
    3 No   3

If yes,
56   Where would you like to live?
      1

57 What would be your main reason for moving?
    1 to be near family   1
    2 because of work   2
    3 to get a better house/flat   3
    4 because you don't like the area *(comment?)*   4
    ....
    5 other   5

58 Are you a member of LARA? *(Residents' Association)*
    1 Yes   1
    2 No   2

59 Do you receive "the Echo"? *(LARA Newsletter)*
    1 Yes   1
    2 No   2

60 Did you read the last one?
    1 Yes   1
    2 No   2

61 Have you ever used the Community Centre?
    1 Yes   1
    2 No   2

62 If no, why not? ....
....

63 If yes, what do you, or members of your household, use it for? *(tick all those mentioned)*
    1 day care/nursery   1
    2 pensioners' club   2
    3 youth club   3
    4 childrens club, playschemes   4
    5 keep-fit classes   5
    6 socials, dances   6
    7 advice   7
    8 gardening club   8
    9 darts club   9
    10 meetings of Residents' Association   10
    11 music/movement, under 5's   11
    12 creche   12

64 About how often do you or members of your household use the Community Centre?
    1 every week   1
    2 twice a month   2
    3 once a month   3
    4 only occasionally   4
    5 never   5

65 When did you yourself last go?
    1 this week   1
    2 during this month   2
    3 one to six months ago   3
    4 within this year   4
    5 never been   5

66 Would anyone in your household use a programme of after school care for children of working parents?
    1 Yes   1
    2 No   2

67 Are there other things you would like the Community Centre to do?
    1 Yes   1
    2 No   2

68 If yes, what things?...
....

69 Has the Housing Action Area affected you and your household?
    1 Yes   1
    2 No   2

70 If yes, how has it affected you?
    1 for good   1
    2 for ill   2
    3 both   3

    (Comment?) ....
    ....

3. MEMBERS OF THE HOUSEHOLD

	A	B	C	D	E	F	G	H
	RESPONDENT							

71 Could you please give me the following details about each person living in your household at this time

NAME
(first name will do)

72 SEX

AGE

73 MARITAL STATUS
s/m/d/w

74 RELATIONSHIP TO RESPONDENT
(e.g. wife, husband, daughter, father, lodger, friend, etc. Also note relationship of other members of the household to each other)

75 Where was each person born?
(Specify in dotted line where possible)

	A	B	C	D	E	F	G	H
1 LARA area	1	1	1	1	1	1	1	1
2 other Battersea	2	2	2	2	2	2	2	2
3 other South London	3	3	3	3	3	3	3	3
4 London north of River	4	4	4	4	4	4	4	4
5 rest of UK	5	5	5	5	5	5	5	5
6 Eire	6	6	6	6	6	6	6	6
7 other Europe	7	7	7	7	7	7	7	7
8 Asia	8	8	8	8	8	8	8	8
9 Africa	9	9	9	9	9	9	9	9
10 Caribbean	10	10	10	10	10	10	10	10
11 North America	11	11	11	11	11	11	11	11
12 Other..	12	12	12	12	12	12	12	12

76 Of those born abroad, how old was each when he or she came to the UK? *(put age or approximate age in years)*

77 How old was each member of your household when he/she finished full-time education? *(put age or approximate age in years)*

78 Have any of you ever attended evening classes?
1 Yes *(tick which)*
2 No

79 Have any of you ever been on day release training?
1 Yes *(tick which)*
2 No

80 Have you or other members of your household any qualifications or certificates? Who has which ones?

	A	B	C	D	E	F	G	H
1 None	1	1	1	1	1	1	1	1
2 CSE	2	2	2	2	2	2	2	2
3 'O'Level/ONC	3	3	3	3	3	3	3	3
4 City and Guilds	4	4	4	4	4	4	4	4
5 Completed Apprenticeship	5	5	5	5	5	5	5	5
6 'A' Level/HNC/Matric	6	6	6	6	6	6	6	6
7 Professional qualification or Degree	7	7	7	7	7	7	7	7
8 Postgraduate degree or diploma	8	8	8	8	8	8	8	8
9 Secretarial/Commercial Certificate	9	9	9	9	9	9	9	9
10 Other...	10	10	10	10	10	10	10	10

211

	A RESPONDENT	B	C	D	E	F	G	H

86 About *how long* does it take each working member of your household to get to work or to school?
(Time for single journey only)

	A	B	C	D	E	F	G	H
1 less than 15 minutes	1	1	1	1	1	1	1	1
2 15 to 30 minutes	2	2	2	2	2	2	2	2
3 30 to 45 minutes	3	3	3	3	3	3	3	3
4 45 to 60 minutes	4	4	4	4	4	4	4	4
5 more than one hour	5	5	5	5	5	5	5	5

87 *How* does each person travel to and from work?
(Tick more than one means of transport if appropriate)

	A	B	C	D	E	F	G	H
1 on foot	1	1	1	1	1	1	1	1
2 by bicycle	2	2	2	2	2	2	2	2
3 own car – alone	3	3	3	3	3	3	3	3
4 own car – shared	4	4	4	4	4	4	4	4
5 regular lift by car	5	5	5	5	5	5	5	5
6 by motor cycle	6	6	6	6	6	6	6	6
7 on one bus	7	7	7	7	7	7	7	7
8 more than one bus	8	8	8	8	8	8	8	8
9 tube	9	9	9	9	9	9	9	9
10 train	10	10	10	10	10	10	10	10

88 About *how much* does travel to and from work cost each person each week?

	A	B	C	D	E	F	G	H
1 nothing	1	1	1	1	1	1	1	1
2 less than £1	2	2	2	2	2	2	2	2
3 more than £1 less than £3	3	3	3	3	3	3	3	3
4 more than £3 less than £6	4	4	4	4	4	4	4	4
5 more than £6	5	5	5	5	5	5	5	5

89 About *how long* has each working member of your household been at his/her present *place* of work?
(Note: this question refers to place of work, not occupation or position)

	A	B	C	D	E	F	G	H
1 less than 1 year	1	1	1	1	1	1	1	1
2 one to 5 years	2	2	2	2	2	2	2	2
3 5 to 10 years	3	3	3	3	3	3	3	3
4 more than 10 years	4	4	4	4	4	4	4	4
5 all working life	5	5	5	5	5	5	5	5

90 How did each person find the work he or she now has?

	A	B	C	D	E	F	G	H
1 just applied at the place	1	1	1	1	1	1	1	1
2 through a friend	2	2	2	2	2	2	2	2
3 through a neighbour	3	3	3	3	3	3	3	3
4 through a family member	4	4	4	4	4	4	4	4
5 from an advertisement	5	5	5	5	5	5	5	5
6 from a Job Centre/Labour Exchange	6	6	6	6	6	6	6	6
7 from a Commercial Employment Agency	7	7	7	7	7	7	7	7
8 other*(specify)*	8	8	8	8	8	8	8	8

91 How long has each *unemployed* member of your household been out of work?

	A	B	C	D	E	F	G	H
1 less than one month	1	1	1	1	1	1	1	1
2 1 to 3 months	2	2	2	2	2	2	2	2
3 3 to 6 months	3	3	3	3	3	3	3	3
4 more than 6 months	4	4	4	4	4	4	4	4
5 never worked	5	5	5	5	5	5	5	5

92 How soon do *you* think each unemployed member of your household can expect to find a job?

	A	B	C	D	E	F	G	H
1 within this month	1	1	1	1	1	1	1	1
2 1 to 3 months	2	2	2	2	2	2	2	2
3 3 to 6 months	3	3	3	3	3	3	3	3
4 more than 6 months	4	4	4	4	4	4	4	4
5 never will find work	5	5	5	5	5	5	5	5

4. EMPLOYMENT / WORK

	A	B	C	D	E	F	G	H
	RESPONDENT							

81 Could you tell me who in your household is:

1   a student
2   working full-time on days only
3   working full-time on shifts
4   working part-time
5   a housewife without paid work
6   retired .... *(job before?)*
7   sick/disabled
8   registered unemployed
9   unemployed, not registered – but looking for a job
10 unemployed, not registered – not looking for a job

A	B	C	D	E	F	G	H
1	1	1	1	1	1	1	1
2	2	2	2	2	2	2	2
3	3	3	3	3	3	3	3
4	4	4	4	4	4	4	4
5	5	5	5	5	5	5	5
6	6	6	6	6	6	6	6
7	7	7	7	7	7	7	7
8	8	8	8	8	8	8	8
9	9	9	9	9	9	9	9
10	10	10	10	10	10	10	10

82 What is the main job or occupation of each member of your household?
(Be as precise as possible. Terms such as Engineer, Clerk, Manager, Storeman should not be used on their own. Write Apprentice, Trainee or Retired if appropriate)

....
....
....
....
....
....
....
....
....
....
....
....
....
....

83 What is the main activity or industry of the place each person works?
(Be precise. Terms such as government, manufacturing, sales, etc. are not enough. Put, e.g. local government, dress manufacture, grocery retail sales, etc.)

....
....
....
....
....
....
....
....
....
....
....
....
....
....

84 Of those in your household who now have paid employment, who is:

1   employee working away from home
2   employed to work at home
3   unpaid worker in family firm
4   self-employed without employees
5   self-employed with 1–25 employees
6   self-employed with more than 25 employees

A	B	C	D	E	F	G	H
1	1	1	1	1	1	1	1
2	2	2	2	2	2	2	2
3	3	3	3	3	3	3	3
4	4	4	4	4	4	4	4
5	5	5	5	5	5	5	5
6	6	6	6	6	6	6	6

85 *Where* does each of these people work?
(Enter students also)

1   at home
2   in Battersea
3   other South London ....
4   other London ....
5   elsewhere ....

A	B	C	D	E	F	G	H
1	1	1	1	1	1	1	1
2	2	2	2	2	2	2	2
3	3	3	3	3	3	3	3
4	4	4	4	4	4	4	4
5	5	5	5	5	5	5	5

5. HOUSEHOLD MACHINERY

(Read across to complete one item at a time.
Tick "yes" answers only.
(Mark more than one user's name if necessary)

93–213

		IS THE ITEM PRESENT?	IS IT USED OFTEN?	WHO USES IT?							
				A RESPONDENT	B	C	D	E	F	G	H
1	Car	1	1	1	1	1	1	1	1	1	1
2	Motorbike/Moped	2	2	2	2	2	2	2	2	2	2
3	Bicycle	3	3	3	3	3	3	3	3	3	3
4	Van or Lorry	4	4	4	4	4	4	4	4	4	4
5	Cooker	5	5	5	5	5	5	5	5	5	5
6	Automatic Oven	6	6	6	6	6	6	6	6	6	6
7	Fridge	7	7	7	7	7	7	7	7	7	7
8	Freezer	8	8	8	8	8	8	8	8	8	8
9	Mixer/Blender	9	9	9	9	9	9	9	9	9	9
10	Pressure Cooker	10	10	10	10	10	10	10	10	10	10
11	Kitchen Scale	11	11	11	11	11	11	11	11	11	11
12	Radio	12	12	12	12	12	12	12	12	12	12
13	TV: Black & White	13	13	13	13	13	13	13	13	13	13
14	TV: Colour	14	14	14	14	14	14	14	14	14	14
15	Stereo Record Player	15	15	15	15	15	15	15	15	15	15
16	Other Record Player	16	16	16	16	16	16	16	16	16	16
17	Tape or Cassette Recorder	17	17	17	17	17	17	17	17	17	17
18	Camera	18	18	18	18	18	18	18	18	18	18
19	Movie Camera	19	19	19	19	19	19	19	19	19	19
20	"Hoover" Vacuum Cleaner	20	20	20	20	20	20	20	20	20	20
21	"Bissel" Carpet Sweeper	21	21	21	21	21	21	21	21	21	21
22	Iron	22	22	22	22	22	22	22	22	22	22
23	Washing Machine, Washer only	23	23	23	23	23	23	23	23	23	23
24	Twin Tub Washing Machine	24	24	24	24	24	24	24	24	24	24
25	Automatic Washing Machine	25	25	25	25	25	25	25	25	25	25
26	Wringer	26	26	26	26	26	26	26	26	26	26
27	Spin Dryer	27	27	27	27	27	27	27	27	27	27
28	Tumble Dryer	28	28	28	28	28	28	28	28	28	28
29	Dishwasher	29	29	29	29	29	29	29	29	29	29
30	Hammer	30	30	30	30	30	30	30	30	30	30
31	Screwdriver	31	31	31	31	31	31	31	31	31	31
32	Hand Drill	32	32	32	32	32	32	32	32	32	32
33	Hand Saw	33	33	33	33	33	33	33	33	33	33
34	Electric Drill	34	34	34	34	34	34	34	34	34	34
35	Electric Saw	35	35	35	35	35	35	35	35	35	35
36	Electric Sander	36	36	36	36	36	36	36	36	36	36
37	Carpentry Bench	37	37	37	37	37	37	37	37	37	37
38	'Work Mate' portable carpentry bench	38	38	38	38	38	38	38	38	38	38
39	Hand or Treadle Sewing Machine	39	39	39	39	39	39	39	39	39	39
40	Electric Sewing Machine	40	40	40	40	40	40	40	40	40	40

6. NECESSARY HOUSEHOLD TASKS

214 Who usually prepares the *main meal* for this household?

....

215–7 Are there others who sometimes prepare the main meal?
1 No   1
2 Yes   2

If yes, who? ....
In what circumstances? ....

218 How much time does it usually take to prepare the main meal? *(do not include oven time)*
1 less than 15 minutes   1
2 15–30 minutes   2
3 30–45 minutes   3
4 45–60 minutes   4
5 more than an hour   5

219 How is the main meal usually taken on weekdays?
1 whole household together   1
2 children and adults separately   2
3 men and women separately   3
4 each person as they come in from school or work   4
5 each person as they feel like it   5

220 Who normally does the routine *shopping*?

....

221–3 Are there others who sometimes do the routine shopping?
1 No   1
2 Yes   2

If yes, who? ....
In what circumstances? ....

224 Where is this shopping usually done?
1 In Battersea   1
2 other South London 2
3 other London 3

225 At what kind of shops is it done?
(Read out list. Tick more than one if necessary)
1 shopping centre   1
2 supermarket(s)   2
3 local small shop/corner shop(s)   3
4 street market(s)   4

226 How does the shopper get there and back?
1 on foot or bike   1
2 private car or motorcycle   2
3 public transport   3
4 taxi   4
5 more than one of these *(specify)*   5

....

227 How often is ordinary shopping done?
1 every day   1
2 every other day   2
3 twice a week   3
4 once a week   4
5 less than once a week   5

228 About how much time does it take every week?
1 less than one hour   1
2 one to five hours   2
3 more than five hours   3

229 Who normally does the main *laundry* in this household? ....

230–2 Are there others who sometimes do the laundry?
1 No   1
2 Yes   2

If yes, who? ....
In what circumstances? ....

233 Where and how is the main laundry usually done?
(Read out list. Tick more than one if necessary)
1 by hand at home   1
2 by machine at home   2
3 at the laundrette: washed only   3
4 washed and dried at laundrette   4
5 dried at the laundrette   5
6 by a laundry or laundry service   6

234 How many times a week is a family wash done?
1 every day   1
2 every other day   2
3 twice a week   3
4 once a week   4
5 less than once a week   5

235 About how much time does it take every week?
1 less than an hour   1
2 one to five hours   2
3 more than five hours   3

7. FRIENDS AND OTHER RESOURCES
(ask about respondent only)

236 How many of the people you know would
you call "close" friends?

1	none	1
2	one or two	2
3	two to six	3
4	six to ten	4
5	more than ten	5

237 Where do your close friends live?
(the number living in each area is not important)

1	in LARA area	1
2	in Battersea	2
3	in other South London	3
4	other London	4
5	other UK	5
6	outside UK	6

238 How did you get to know them?
(the number in each category is not important)

1	because he/she lives nearby	1
2	through connections at work	2
3	doing business with them *(e.g. tradesmen, teacher, etc).*	3
4	because of family ties	4
5	through the children	5
6	at school or college	6
7	other	7

239 When was the last time you had contact by
visit, phone or letter with a close friend?
(Note special occasion where mentioned)

1	this week	1
2	during this month	2
3	one to six months ago	3
4	within this year	4
5	more than a year ago	5

240 How were you in contact with him or her?

1	visit from him/her	1
2	visit to him/her	2
3	phone call from him/her	3
4	phone call to him/her	4
5	letter/card from him/her	5
6	letter/card to him/her	6

241 What is your religion?

1	C of E	1
2	Methodist	2
3	Catholic	3
4	other Christian	4
5	Jewish	5
6	Moslem	6
7	Hindu	7
8	Sikh	8
9	other	9
10	no religion	10

242 Do you attend religious services?

1	Yes	1
2	No	2

243 If yes, about how often?

1	once a week	1
2	once a month	2
3	two or three times a year	3
4	once a year	4
5	for special events only	5

244–
250 How often during the past year have you
used the following services?

	1 once a week	2 once a month	3 two/ three times	4 once in the year	5 whenever a crisis came up
Social Services	1	2	3	4	5
Job Centre	1	2	3	4	5
Hospital or Clinic	1	2	3	4	5
Advice Centre	1	2	3	4	5
Counselling Service	1	2	3	4	5
Police	1	2	3	4	5
Dept. of Health and Social Security	1	2	3	4	5

251 How long have you lived in Battersea?

1	less than a year	1
2	one to five years	2
3	five to ten years	3
4	ten to twenty years	4
5	more than twenty years	5
6	since birth	6

8. FAMILY AND RELATIVES outside this household

252– *Single households ask:* **Where was each of**
255 **your parents born?**

All other households ask: **Where was each of**
your parents and your partner's parents born?
(Note: this applies only to parents not living
in this household)

	OWN MOTHER	OWN FATHER	PARTNER MOTHER	PARTNER FATHER
1 LARA area	1	1	1	1 ....
2 other Battersea	2	2	2	2 ....
3 other South London	3	3	3	3 ....
4 London North of River	4	4	4	4 ....
5 other UK	5	5	5	5 ....
6 Eire	6	6	6	6 ....
7 other Europe	7	7	7	7 ....
8 Asia	8	8	8	8 ....
9 Africa	9	9	9	9 ....
10 Caribbean	10	10	10	10 ....
11 North America	11	11	11	11 ....
12 other	12	12	12	12 ....

256– **Are they all still alive?**
263

1 Yes

2 No   If not, what year did each die?

1	1	1	1
2 .... (yr)	2 .... (yr)	2 .... (yr)	2 .... (yr)

264 **Of all your relatives, apart from parents and**
children, is there any one who is specially
important to you or your household?

1 Yes — 1

2 No, no other relatives at all — 2

3 No, no one is specially important — 3

4 No, all my relatives are equally
important — 4

265– **If yes,** *how* **are they related to you or your**
270 **family?**
(write in the columns marked special relatives:
male/female cousin; maternal/paternal aunt/
uncle of self or partner etc. Include "not a
real cousin", "like an aunt", "godmother"
etc. if reported as such)

SPECIAL RELATIVES

271– *Where* **does each of your absent parents or special**
280 **relatives live?**

	PARENTS				SPECIAL RELATIVES					
	OWN MO.	OWN FA.	PTNR. MO.	PTNR FA.						
1 Battersea	1	1	1	1	1	1	1	1	1	1
2 other South London	2	2	2	2	2	2	2	2	2	2
3 other London	3	3	3	3	3	3	3	3	3	3
4 other UK	4	4	4	4	4	4	4	4	4	4
5 outside UK	5	5	5	5	5	5	5	5	5	5

281– **When were you last in contact, by visit, phone or**
290 **letter, with each of them?**
(if special occasions are mentioned, please note)

1 this week	1	1	1	1	1	1	1	1	1	1
2 during this month	2	2	2	2	2	2	2	2	2	2
3 one to six months ago	3	3	3	3	3	3	3	3	3	3
4 within this year	4	4	4	4	4	4	4	4	4	4
5 more than a year ago	5	5	5	5	5	5	5	5	5	5
6 out of touch altogether	6	6	6	6	6	6	6	6	6	6

291– **How were you last in contact with each of them?**
300

1 they visited here	1	1	1	1	1	1	1	1	1	1
2 respondent visited them	2	2	2	2	2	2	2	2	2	2
3 phone call from them	3	3	3	3	3	3	3	3	3	3
4 phone call to them	4	4	4	4	4	4	4	4	4	4
5 letter/card from them	5	5	5	5	5	5	5	5	5	5
6 letter/card to them	6	6	6	6	6	6	6	6	6	6

301 **Do you have children who no longer live with you?**

1 Yes *(complete next page also)*

2 No *(leave out next page)*

8. continued: CHILDREN

(Ask only those who have children no longer living with them)

302 How many sons do you have?   ....

303 How many daughters do you have? ....

304— When was each born?
309 *(put the first name and year of birth of each on a dotted line at the top of one of the columns)*

310— *Where does each of your absent children live?*
315 *(Specify where possible)*   ....

    1 Battersea
    2 other South London
    3 other London
    4 other UK
    5 outside UK

1	1	1	1	1	1
2	2	2	2	2	2
3	3	3	3	3	3
4	4	4	4	4	4
5	5	5	5	5	5

316— *When* were you last in contact by visit, phone
321 or letter with each of them?

    1 this week
    2 during this month
    3 one to six months ago
    4 within this year
    5 more than a year ago
    6 out of touch altogether

1	1	1	1	1	1
2	2	2	2	2	2
3	3	3	3	3	3
4	4	4	4	4	4
5	5	5	5	5	5
6	6	6	6	6	6

322— *How* were you last in contact with each of
327 them?

    1 he/she visited here
    2 respondent visited him/her
    3 phone call from him/her
    4 phone call to him/her
    5 letter/card from him/her
    6 letter/card to him/her

1	1	1	1	1	1
2	2	2	2	2	2
3	3	3	3	3	3
4	4	4	4	4	4
5	5	5	5	5	5
6	6	6	6	6	6

C Data processing

The objective of data processing has been described as the 'capture and transforming of data into useful information and the transmission of this information to...specific individuals or groups'.[2] The definition makes the distinction between data and information. Data are the raw materials relating to the observed activities which become information when correctly processed. The information produced allows the interpretation and analysis of the subject under study to be completed.

When a computer is used in data processing the operation is broken into several stages. In the case of the Battersea survey five stages were involved:

1) The questionnaires were completed and rechecked in the debriefing of the interviewers (Appendix A).

2) The data from the questionnaire were transferred to computer coding sheets by trained coders.[3]

3) The data was punched onto cards (i.e. transferred to a machine processible form).

4) The data was input into the computer and checked and cleaned before it was structured for analysis.

5) Preliminary analysis (i.e. the tabulation) of the data was carried out with the help of SPSS.[4]

During the preparation and processing stages, a series of operations were carried out to ensure that the information produced from the data was error free and in a form which aided analysis. Errors can enter the data set at the collection, coding, punching, editing or file construction stages of the process but there are standard procedures for dealing with them. The Neighbourhood Survey however, generated problems peculiar to itself.

At the design stage there was the problem of constructing a questionnaire which could be administered by lay interviewers who were not familiar with complex questionnaires, coding frames or multiple instructions, and yet would yield high quality information. On both counts the questionnaire (appended) was successful.

During its administration, several important manual error checks were carried out as part of the debriefing exercise (Appendix A). In 10 per cent of the cases, a second interview was carried out by a different interviewer and the questionnaires were checked for the quality of information and consistency between the two interviewers.

The coding operation was carried out in two parts. The more difficult sections, those containing a large number of possible answers, had to be handled by one or two closely supervised coders but the main part of the operation was performed by a team of coders. The main group consisted of ten second year town planning students who had previous experience of coding street surveys and had recently coded a large and complex questionnaire. Consequently, they were familiar with the principles of coding and required specific rather than general instruction in this area.

A special coding form was produced to overcome the problems of the questionnaire format. The codesheet was designed to give the maximum amount of information possible to the coders by converting standard Fortran coding forms into a combined instruction sheet and coding form. Instructions and additional codes were printed adjacent to the columns they related to and the number of the question was printed over the top of the column into which the response was to be coded. The form and sample questionnaires were used to train the interviewers before they began work. The same procedure was used for the difficult sections except that supervision was intensified.

When the coding stage was finished, 10 per cent of the coding sheets were fully checked by the data processer. An average of between three and four transference coding errors were found on each sheet out of a total number of entries varying between 200 and 500 per questionnaire. This was an acceptable error rate for this stage because many of these errors were of the type which would be detected by subsequent machine checks. The 10 per cent sample check was primarily concerned with ensuring that there had been no consistent misreading or misapplication of the instructions. In fact only one such case arose, and all the questionnaires handled by that individual coder were rechecked and corrected by the data processer. At this point the data were punched on computer cards. Punching errors were minimised by a standard 'verification' check. This is done by overpunching the cards using a special facility

on card punches.   If an attempt is made to punch a
new hole on the second run then the machine stops so
that the card can be checked.

The data from the punched cards was then input into
the computer and transferred to magnetic tape and disk
for ease of access and manipulation.   Before the analysis,
it was necessary to make a further series of checks,
this time using computer software.   Again, these checks
were to ensure the consistency and accuracy of the
data, but they also checked the data for logical consistency (e.g. that no three year olds were recorded as
married).

This work was done at the University of London Computer
Centre using SNUFF editing system to amend and change
the data.[5]   Most of the editing work comprised two
types of machine checks:-

1) The use of packages such as SCAN[6] and SORT/MERGE.[7]

2) The use of FORTRAN[8] programmes specifically written
to overcome individual problems.

The SORT/MERGE package was used to ensure that the
data were correctly ordered.   This was followed by
a SCAN check to verify that the coded number in each
and every column was within the limits permissible
for the relevant variable.

The second series of machine checks required individually
written Fortran programmes designed to check the logical
consistency of the data.   For example, it was possible
to ensure that there were no married persons aged fifteen
or less, or people born abroad who, according to the
data set, had also lived in Battersea all their lives.
In addition to these checks, the clerical assistant
working on the survey made systematic visual checks
of frequency runs and cross tabulations when the data
set was being run on the computer.   Any apparently
abnormal groupings were noted and checked against the
original information.

Two data sets were eventually set up to be used in
the analysis of the survey data.   One of these was
a subset of the other.   This dual structure was adopted
so that the unit of analysis could be shifted easily
from the individual to the household.   The main data
set contained all the coded information from the questionnaires and some data which was coded separately and
added later.   It comprised 446 cases with 16 cards
per case.   The 327 questions in the questionnaire
generated 872 variables in the main data set.   The
late coded and extra variables constructed by recoding
existing variables were:

1) Father's birthplace
2) Mother's birthplace

3) Size of family
4) Number of employed in the household
5) Relationship to head of household
6) Variables from Section 1B.

In each case the data were coded, punched and cleaned as before. The file containing the additional data was then merged with the main file so that the additional data entered the main data set as extra card images.

Six other variables were also necessary to the analysis. These were constructed using SPSS data modification cards and are therefore part of the SPSS set up and not a permanent part of the data set. They are:

E.D. - A variable representing the households in each 1971 Census Enumeration District. This was created by recoding the identification number of each household into an ED number.

STREET - As above but for the street in which the household was set.

NEWAGE - New age is calculated by subtracting the age of arrival in UK, (Q76: variable AGEARR) from the chronological age (Q72: Variable AGE).

SOCLAS - A variable representing social class, as defined in the 1971 census, was created. Social classes are groups of occupations which were produced by a simple recoding procedure.

SEG - A variable representing socio economic group. SEGs were created by grouping occupational classifications in combination with job status.

PMETH - A variable representing ethnic origin, defined by the birthplace of the individual and the individual's mother and father in combination.

There was a severe limitation involved in using SPSS 7.0 to analyse the neighbourhood survey data set. The DO REPEAT statement, which allows tasks to be performed any defined number of times, can only be used in isolation, i.e. one DO REPEAT statement has to be completed before another can be started. In programming language, this means that do-loops cannot be nested inside one another; in ordinary terms it means that a file structure used for the analysis of data at the household level is not suitable for analysis at the individual level because data on individuals cannot easily be abstracted from household data.

To overcome this problem a second data file was constructed as a subset of the main data file. This file, known as the demographic file, was designed to permit straightforward analysis of data relating to individual members of the household. It contained only the information which applied to all individual members of the household: the demographic information itself (Qs 71-80), additional individually based information (Qs 81-92) and Section Five, the section on household machinery and its uses. The same variables were added to this data set as were added to the main data set. The demographic file was always treated as a subset of the main data set and was not edited.

Overall the data processing exercise was continually refined and largely successful. Two comprehensive data sets were produced which provide a basis for analysis. Fuller experience than it is appropriate to set out here has produced guidelines for the data processing of further surveys and we may expect that a repeat exercise will be less time consuming.

NOTES

(1)   This section was compiled by Ray Webster.

(2)   V. T. Dock and E. Essick, 1978: 4.

(3)   Most of the answers to questions were written in a coded form on the questionnaire, although the answers to the open ended questions had to be coded at this point.

(4)   SPSS: Statistiscal Package for the Social Sciences is a widely used program for handling and analysing social science data. See Nie et al 1975.

(5)   SNUFF: An Editor for Interactive or Batch use. ULCC Bulletin B2.7/3.

(6)   SCAN: A Data Verification Program. ULCC Document GOI SCAN.

(7)   Simple use of SORT/MERGE. ULCC Bulletin B5.1/1.

(8)   Fortran: FORmula TRANslation) the computer language used throughout the data processing exercise.

Bibliography

Apter, D.E., (1964), 'Ideology and Discontent' in D.E. Apter (ed) Ideology and Discontent, The Free Press, Glencoe, Illinois.

Better Homes - The Next Priorities (1975), HMSO, London.

Blau, P.M., (1964), Exchange and Power in Social Life, John Wiley and Sons Inc., New York

Booth, C., (1889-91), Labour and Life of the People, Three Volumes, Williams and Norgate, London.

Booth, C., (1902-3), Life and Labour of the People in London, Seventeen Volumes, Macmillan, London.

Booth Manuscripts, (no date), Group B, notebook B.62. (British Library of Political and Economic Science).

Bott, E., (1957), Family and Social Network, Tavistock, London.

Bourdieu, P., (1977), Outline of a Theory of Practice, Cambridge University Press, Cambridge.

Brown, K.D., (1976), 'London and the Historical Reputation of John Burns', London Journal, vol.2, no.2.

Brown, K.D., (1977), John Burns, Royal Historical Society Studies in History, London.

Census of England and Wales,(1921, 1951, 1961, 1971), HMSO, London.

Census of England and Wales,(1961, 1966, 1971), Ward Library Data Small Area Statistics (Unpublished).

City of Bradford Metropolitan District Council, (1979), National Dwelling & Housing Survey Interview Outcome Data (Unpublished).

Clark, C., (1958), 'The economics of housework', Bulletin of the Oxford Institute of Statistics, vol.20.

Craig, F.W.S., (ed) (1971), Greater London Votes I, Political Reference Publications, Chichester.

Craig, F.W.S., (ed) (1972), Boundaries of Parliamentary Constituencies 1885-1972, Political Reference Publications, Chichester.

De Lange, D.J. and Kosmin, B.A., (1979), Community Resources for a Community Survey, Board of Deputies of British Jews, London.

Deakin, N. and Ungerson, C., (1977), Leaving London, Heinemann, London.

Dennis, R., (1978), 'Changing South London', in Hugh Clout (ed) Changing London, University Tutorial Press, Slough.

Department of Employment Gazette, (1975, 1978, 1979, 1981), Volumes 83, 86, 87, 89, HMSO, London.

Department of the Environment, (1975), Circulars 13/75 and 14/75, HMSO, London.

Department of the Environment, (1979), National Dwelling & Housing Survey, HMSO, London.

Do ck V.T. and Essick, E., (1978), Principles of Business Data Processing, Science Research Associates, New York.

Elias, N. and Scotson, J.L., (1965), The Established and The Outsiders, Frank Cass and Co. Ltd., London.

Firth, R., (1951), Elements of Social Organisation, Watts and Company, London.

Firth, R., (1956), Two Studies of Kinship in London, London School of Economics, Monographs on Social Anthropology, no.15, Athlone Press, London.

Firth, R., (1964), Essays on Social Organisation and Values, Athlone Press, London.

Flett, H., (1979a), 'Bureaucracy and Ethnicity' in S. Wallman (ed) Ethnicity at Work, Macmillan, London.

Flett, H., (1979b), 'Dispersal policies in council housing: arguments and evidence', in New Community, July.

Gans, H., (1962), The Urban Villagers, Free Press of Glencoe, New York.

Gellner, E.A., (1982), Language, State and Culture, 6th Radcliffe Brown Memorial Lecture in Social Anthropology, British Academy, London.

Gershuny, J.I., (1979), After Industrial Society?, Macmillan, London.

Gershuny, J.I. and Pahl, R.E., (1980), 'The Hidden Economy', in New Society, vol.51, no.900.

Gershuny, J.I. and Thomas, G.S., (1980), Changing Patterns of Time Use, UK, 1961-1975, University of Sussex: Science Policy Research Unit (SPRU) Occasional Paper no.13.

Gershuny, J.I. and Thomas, G.S., (1982), Changing Times: Activity Patterns in the UK 1937-1975, OUP (in press).

Harrisson, T., (1976), Living Through the Blitz, Penguin, Harmondsworth.

Henry, S., (1978), The Hidden Economy: the Context and Control of Borderline Crime, Martin Robertson, London.

Jahoda, M., Lazarsfeld, P. and Zeisel, H., (1972), Marienthal: the sociography of an unemployed community, Tavistock, London.

Jay, D., (1980), Change and Fortune: A Political Record, Hutchinson, London.

Kent, W., (1950), John Burns: Labour's Lost Leader, Williams and Norgate, London.

Kosmin, B.A., (1979), 'J.R. Archer (1863-1932): A Pan-Africanist in the Battersea Labour Movement', New Community, vol.vii, no.3.

Kosmin, B.A. and De Lange, D.J., (1980), 'Conflicting Urban Ideologies', in The London Journal, vol.6, no.2.

LARA Echo, (1978), no. 39, December.

Leach, E., (1967), 'An anthropologist's reflections on a Social Survey', in O. Jongmans and P. Gutkind (eds) Anthropologists in the Field, Van Gorcum and Company, Assen.

Linklater, A., (1980), An Unhusbanded Life - Charlotte Despard: suffragette, socialist and Sinn Feiner, Hutchison, London.

London Housing Research Group, (1979), 'How reliable are the National Dwelling and Housing Survey Results for the London Boroughs?', London, June.

Louvaine Action Plan, (1975), A Report by Louvaine Area Residents' Association (Unpublished).

McCulloch, J.R., (1866), A Dictionary: Geographical, Statistical and Historical of the Various Countries, Places and Principal

Natural Objects in the World, vol.I, Longmans, Green and Co., London.

Meissner, M., (et alia) (1977), 'No Exit for Wives', Canadian Review of Sociology and Anthropology, vol.12, no.4, Part 1.

Metallurgicon Local Directory (1867), London.

Morrey, C.R., (1976), The 1971 Census: Demographic, Social and Economic Indices for Wards in Greater London, Greater London Council, London.

Moss, L. and Parker, S.H., (1967), The Local Government Councillor, (Maud Committee, vol.2), HMSO, London.

New Survey of London Life and Labour, (1933-5), Nine Volumes, King, London.

Nie, Hull, Jenkins, Steinbrenner and Bent, (1975), Statistical Package for the Social Sciences, (2nd Edition), McGraw Hill, New York.

Patterson, S., (1968), Immigrants in Industry, Oxford University Press, London, for the Institute of Race Relations.

Price, P., (1972), An Imperial War and the British Working Class, Routledge, London.

Registrar General's Statistical Review for England and Wales for 1938, (1940), HMSO, London.

Rhodes, G., (ed) (1972a), The New Government of London: the first five years, Weidenfeld & Nicholson, London.

Rhodes, G., (1972b), The Government of London: the struggle for reform, Weidenfeld & Nicholson, London.

Robinson, J., (1977), Changes in America's Use of Time: 1965-1975, Communications Research Centre, Cleveland State University, Cleveland, Ohio.

Sanders, W.S., (1927), Early Socialist Days, Hogarth, London.

Skeffington Report, (1969), Report of the Committee on Public Participation and Planning: People and Planning, HMSO, London.

Smith, D.J., (1977), Racial Disadvantage in Britain: the PEP Report, Penguin, Harmondsworth.

Stenton, M. and Lees, S., (1979), Who's Who of British Members of Parliament, Volume III, 1919-45, Harvester Press, Brighton.

Szalai, A., (1972), The Use of Time, Mouton, The Hague.

Thompson, P., (1967), Socialists, Liberals and Labour, Routledge, London.

Thorns, D., (1973), Suburbia, Paladin Books, London.

Town and Country Planning Act, (1968), HMSO, London.

Townsend, P., (1979), Poverty in the UK: a Survey of Household Resources and Standards of Living, Penguin, Harmondsworth.

University of London Computer Centre, Bulletins B2 7/3, B5 1/1. Document G01 SCAN, (Unpublished).

Wadel, C., (1979), 'The Hidden Work of Everyday Life', in S. Wallman (ed), Social Anthropology of Work, A.S.A. Monographs in Social Anthropology no. 19, Academic Press, London.

Wallman, S., (1974), 'Kinship, a-Kinship, anti-Kinship; variations in the logic of kinship situations', in E. Leyton, (ed) The Compact: selected dimensions of friendship, Memorial University I.S.E.R., St. John's, Newfoundland, and in J. Hum. Evol. 1975, vol.4, no.5.

Wallman, S., (1975), 'A Street in Waterloo', New Community, vol.iv, no.4.

Wallman, S., (1978), 'The Boundaries of "Race": processes of ethnicity in England', MAN, vol.13, no.2.

Wallman, S., (1980), 'Introduction' to S. Wallman (ed) Social Anthropology of Work, Association of Social Anthropologists, Monograph no.19, Academic Press, London.

226

Wallman, S., (1983), Eight London Households, Tavistock, London.
Wallman, S., Dhooge, Y., Goldman, A. and Kosmin, B.A., (1980), 'Ethnography by Proxy: strategies for research in the inner city', ETHNOS 1-2, Stockholm.
Watson, J.L., (ed) (1977), Between Two Cultures, Blackwell, Oxford.
Whyte, W., (1955), Street Corner Society, Chicago University Press, Chicago.
Williams, G.R., (1975), London in the Country, Hamish Hamilton, London.
Williams, R., (1973), The Country and the City, Chatto and Windus, London.
Woodhouse, M. and Pearce, B., (1975), Essays on the History of Communism in Britain, New Park, London.
Wrigley, C., (1974), 'Liberals and the desire for working class representation in Battersea 1886-1922', in K.D. Brown (ed) Essays in Anti-Labour History, Macmillan, London.
Wrigley, C., (1977), The First World War and its Aftermath: Changes in the Battersea Labour Movement 1914-1919, Battersea and Wandsworth Labour and Social History Group, London.
Wrigley, C., (1977), Battersea Republicans and the 1902 Coronation, Battersea and Wandsworth Labour and Social History Group, London.
Young, M. and Willmott, P., (1957), Family and Kinship in East London, Penguin, Harmondsworth.
Young, M. and Willmott, P., (1960), Family and Class in a London Suburb, Routledge and Kegan Paul, London.
Young, M. and Willmott, P., (1973), The Symmetrical Family, Routledge and Kegan Paul, London.

Index of names